101 PAT-DOWNS

101

Pat-Downs

An Undercover Look at
Airport Security and the TSA

SHAWNA MALVINI REDDEN

POTOMAC BOOKS

AN IMPRINT OF THE UNIVERSITY OF NEBRASKA PRESS

All rights reserved. Potomac Books is an imprint
of the University of Nebraska Press.
Manufactured in the United States of America.

Library of Congress Cataloging-in-Publication Data
Names: Redden, Shawna Malvini, author.
Title: 101 pat-downs: an undercover look at airport
security and the TSA / Shawna Malvini Redden.
Other titles: One hundred one pat downs: an undercover look at
airport security and the Transportation Security Administration
Description: Lincoln: Potomac Books, an imprint of
the University of Nebraska Press, 2021. | Includes
bibliographical references and index.
Identifiers: LCCN 2020038639
ISBN 9781640123625 (Hardback)
ISBN 9781640124622 (ePub)
ISBN 9781640124639 (mobi)
ISBN 9781640124646 (PDF)
Subjects: LCSH: Aeronautics, Commercial—Security
measures. | Aeronautics, Commercial—Passenger
traffic—Security measures. | Airports—Security measures.
| Airports—Management. | Airports—Employees—
Safety measures. | Terrorism—Prevention.
Classification: LCC TL725.3.S44 R44 2021
| DDC 363.28/760973—dc23
LC record available at https://lccn.loc.gov/2020038639

Set in Lyon and Proxima Nova by Laura Buis.
Designed by N. Putens.

For my Marm, who taught me to love books.
And for Tim. Because I promised warbirds, didn't I?

Contents

Illustrations

Acknowledgments

Extreme gratitude to everyone who helped make this book possible—first and foremost, the officers, travelers, and crewmembers who shared their stories. Thank you for trusting me and letting me experience your world.

Huge thanks to my agent, Jessica Alvarez of BookEnds Literary, for believing in this project and supporting me.

Gratitude to the editorial team at the University of Nebraska Press for bringing this book into the world. Deep thanks to Sandy Crump for her expert editing.

Love and appreciation to my support system: My family, especially my husband, Tim (aka #Review2Husband), the best, most brutal editor on earth; Marm and Brenda for believing I can do anything; Jeanne for being my enthusiastic champion, wine unicorn, and cheerful editor; Geeta for reasons, especially your wisdom, daily check-ins, and cheese appreciation; Amy for listening, understanding (everything), and always making me laugh; Katie for being the best writing buddy for life; Elizabeth for your friendship and spectacular suggestions, especially for being the first to say, "This sounds like a book"; Mandy for the "book day ice cream" delivery, without which I could've never persevered; and Kristin for shouting, "FIFI!" at regular intervals. And all of the people I'm sure I'm forgetting.

Special appreciation to friend and mentor Dr. Sarah Tracy, for your cheerful support, for giving me the tools to make this research journey possible, and for tolerating my TSA talk for the last decade.

Thanks also to my students at Sacramento State University, who have cheered me on during the whole book process and not complained (too much) when it took me awhile to grade their papers.

101 PAT-DOWNS

Introduction

Going Undercover in Airport Security

August 16, 2009.

"Ma'am, do you know why I pulled you over?"

Tears streaming, I blubber, "No." Panic-wiping snot from my nose, I fumble for my license and registration. "Was I speeding?"

"No. You made an illegal U-turn."

"Are those not allowed here?" I choke out.

He explains that U-turns are fine, except in front of big signs with the U-turn symbol crossed out in red, like the one in front of the *police station* where I am now stopped.

I burst into fresh tears.

Surveying my California documents, he asks where I live.

"I don't know!" I wail. And it is true. Having relocated to Mesa, Arizona, from Sacramento only twenty-five hours before, sans smartphone—my Blackberry 8320 doesn't have GPS or a maps app—I've been trying to find my apartment for *hours*.

"Ma'am, have you been drinking?"

When I can speak coherently, I explain that the puffy, bloodshot eyes are because I just dropped my fiancé off at the airport and don't know when I will see him again. I share that I'm starting a doctoral program at Arizona State tomorrow, that I moved to Arizona yesterday and can't remember my address, only that my apartment is somewhere on Gilbert Avenue. I admit that I've been trying to get home from the airport, driving in an unfamiliar city at night, for two hours now.

As the story tumbles out, the officer realizes I am distraught, not drunk. After some reassurance, he lets me go with a warning and gives me directions to my new home—on this same street, but twenty-five minutes in the opposite direction.

Thus was the beginning of my new life in the desert, one where I'd be separated from my home, almost-husband, and dog for several years. One filled with travel and textbooks. But one where I'd never again get lost on my way home from the airport.

I had no way of knowing then that the airport would become so central to my life—that I would spend many thousands of dollars and *years* investigating it. That I would get to know its employees and its characters personally. And that at least one visit to the airport would end with a near-death experience.[1]

But I'm getting ahead of myself. Let me go back to my first momentous airport experience, the last time someone walked me right up to the gate for a flight.

September 2000.

I was eighteen years old and flying by myself for the first time.

The phone had rung at 6:00 a.m. the day before, shattering the predawn silence in the apartment I shared with my dad and stepmom in a suburb of Sacramento, California. Dripping wet from the shower, I'd run to grab the phone from its cradle in the kitchen to spare the rest of the household an excessively early wake-up call.

It was my best friend Heather on the line, offering me admission to the same small liberal arts college she was attending. Really. No joke. Heather worked in the development department at her school, Union College, and had convinced the recruiters that they needed me. The financial aid and admission details would be worked out when I arrived, she said. A dorm room and roommate awaited two doors down from hers. There was even a free plane ticket available. I just had to agree and hop on a plane to Lincoln, Nebraska, *the next day*.

For various financial and family reasons, I was not planning to attend college like the rest of my friends, despite graduating near the top of my class, with scholarships and honors. Instead, I was toiling as a file clerk in the dank basement of a financial planner's office. In what I think back on as my best, most risky decision ever, I quit my job, applied for a credit card, and started packing. I had no money and no real plan, just a burning desire to escape the drudgery of my dead-end job.

The next day, I dragged two suitcases and a military duffel, all borrowed, to Sacramento International Airport, where I met my little sister and mother. Waiting for my United flight to board, we sat in leatherette chairs, metal arms partitioning us as we said awkward, unexpected goodbyes. For the first time in my eighteen years, I had no idea when I would see them again.

With red-rimmed eyes, Mom handed me some of her tip money from the hair salon, offering tender words and wishes of good luck. I asked her to take my unfinished copy of *War and Peace* back to the library. My sister Brenda gave me a shoebox wrapped in magazine pages featuring pictures of Degas ballerinas, the whole interior scrawled with our favorite inside jokes. The box held mementos and letters from her and our little sister, Emily, that had me crying halfway to Lincoln.

As it turned out, one Nebraska winter was quite enough for this California girl, and I transferred to a sister school of my Midwest college. Exactly one year and ten days later, on September 11, 2001, I was in Walla Walla, Washington, preparing to start my sophomore year at a new university. When I awoke late that morning in an unfamiliar bed at a friend's house, both planes had already hit the Twin Towers. I was so disoriented that at first I thought the news was a horrible prank. I didn't realize that the world had fundamentally changed.

As I think about how September 11 changed flying forever—the terrorist attacks would spawn the Transportation Security Administration (TSA)—I can't imagine what it would have been like if I'd had to say goodbye to my family in the main airport terminal, before going to my gate. Or if I'd had to go through security on my own, bawling my brains out as an eighteen-year-old kid, having only flown once before and never by myself. Or if I'd had to juggle my box of mementos through the checkpoint, cramming them into a gray bin with my shoes and belt and jacket, only to find out when I got to the gate that, according to FAA regulations, I had too many carry-ons.

Although I missed what some call the golden age of flying, when security was nonexistent, flight attendants were "stewardesses," and flying was a dress-up occasion, I do remember a more humane era. I recall when airport security was just a two-minute excursion through the metal detector, not the complex, cumbersome, technology-driven, invasive, emotional, and sometimes enraging process it is today.

Nearly nine years after waking up in Walla Walla, I embarked on a three-year odyssey to understand airport security and figure out why exactly the TSA persists.

Thursday, August 20, 2010, Sky Harbor International Airport, Phoenix, Arizona.
Now in my second year in a doctoral program at Arizona State University, I've survived the first week of school and am heading back home to California. I still don't realize how important the airport will become, although I plan to fly back and forth regularly between Tempe and my new husband in Sacramento. Seriously new. We only returned from our honeymoon two weeks ago and, after eight days of cohabitating as a married couple, made the drive to the desert so I could start year two of my program. Leaving Tim at the airport that second time wasn't easy, but at least it wasn't as traumatic as the first.

Now, a week later, I'm back at Sky Harbor. I live with a roommate who's just dropped me off at the dark curbside of Terminal Four, where cigarette smoke mixes with hot asphalt, radiating in the 110-degree heat.

Tugging my red rolling carry-on suitcase, I walk through the first sliding door and into the cool terminal. Several months have passed since my last commercial flight in May, but Sky Harbor still feels like a second home. I spent a lot of time here during the previous year, traveling to and from Sacramento every two weeks, keeping a long-distance engagement afloat. Bypassing the ticket area, I take the escalator to security, hoping for a short line.

Travelers visit on the second floor, smiling between bites of ice cream and sips of coffee, as flight crews gab in line at Paradise Bakery. Pauses punctuate the conversations as every few minutes, the overhead security announcement loudly reminds us to avoid transporting items from strangers. As I beeline to the security checkpoint for Terminal C, I wonder if anyone actually listens to the messages. I don't like to talk to strangers at the airport, let alone receive packages from them.

With mild trepidation, I approach the transportation security officers (TSOs) checking boarding passes. I hold my temporary California identification, a photo-less folded piece of DMV printer paper. I've just changed to my married name, and I worry about getting hassled or not being allowed to fly because I lack official photo ID. I've been fretting about the temporary document for a couple of weeks, rehearsing how I'll explain myself. But the TSO doesn't bat an eye. Nor will they for the next ten flights I take before my new driver's license arrives. I start to wonder how closely they examine documents, especially, I imagine, for people who look like me: nonthreatening.

I walk away from the ID checker a little lighter in spirit—a newlywed heading home!

After getting barefoot, I hoist my suitcase, purse, and shoes onto a conveyor belt to be screened. Expecting my carry-on to pop through the X-ray machine quickly, like usual, I hop from one bare foot to the other. Annoyed, I worry with a hypochondriac's flare about what organisms my toes are touching.

The TSA started requiring passengers to remove their shoes before walking through the metal detector in 2006. Without shoes I feel vulnerable and uncomfortable. I have one less layer of protection and decreased mobility, and it feels like the TSOs, in their heavy boots, have so much more power. Can I be the only one who feels this way?

A shrill "BEEP, BEEP, BEEP!" jars me and I look up to see accusation and irritation in the eyes of a female TSO.

"Is this your bag?" she demands with a huff, an eyebrow raised at my candy-apple-red suitcase.

As I nod, she peels back the zipper without asking permission. I watch as dirty laundry gets tossed about while she digs for whatever I must be smuggling. I note the amusement of onlooking TSOs and sympathetic glances from rubbernecking passersby.

I stand barefoot and waiting, embarrassed and uncertain. Although I press a few boundaries in security as a frequent flier—for instance, never taking my liquids and gels out of my suitcase unless forced—I am primarily a rule follower. Being pulled out of line feels awkward. Watching my things get rifled through? Mortifying. I am taken aback by how adversarial the woman appears. The scowl. The huffing. *What did I ever do to you, lady?* During the interaction, I am acutely attuned to the reactions of passengers and other employees.

The cause for my security stop? An errant corkscrew/cheese knife contraption, something I'd picked up at a B and B on our honeymoon. She tells me I can take the item to my car (which is not at the airport) or they can throw it out.

"I'm going to need to pat you down now," she informs me flatly, but again without asking permission.

Chagrined for having forgotten the flimsy corkscrew and annoyed that the silly memento was confiscated, I now perceive a change in the TSO's manner.[2] Although she does not converse or make much eye contact, my lowered threat level seems to have diffused her aggressive demeanor.

She conducts the screening with an air of casual routine, perhaps let down at the false alarm. It's really no big deal, just quick swipes with the back of her hands, but I'm still disgruntled.

I leave for my gate after ten minutes, feeling aggravated and exposed. The TSA's purpose is to find wrongdoing and prevent terrorism. To do a good job as a TSA employee means to find a certain number of items or threats from day to day. The TSO I met seems almost disappointed that my stop has amounted to naught. How often do TSA agents find something of substance? Although she seems relieved, I wonder how irritating it is to waste time on fruitless screenings like mine. In retrospect, I realize that I found it frustrating because of the inane nature of the rules. Knives/corkscrews are verboten, but long, sharp knitting needles and small scissors up to four inches are allowed? The rules seem arbitrary.

Feeling vulnerable and angry about having no control over having my person and property searched, I start thinking about the emotions involved in airport security. How do emotions influence interactions between employees and travelers at airports? How did my mix of embarrassment and anger shape how I responded to the TSO who was feeling her own suspicion, relief, and annoyance?

Although this was a fairly routine interaction, it would only have taken a small escalation of emotion to spur serious consequences. For example, had I caused a scene and yelled at the woman (as I've seen others do), I might've been kicked out of the airport or even arrested for threatening security.[3] Of course, positive outcomes were possible as well. For instance, instead of meeting me with immediate accusation and irritation, the officer could have stayed neutral until she found the problem or used humor to put me at ease. In that case, I might've left laughing instead of angry and plotting to learn more.

However, my irritation caused me to start questioning: How do TSA officers and passengers interact? That simple question would shape the next few years of my life as I used it to launch an academic research career.

Allow me to explain.

After graduating from Walla Walla College, I worked in health care communication and marketing, first in a small rural hospital and then in the corporate office of a multistate health care system. Like anyone who starts to hate the limitations of their job, I began looking for ways to grow. For me the best and safest one was grad school. Unlike when I made my first foray into higher education, this time I had a solid career foundation, a steady paycheck, and a plan to be methodical about professional advancement.

Fast-forward three years.

While finishing my master's degree in communication studies at California State University, Sacramento, I decided I wanted to become a college professor. My program offered student teaching opportunities, and as I taught public speaking, I quickly realized the classroom felt like home. With every earnest and idealistic fiber of my young being, I left the Cal State system wanting to make a difference in the lives of students, just like my professors had done for me. I didn't fully understand that I would need to become a researcher first.

A researcher? What does that even mean?

Coming from working-class roots—hairdresser mom, mechanic dad—I was the first person in my immediate family to finish college, let alone strive for an advanced degree. The master's was somewhat understandable to my family: "going back for an MBA" had become increasingly common as the housing-bubble-bursting economy tanked and the job market contracted. But a PhD? Why on earth? Because I'd gotten engaged just after my MA graduation, I was asked with annoying regularity why I should go on for the doctorate (as if an MRS. would preclude my desire for the PhD).

I started to see that "ivory tower" and "pie in the sky" stereotypes about academia and academics endure because most people don't realize what graduate school is about, and lots of us egghead types can't explain it without making people's eyes glaze over.

In short, advanced degrees—at least the terminal type (which means "as far as you can go," not "you're going to die")—are about creating new knowledge, thinking innovative thoughts, making novel connections between theories or contexts, and sharing these ideas with others. In particular, terminal degrees require students to generate unique and meaningful claims about the world that help advance a particular discipline or field. For me, that has largely manifested in performing research to understand communication in organizations and making recommendations to improve policy and practice.

Still sounds vague and esoteric, right? That's what I thought during my first year as a doctoral student at Arizona State University's Hugh Downs School of Human Communication. It wasn't until I took Dr. Sarah Tracy's qualitative methods course during my second year that I began to under-stand how I could "build new knowledge." And damn if it wasn't one of the hardest, most painful, most rewarding lessons of my life.

Our first assignment was to learn how to do fieldwork and participant observation, which is essentially recording the sights, sounds, smells, feelings, and conversations in a particular setting (like the airport). Professional people watching, if you will. Dr. Tracy taught us how to make meaning from our field notes (and how to use other methods such as interviewing).

My classmates examined a wide range of contexts and dynamics. Kristin shadowed and interviewed veterinarians, watching how they interacted with pet owners during routine and emergent situations. Tim (a classmate, not my husband) worked with homeless youth, using his position as director of a nonprofit outreach center to understand the kids' lives on the street and to advocate for them. Gino interviewed bereaved parents and learned about the challenges they face in communicating at work after losing a child.

Me? I studied airport security.

Those tumultuous emotions I felt when my bag was searched, my corkscrew confiscated, my body patted down? I learned how to connect those feelings and the resulting interactions to communication and organizational theories.[4] I related rude passenger behavior to American expectations of customer service and the paradigm of "the customer is always right."[5] I linked TSOs' aggressive behavior to the ability to exercise power over passengers.[6] After six months of observing and interviewing passengers in the airport, I even coined a new theoretical concept—"emotional taxes"—to refer to the emotions we are required to "pay" in compulsory interactions like airport security screenings.[7]

In Dr. Tracy's class and throughout our subsequent mentor-mentee (now, friend and colleague) relationship, I learned that I could use my research tools—conversation, observation, interview, historical analysis—to develop ideas that would help people actually communicate better. And in the case of the TSA, perhaps these ideas would make flying and working in airports easier for all involved.

For three years I worked "under cover," flying in and out of airports around the country, engaging with travelers and TSOs alike. I asked questions at the airport, then formally interviewed passengers and security officers privately. And I watched, recording every important interaction in my field notes, from TSOs cracking jokes to passengers in line who were going mildly bonkers when their water bottles were confiscated.

I started out dying to know why passengers put up with invasive screening. I lost sleep wondering how on earth TSOs get through the day dealing with so much passenger disrespect and anger. I pondered what the powers that be who created the TSA in the first place were smoking.

Over the months and years, I found that the answers to my questions were much more complicated than my early suppositions. And the answers involved a formidable combination of identity, emotion, history, politics, power, profit, and several levels of social discourse. I met mission-oriented TSOs who described their jobs with reverent commitment and others who lived up to every lazy, deviant stereotype the media has to offer. And I ran into every type of passenger on the planet, from entitled business travelers to parents with toddlers to the hot mess, travels-once-a-year, can't-figure-out-how-to-get-through-the-security-checkpoint-without-crying flier.

As a communication scholar who has been studying the TSA for more than a decade, I have explored how identities emerge through emotional interactions—in other words, how people act and what aspects of their identities they portray during emotional situations.[8] For instance, when people get into angry altercations, do they communicate the same sense of self as when conversations are less heated? To understand these ideas, I looked at the micro-, meso-, and macro-level discourses that people use to make sense of their experiences.[9]

At the *micro* level, social discourse includes conversations, interpersonal communication, email, text messages, social media posts—the talk and text we use in our everyday lives. *Meso* refers to the organizational level, where social discourse occurs through policies and procedures that span across the organization; in this case, procedures such as how to conduct a pat-down. *Macro*-level discourse involves larger social narratives that structure societies and cultures, and assumptions that permeate the broader social sphere. Think about how the idea that "the customer is always right" structures interactions between service providers and patrons, for instance. And consider how you probably don't feel like a customer with rights in airport security.

Through airport stories and interviews, this book shows that passengers grasp interpersonal and social discourses, including the horror stories they hear from friends and the pop culture portrayals of the TSA on shows like *South Park* and *Saturday Night Live*.[10] TSOs, on the other hand, are more heavily influenced by their everyday experiences with passengers and by organizational discourses that promote rule enforcement, patriotism, and duty. Using firsthand experiences of passengers and security officers, contextualized with history, policy, and research, *101 Pat-Downs* helps explain why the experience of working in and traveling through airports is more uncomfortable than it needs to be.[11]

Throughout this book, you'll meet common "characters" of airport security. You'll see the human face behind the stereotypically gruff TSO exterior and understand why so many passengers feel nervous inside TSA checkpoints. Tracing the main elements of security, along with a quick history of how the TSA came to be, the book demonstrates why certain security protocols such as shoe removal and advanced imaging technology now appear commonplace, and how acceptance of these procedures allows the TSA to intensify security protocols largely without being questioned. Throughout are insights into the complex historical environment of airport security and practical tips on how to navigate the security process.

As two million people fly commercially every day in the United States, and every single passenger must interact with members of airport security, *101 Pat-Downs* is a perfect traveler's companion for dealing with what one TSO interviewee described as the nation's "second most hated government agency" (after the IRS, that is). *101 Pat-Downs* is the first book to look at airport security from a critical observer's perspective, showing the hilarious, horrible, and mundane sides of the TSA while offering suggestions for making communication easier. Readers can apply takeaways from the book to other emotionally charged situations where we are forced to communicate with authority figures, such as traffic stops, court appointments, and doctor visits.

Pro Travel Tip #1:

Leave the Guesswork for *Jeopardy*

Curious or worried about an upcoming trip through airport security? Don't bring shame upon your family by waiting until you get to the airport to ask questions. The TSA has a fairly comprehensive website with tons of information about policies and procedures. Understanding the policies and your rights as a passenger is key, especially if you get into a disagreement with a TSA officer.

1

From the Golden Age of Flying to Security Theatre in Ninety Days Flat

How September 11, 2001, Changed Airport Security Forever

January 3, 2020.

"Are you doing 'dry January'?" Dave asks.

"Perhaps," Theresa replies, wryly, raising her glass of Sancerre.

We're sitting around a friend's dining room table, doing post-holiday catch-up: What did Santa bring? How long are the kids' college breaks? How many bottles of champagne for New Year's Eve?

I'm playing with someone's tabletop curling game, pushing miniature weighted stones across a plastic sheet, when our friend John asks, "How's the book going?"

Like any good writer, I lie about my progress and divert attention to other topics. I ask, "Anyone have good TSA stories for me?"

Somehow the question makes us travel back in time almost two decades—to September 11, 2001.

Tom jumps in, "Matt called me at work and said 'I'm okay.'" He explains how he was working a long shift during his emergency medicine residency in Albany, New York. He had no idea what his brother, Matt, a pilot for Delta at the time, was talking about.

Around the table, everyone starts telling their 9/11 stories. Dave was heading to Rotary at 7:15 a.m. (Pacific time), and by then the first plane had already hit.

Deb mentions how her friend was a flight attendant who called in sick that day and otherwise would have been on one of the planes.

"I was driving to Sacramento from Tulare," Tim says, referencing his long drive up I-5 through Central California. "I'm watching the truckers and their body language changed. They started hunching over their steering wheels. I could see them all talking nonstop. I knew something was going on."

"I flew home on Flight 93 the day before," John pipes up. My head whips over to him, the expression *Seriously?* on my face.

"He was actually scheduled on the 9/11 flight," his wife Theresa clarifies. "We have the receipt." John had been in New York on business on September 10. His dinner meeting cancelled, so he packed up and went to the airport to catch the same flight, only one day earlier.

"He never returned my call," John said of his dinner companion, not needing to explain that the missed call meant he got to see his children grow up.

Later, Theresa would tell me John was antsy to get home because she was about to deliver their third child. "To this day, our youngest daughter says, 'My dad is here because he wanted to see me,'" Theresa said.

The atmosphere of our "game night" suddenly turned heavy, each of us recalling where we were—physically and emotionally—during the attacks.

What struck me was not only my own memories of being in Walla Walla at the time, but also how the college students I currently teach are further and further removed from even *knowing* about 9/11, let alone remembering it or feeling its impacts.

Freshmen entering college since 2019 were not even alive when the planes hit the towers and nearly three thousand people died in coordinated terrorist attacks in three states. They take for granted what air travel is like today. For them, the TSA has always existed. But for most of the population, while we may have acclimated to security procedures, we can remember the times before, when airport security was not much more than a security guard and a metal detector.

The September 11, 2001, terrorist attacks dramatically changed the face of commercial air travel in the United States. Not only did they devastate the aviation industry with multibillion-dollar financial losses, they also spawned the creation of the Transportation Security Administration (TSA), forever changing what it means to fly in the United States and beyond.

With the advent of the TSA, airports abruptly transitioned from maintaining their own private security forces (contracted for by the airlines) to integrating federal officers into their domains.[1] Enacted by Congress and signed into law by President George W. Bush in November 2001, the newly commissioned TSA began hiring thousands of officers to staff airports and systematizing security screening across the country.[2]

Many but not all officers came from the pool of twenty-eight thousand private security guards already in place. Although it took the TSA a year to hire the approximately forty-five thousand people necessary to staff airports and meet White House mandates, new regulations made it immediately clear that air travel as America knew it would never be the same.[3]

In the months following 9/11, security lines that had once been but brief formalities blossomed into lengthy queues that moved by the inch. Airlines cautioned passengers to arrive at least two hours prior to domestic flights and prepare for heretofore unheard-of scrutiny of their bodies and baggage. The list of prohibited carry-on items grew steadily. Constantly changing, the carry-on rules appeared capricious, with toy weapons and most sporting equipment banned but items like ice skates allowed. In response to outrageously long lines, airlines established VIP security queues for frequent fliers, but these were abolished by the TSA in 2002 before again being reinstated as a government revenue function years later.[4]

In the year after 9/11, passengers learned that they could no longer walk into the terminal area without a boarding pass. Although modern travelers now take this restriction for granted, it dramatically changed the culture of going to the airport.

No longer could tearful reunions or goodbyes take place near the gate. People watching for pleasure soon morphed into terrorist spotting, with passengers being continually admonished to keep their eyes open for suspicious happenings. These directives, which still play on recorded loops over airport public address systems, served as an early iteration of the Department of Homeland Security's "If You See Something, Say Something" campaign, which encouraged passengers in all transportation settings to report suspicious activity, people, or packages.

During the early aftermath of 9/11, new security measures were accepted by a terrified flying public who demanded that the government do something to ensure safety and restore confidence in commercial aviation. Acceptance of these processes also set the stage for passengers and TSOs to develop the identity performances—in other words, the identities they portray in emotional situations—that are of interest in this book.

Before 9/11, airport security costs were measured in the millions of dollars. Today the costs factor in the billions. In 2000 the Government Accountability Office estimated that U.S. airlines spent $448 million on security, or seventy-five cents to screen each passenger and the passenger's luggage.[5] A decade later, airlines paid $7.4 billion for security, not including the $2.1 billion from the September 11 Security Fee paid directly by consumers.[6] Together these equate to $15.09 per passenger. Not adjusting for inflation, these figures suggest that it became twenty times more expensive to administer security after the advent of the TSA.[7]

Despite critiques, TSA officials reckon nearly twenty years of safe skies worth the costs. However, opposing viewpoints cite the historical rarity of terrorist attacks and the vast TSA expenditures that have netted *zero* terrorist plots foiled.[8] Scholars of foreign and defense policy estimate that the risk of a U.S. citizen dying in a terrorist attack is one in 3.5 million, and that deaths by Islamic extremists (outside of war zones) account for between two hundred and four hundred deaths annually *worldwide*, the same number of people who die in bathtubs every year in the United States.[9] Furthermore, the TSA blog's annual "Top Good Catches" and "Week in Review" posts feature confiscated weapons and contraband, including live animals, but not, to date, any terrorists.

During my interviews with passengers, I asked what they thought of the TSA's mission. In conversation with "Kristine," a freelance travel photographer, I said, "I'm going to read you the mission statement of the TSA."

She replied, "Oh, this should be good," like she was gearing up.

"'The TSA's mission is to protect the nation's transportation systems to ensure freedom of movement for people and commerce.' What do you think of that mission statement?" I asked.

After a long pause, Kristine answered, "They see themselves as law enforcement and that mission statement goes right along with that."

"What do you mean by that?" I asked.

"To protect," Kristine said. "When they're talking about 'protecting the free movement of people and commerce,' they're not talking about me, the individual. They're talking about our nation as a whole, it feels like."

Another passenger, "Sue," a public relations executive, agreed.

"I would say they exemplify that mission very well and I think it probably explains why they don't seem very humane in their treatment," Sue said.

"They're not there for us, they're there for transportation," Sue continued. "They're there to keep the system running smoothly. They're there to make sure no terrible things happen at the airport. I realize that, but I think when it comes to how they interact with people, they should try to treat people as people."

So many of the conflicts and challenges with airport security stem from this tension . . . individual feelings versus systemic concerns for safety.

"You said, 'They're not there for us.' How do you feel that your role as a customer in airport security differs at the airport versus as a customer in other service interactions? At the grocery store or the mall, or wherever?" I asked Sue.

"Well, at the airport, I might be a customer of a specific airline. I might be somebody who is helping to pay their salary, because if I wasn't flying, they wouldn't be getting a paycheck—not me personally, but everybody. But I think that relationship is so indirect that it probably doesn't play a factor in their [TSA officers'] minds," Sue explained.

"I do think there's that reality that if I offend them in any way, they can exercise authority to harass me . . . what I call harass," Sue continued. "Send me into further screening, or further testing, or hold me in a room for questioning, or kick me out of the airport, or blacklist me from flying." And indeed, she is 100 percent correct in assuming that the TSA has the power to delay or limit her ability to fly.

"I honestly believe that I'm not viewed as a customer by them," Sue said. "I'm viewed as a potential security threat. I think that's drastically different than if I were to go to a supermarket and ask for a tomato."

This line of thinking is why I find airport security an interesting context for examining communication. It's one of the few places where the customer service script is flipped and we encounter compulsory interactions with steep differences in power between us and the folks in charge (the folks who, as Sue said, could arbitrarily decide to punish us if they chose to). Whereas Americans endorse a "the customer is always right" mentality, the fact is that we are not customers when we are in airport security. Like Sue said, we're potential threats.

That tension accounts for so many of our challenging feelings in security. We're not customers, and rationally we might know that. But throughout the stories in this book, you will see that many of us are so used to a basic level of customer service in most organizational encounters that being treated with suspicion is a new and difficult experience (for the more privileged of us, anyway).

"How does that difference make you feel?" I asked Sue, encouraging her to reflect on the security-versus-supermarket comparison. "Are you okay with it, or do you find it frustrating?"

"Well, like I said, I think that's the distinct difference between flying pre-9/11 and post-9/11," Sue said. "It wasn't like that before, as you probably remember. The TSA was hardly even a blip on your screen when you were flying. You just went through the scanner real quick and went on with your flight. Now you have to plan ahead for TSA. You have to get there [early], saving at least one hour to deal with TSA."

"It's strange," I remarked. "TSA didn't even exist before 9/11. They were created as a result of it."

"Yeah, it wasn't TSA." Sue caught herself. "They had security. You still had a metal detector you had to walk through or whatever."

"It's so crazy how much has changed," I added, thinking about the luggage limitations, invasion of privacy, and technologies involved in modern airport checkpoints.

"It makes sense to have security," Sue said. "I get the justification. I get the fear mongering, but there are people I fly with that strongly believe in TSA's mission, because they are huge xenophobes or they are huge jerks. They honestly believe people are out to 'get them' on airplanes."

Here Sue referenced the Islamophobia that has persisted in the United States since 9/11—the fear of Muslim people that has translated to fear of many brown people, especially those of Middle Eastern descent or appearance. And this is a relatively new fear related to air travel and security.

Decades earlier, for instance, folks harbored legitimate concerns about airplanes being hijacked. In the 1960s and 1970s, hijackings were a regular occurrence. In fact, according to Brendan I. Koerner's book *The Skies Belong to Us*, more than 130 American airplanes were hijacked between 1968 and 1972.[10] As a response to these "skyjackers"—who usually demanded to be taken to specific locations, like Cuba, or wanted massive payouts—airlines started to embed security in airports in 1973. But security was cursory—a metal detector and a security guard.

Fast-forward nearly thirty years and the fear is not of hijacking per se but of suicide missions.

"But I feel like the possibility of that happening is probably so slim. Maybe I'm naive, I don't know," Sue added.

"I would like to believe that it is slim," I commented, and we both laugh.

"As much as I fly, I hope so too," Sue said.

While many take issue with TSA policies and practices, most concede that airport security is a necessary evil. In the following chapters, we'll explore how this necessary evil or, said differently, this safety mechanism, influences people—passengers and airport security officers alike.

Pro Travel Tip #2:

Don't Even Joke about Blowing Up an Airplane

While the September 11, 2001, terrorist attacks might seem like a long time ago, airlines and airport security take even joking threats about blowing up airplanes seriously. In 2018 a man was removed from a flight for joking about blowing up the plane, and in 2014 a teenage girl in the Netherlands was arrested for tweeting a bomb threat to American Airlines. The fourteen-year-old was later released without charges.

2

"My House, My Rules"

On Stereotypical Transportation Security Officers

September 25, 2010.

Oh my god, I am busted! As the transportation security officers, or TSOs, start to surround me, I wonder: *Is this the day I get arrested in the name of research?*

I've been standing in the unused family/medical boarding line in Security Checkpoint C, watching passengers and TSOs in the busy general boarding line for the last twenty-five minutes. It's one of the few times I'm at the airport without plans to travel. I'm there to fulfill an assignment for my qualitative methods class—four hours of focused observation in my research context.

I started observing security an hour ago, hiding behind a large potted palm at the edge of the checkpoint, bemused at the gloriousness of human nature. The large security checkpoint was quiet at first, and approaching passengers were dragging their luggage through dozens of empty security rows to get to the TSA ID checkers. That is, until an elderly couple, to save a few steps, cut underneath the tape between the stanchions that marked the line. Then everyone else started following suit.

I snickered at a group of twenty-somethings who tried to emulate the couple by ducking under. Their bulky backpacks snagged the tape, breaking it away from the stanchions. Peals of laughter lightened the atmosphere for a moment. Noticing this, a few older folks carefully removed the tape from the stanchions and walked through upright. I waited for a TSO to tell them not to mess with the tape, but no one did. Still, others tromped around the "right" way, some throwing withering looks at the "cutters" ahead.

The line-ducking passengers clustered, all chatting and laughing, but I couldn't make out their dialogue from twenty feet away. Since such levity is terribly unusual for the security scene, I wanted to better understand their joy. So I edged closer to the security line, watching the casual weekend travelers and furiously jotting observations in my spiral notebook.

It felt awkward to just stand there staring at the line, so after a few minutes I scooted right up into the unused family/medical lane. It's adjacent to general boarding and skirts along a six-foot metal and frosted glass wall, which conveniently obscures me from the closest TSO, who is checking IDs and tickets. This is where the TSOs will soon pounce.

Now, leaning against the wall and feeling less exposed, I'm watching passengers proceed through the line—the friendly Southern belle gliding away in lime green loafers and crisp khakis, carrying a Coach purse; the boisterous Texan who bounces as she forks over her driver's license; the burly biker-esque fellow whose bold black tats clash with the stuffed pink unicorn he's carrying for his daughter and the creamy leather of a wifely purse draped over his arm.

I'm paying special attention to how emotional expressions pass nonverbally between passengers and TSOs. I see the stoic-looking TSO who seems to catch the bubbly Texan's smile, only to lose it after encountering three stone-faced passengers in a row. I watch previously excited passengers go rigid and get annoyed when they offer documents to a slack-faced TSO who doesn't return their grins, and I see a nervous-looking passenger relax when she encounters a smiling officer. I start to contemplate how emotional expressions are reciprocal—each person influencing the other—and make notes on what will eventually become my first published research paper.[1]

Feeling self-congratulatory about my prime observing spot, I'm scrawling page after page of notes when I notice a wiry man in his late thirties sporting a rockabilly bouffant and looking at me quizzically, and then a too-pale-to-be-from-Arizona woman glaring at my notepad.

My scribbling continues, but a few minutes later I detect two extra TSOs walking around the check-in area. I've seen officers observing the line from that vantage during previous visits, so I don't think much of it until I notice them noticing me. *Uh oh.*

I pretend not to see the agents as they walk toward the general boarding line, stopping to confer. But they about-face and, not too casually, trek back around the line in opposite directions. My heart thuds.

The TSOs approach, entering the line I'm in from opposing sides. I'm trapped. My notes become incoherent squiggles.

"Do you need assistance?" one of them, a woman with dark hair pulled into a tight bun, asks.

Looking past her, I notice the TSOs at the document station aren't checking IDs. The line no longer shuffles by. *Did they really stop the security line . . . because of me?*

My cheeks are on fire. I can feel my chest turning a strawberry color as my heart starts racing and my palms go damp.

"I'm a student doing a research project for school," I stammer, explaining that I study communication at Arizona State and am observing the line to better understand social interactions and emotions.

She looks relieved as I offer to show my school ID. *Why didn't I wear an ASU T-shirt??* I silently yell at myself, ignoring the fact that I don't even own one.

With as much innocent cheerfulness as I can muster, I ask if I can stay put and watch the line. I promise to move if anyone needs to actually use the family/medical line.

"I don't know how much they will want you right here," she replies. "You better move back."

"Is it possible to speak with your manager and ask permission?" I inquire politely. "I'm happy to explain everything."

Now *she's* nervous, repeating her admonition that "they" will not want me around and that I should move back out of the line. I'm struck that she doesn't tell me to leave or give me permission to stay, but says I can "just see what happens."

I stand in place for a few minutes, feigning nonchalance even though I'm now sweating through my black Target T-shirt. She disappears, presumably to deliberate with other agents.

Realizing the line is *still* not moving, I lose my resolve and move back near the potted palm across from the checkpoint. I'm flying home in five days and have no desire to get added to the Do Not Fly list.

While pretending to take notes—I can barely breathe at this point—I see two different male TSOs standing near the observation spot I vacated just moments ago, heads together. A sheriff's deputy joins them, no one making eye contact with me.

Meanwhile, the stalled line starts to fill up. No one's cutting under now. There are only three ID checkers, while two extra TSOs stand by, chatting. I realize the X-ray screeners are backed up and the ID checking has stopped because there is no room for people to move in the enclosed security area. But did it slow down because half of the TSOs are away from their posts and worried about me? I'm mortified. All of my insecurities as a life-long rule follower are making me feel guilty, even though I haven't done anything wrong, technically.

Now the original pair of TSOs who corralled me earlier, a baby-faced man who's probably in his thirties despite looking like a teenager and his early forties bun-rocking counterpart, join the group standing near my old observation spot. They appear to be talking about me; I feel their eyes flick my way now and again. I observe them alternating positions, arms behind their backs, then hands on their hips, then hands in their pockets. They seem casual and jokey, toothy smiles visible from twenty-five feet away. I'm glad they're having fun while I'm recovering from my mini coronary.

While the female agent takes a phone call, I continue to act calm, pretending I don't notice them noticing me still noticing them.

A few minutes later, the original pair of TSOs approach *again*.

"How long will you be?" asks "Baby Face," his doughy cheeks as red as mine feel.

"A few hours," I reply.

"Whoa!" they exclaim, in startling unison, showcasing nearly identical expressions of shock.

I laugh and then they laugh, and then we all chuckle as I joke about not wanting to get arrested or placed on the no-fly list. They say I aroused suspicion when passengers reported my notetaking activities to the ID checkers. *See something, say something, eh?* I re-explain my project and they both suggest I go downstairs to the check-in area instead.[2]

We chat a few moments longer, and I try to ingratiate myself enough to ask for an interview. When I ask once more if I can speak to a supervisor and request permission to observe, they both ignore me, suggesting yet again that I go to another area of the terminal. Although they are surprisingly pleasant, it's clear that I am absolutely not welcome here, even in a public area of the airport, next to a permanent seating area.

Rather than cause more of a scene, I leave the checkpoint, my mind racing with questions. First, I was not actually noticed by TSOs but by passengers who reported my *suspicious* notetaking. How well do officers pay attention to the area outside of their immediate purview?

Second, in the original confrontation, the bunned TSO said "they" wouldn't want me standing so close. Who are "they"? Obviously powers-that-be in the TSA, but even as an officer, she did not see herself in a group with power? Likewise, the TSOs would not consider allowing me to speak with higher-ups. Too much hassle? Fear of management? A cover-your-ass response because they hadn't been the first to notice me?

Third, the reaction to a seeming "threat" was immediate, but it was not aggressive. All of the TSOs who approached were respectful and not hostile. They could have demanded I leave at any time, but they didn't. I was offered assistance, not grilled about my activities. Had I not disclosed my project, would they have remained as relaxed? Undoubtedly I can thank my nonthreatening young, white, female body for their chill approach, but even still, I feel *so* uncomfortable. I can only imagine the response if I was a "suspicious" notetaking man or person of color.

This experience both confirms and complicates what I understand about "typical" TSA officers. On one hand, an unknown person without a ticket was able to hang out in a security line for twenty-five minutes without being noticed by an employee. That seems aligned with media portrayals of TSOs as either lazy or ineffective or both. But on the other hand, the interactions challenge some of the portrayals of TSOs as power-hungry authoritarians lording over their fiefdoms. These officers seem tentative, and they have very clearly distanced themselves from authority. I wonder if their demeanor has to do with the fact that I was not breaking a specific rule. Random student observers don't seem to be covered in their standard operating procedures. Maybe my presence evoked a "that does not compute" error message because there is no clear rule to follow?

All I know is that I *must* talk to some TSOs one-on-one. And I need to ditch my trusty notepad. Apparently pens and paper look *really* shady at the airport. I switch to emailing/texting/calling myself to record observations. For the following several years, no one will look twice if I appear completely absorbed by technology.

Formally talking to TSOs turns out to be much harder than I imagined. Although I chitchat with TSOs every time I fly—usually while they're patting me down or processing my belongings—getting any of them to agree to a formal interview seems impossible.

I create business cards noting my position as a doctoral candidate/ researcher and start handing them out around airports. I ask TSOs for interviews when I see them hanging around in the terminal, taking the parking lot shuttle, or on break in airport eateries. Because of my research ethics requirements—namely, not interrupting security protocol (again)—I avoid inquiring during security screenings because I do not want to distract officers or delay service at checkpoints. But I talk to them every other chance I get. So I'm annoyed, surprised, and worried when my efforts net *zero* interviews.

But after making contact with one TSO in a large Southern California airport, I think I've finally struck gold.

I meet "Sally" during a routine pat-down. I first see her checking tickets and IDs at the head of a slow-moving line. She stands out because she looks miserable. Short, white, and wrinkly, she has graying dark hair slicked back into a tight tail. I imagine that many of her wrinkles have come from scowling when passengers don't move fast enough or don't have their IDs ready. She hollers, "Look at the line and move forward already!" to an unfortunate soul ahead of me, who startles at her imperious tone. Impatient passenger that I am, I was thinking the same thing, but coming from a cranky-looking TSO, the command seems especially harsh.

A few minutes later, Sally moves from the document checking station into the checkpoint. I watch her stomping around, a red watch positioned over blue gloves, her hands opening and closing at her sides in a gesture that exudes impatience. She trudges from line to line, shifting bins, telling passengers what to remove from their pockets, ostensibly "helping" people through the line. "Gruff" doesn't begin to cover it. She doesn't yell, but her puckered face, sallow complexion, and sour tone intimidate, even though she can't be more than five feet tall.

Meanwhile, I step up to hand my documents to a forty-something TSO with eyes that peer through thick, dark frames. He studiously contemplates my license, glancing back and forth from boarding pass to license, slowly pronouncing my full name—Shawna Kristine Louise Malvini Redden—lingering over the syllables before pointing out that my license expires in four years. I nod, discomfited.

He analyzes my license *again* for a long moment and says, "Your smile is prettier in person."

As he speaks, his eyes bore into mine. My skin is crawling by the time he hands back my documents, his fingers purposely brushing mine. I feel his gaze linger as I walk into the checkpoint and I worry for a minute that the creepster was memorizing my address. *So grateful I'm not a local.*

While I wait to put my carry-ons on the conveyor belt, a tall male TSO comes out from behind the advanced imaging machine and bellows at the younger officer directing traffic. "Pockets, Garcia, pockets! Every one of them had something in their pockets." His voice oozes annoyance at young Garcia, who rolls his eyes in turn. Every time someone steps into the machine with something in their pocket, the whole screening process has to stop. No wonder the lines are moving like molasses today.

I ask to opt out of the advanced imaging. Garcia tells me the scanner is not an X-ray machine, that unlike most major airports (he names a few), this one uses radio waves, not radiation. I smile, nod, and say thank-you for the information but remain committed to opting out. Sometimes I argue, but I was not in the mood after my creeptastic interaction earlier. In fact, I'm startled by all of the TSO caricatures today—the gruff and intimidating TSO, the potential sexual predator, the apparently gives-no-shits loafer Garcia, who parrots TSA talking points without doing his actual job.

Awaiting my pat-down, I watch my purse and laptop go through screening and languish unattended. I look up to see Sally, the grumpy TSO, stalking toward me with an intense glare. Of course. Asking if I have any metal or a belt on me (no and no), she allows me through the side gate and asks me to point out my things. She grabs them and we walk over to a screening area downstream from the checkpoint.

Sally invites me to sit while she puts on new gloves and tests them for residue of explosives prior to beginning my pat-down. I've only had one other TSO pretest gloves, ostensibly to check for a false positive before starting the screening. She gave me a horrendously invasive pat-down, so I feel a pang of worry.

Happily, the nerves were unnecessary. As she starts, Sally compliments the intricate *mehndi*, or henna tattoos, on my left hand. I share how that I attended my best friend's Indian wedding over the weekend and that many of the women had mehndi inked on their left hands in a tradition that wishes good health and prosperity for the bride.

We speak of the rituals involved in an Indian wedding and how elaborate they are compared to American celebrations. She gasps when I mention that the priest required a litany of items for the ceremony, including mangos, coconuts, rice, barley, butter, and cash, and how everything had special symbolic meaning. Sally shares that her daughter is dating an Egyptian man who wants to get married and she wonders about Egyptian wedding customs. I'm startled when she admits surprise at his interest in her daughter, whom she describes as not conventionally pretty, carrying extra weight, and the mother of a hostile tween daughter.

"My granddaughter hates the guy," she says.

"Don't twelve-year-olds hate everyone?" I ask with a smile. Sally chuckles, agreeing enthusiastically.

I realize in talking to Sally that she does not display a lot of emotion through her face but acts friendly enough overall. In that few minutes, we share some laughs and pieces of ourselves, adding a little buoyancy to our days, which definitely helps me erase some of the earlier unease. I wonder how many people stereotype her as unfriendly, like I did initially, but do not get a chance to change their opinion because they are too afraid or uncomfortable to talk to her.

An hour later, I'm halfway through a burrito when I see Sally enter the food court with a coworker who's even crankier looking and shorter than she is. I'm embarrassed when I realize that in my earlier observations, I had thought they were the same person. The shorter woman was actually the one who hollered, stomped, and acted so frustrated with passengers.

I watch as the women approach a burger joint. A sign on the register says "cash only." Sally apparently has none, so her friend offers to buy her a cheeseburger. Sally sits while her friend, whose gravelly, harsh voice reminds me of Roz from *Monsters, Inc.*, orders.

While "Roz" buys lunch, Sally calls to her, "Are you on break?" (I presume she is asking whether Roz is "on break," as opposed to "on lunch," to find out how much time they have.)

"*Yes*, I'm on break," Roz snaps, gathering packets of ketchup.

"Don't bite my head off," Sally replies, jovially. "I'll smack ya."

"I'm leaving in five days, anyway," Roz says.

"Don't rub it in my face. Then I'll really smack ya," Sally retorts.

For vacation? For another job? I'm so curious!

Despite Roz's sharpness, the exchange between the two flows with the familiar banter of good friends. As they eat, Sally pulls out a tablet—bigger than an iPhone but smaller than an iPad and starts scrolling while Roz watches, mildly curious.

"Everyone's on Facebook," Sally says. "You gotta go on there."

Roz demurs, explaining how she doesn't care what everyone is doing every second of the damn day. I can practically hear the unspoken "kids these days" critique. Sally admits she likes to spy on people, especially her granddaughter.

After a bit, Sally and Roz start talking about heading back to work. I wolf down the rest of the burrito I've been ignoring while typing field notes and psych myself up to approach their table. Despite my pleasant rapport with Sally in the terminal, Roz's presence fills me with nerves. I'm not normally one to interrupt people or talk to strangers without a good reason. But I suck it up, gather my things, and march over as they stand to leave. I introduce myself, hand Sally a business card, and explain that I'd love to interview her about her work. I tell her she can contact me any time at her convenience.

"About the TSA?" Sally asks, at first surprised and now shrinking back, our friendly exchange earlier apparently forgotten. She seems to withdraw— not quite afraid, but definitely wanting to put distance between us.

I confirm, feeling like one of those clipboard-holding canvassers, only instead of harassing people to sign a Greenpeace petition, I'm pleading with them to help save my research.

"I'll have to ask my supervisor," Sally replies, her palms out in a "stop" gesture, as if to deter me.

"Of course. No problem," I say, reiterating that I want to speak with her about interactions with passengers, not about her job duties specifically. Not about anything secret that could get her into trouble. I'll find later that a lot of TSOs assume I'm a reporter trying to do an expose on the TSA.

She seems a bit shocked that I'm interested in her, and now she moves away from me as quickly as possible. Roz, meanwhile, stares at me with a smirk on her face. I know Sally probably won't contact me, but her nervousness seems noteworthy.

"I'll have to ask my supervisor" is a refrain I'll hear repeatedly as the years go on. Most are phrases used to blow me off, but every so often a TSO will actually consider my interview request. And I encourage them to ask permission, offering to speak with supervisors and provide documentation about my project. I may be undercover in observation mode, but I'm not running a fully covert operation. Still, no one agrees to speak with me.

I start to feel desperate—I've got a dissertation to finish after all. I've already written to two major airports in two states requesting formal permission to interview and observe. Both requests go unanswered. I sign up to volunteer at one airport and that doesn't work out. I even apply for a TSO position at my home airport. The application process is extensive and I meet all of the basic conditions—I'm a U.S. citizen of appropriate age with no drug or health problems, no criminal history, no defaulted debt, fluent in English, and with a high school diploma. In the ten-phase hiring process, I stall out at phase three, according to the online application tracker, and never get a call. The tacit rejection rankles.

Worrying that no TSOs will ever talk to me and my research will fail, I take to social media: Do I know anyone who knows any TSOs? And it turns out I do. A college friend works at a preschool where one of the dads happens to be a TSO. And he agrees to an interview.

I am psyched.

The day of the interview arrives and I'm a five-foot-eight bag of nerves. I drive to the TSO's house—a modest two-story wedged in between two other houses, small lawns littered with leaves, on a street packed with cars. It's near the freeway and along the airport's flight path; I hear jets overhead constantly.

I'm meeting with "Skeet," who describes himself as a federal officer who's "about thirty" and Caucasian. He directs me to a comfortably lumpy sectional in an entryway alcove covered with the detritus of small children—toys, crayon artwork, miniature shoes. I move a pink fuzzy blanket aside and take a seat across from him, setting my digital recorders (one primary, one spare) between us.

A military veteran, Skeet depicts his four years with the TSA as a continuation of his eight years of service. His work day starts at 4:00 a.m. with a team briefing about world and regional events related to air security, as well as any local and national policy updates.

His appearance and demeanor remind me of Neal Gamby, Danny McBride's sweater vest–wearing, whistleblowing, disciplinarian character on the HBO comedy *Vice Principals*. Gruff but a little goofy, they both seem to take themselves and their jobs very seriously.

Shuddering at the thought of his 2:00 a.m. wake-up, I ask, "What does it feel like to work at the airport?"

"At first it's . . . I want to say glamorous, because that's the first word that popped into my head," Skeet says. "But it's not really glamorous. It's like, 'This is all new and exciting.'"

I think of the early days at a new job and imagine working at the airport must be nerve-wracking but fun in the beginning.

"[But] I thought the TSA had more power," Skeet admits. "When I was going through airports [as a passenger], I was a little more [frightened] of TSOs. They have a badge, and they're in uniform just like a lot of cops. I guess [I had] the whole mindset of, 'Hey, the cops are out to get us' type of a thing and TSOs must be too. And then after I started working, I realized they don't have as much power as I thought."

The impression of TSOs being all-powerful will be echoed repeatedly in my research by passengers who seem afraid of getting things wrong and having TSOs punish them.

Skeet goes on to discuss how being a TSO isn't about getting passengers in trouble, but rather helping them through security while enforcing rules that are out of his control.

In my subsequent interviews, I'll hear nearly every TSO lament "the rules" and how they can be constraining, especially in the hands of the micromanagers above them.

When I ask about having to implement rules, I expect stories of frustration, but Skeet laughs. "The madder people get, the more fun we [have]."

"What do you mean by that?" I probe, chuckling a little in surprise.

"Have you ever been to McDonald's at 10:01?" Skeet asks.

"When they close?"

"No. Ten o'clock in the morning when they've stopped serving breakfast," Skeet clarifies. Our conversation is taking place before McDonald's changed its forty-three-year tradition of only serving breakfast until 10:00 a.m. sharp. "You go in there and say, 'I'm ready for breakfast.' Then they are like, 'I'm sorry. It's 10:01. We don't serve breakfast anymore.' You get so upset, 'But, it's *one* minute after!'"

I'm now cracking up as I remember arriving minutes late for an Egg McMuffin and feeling hateful and hangry at employees who would not make an exception.

"Think of that related to somebody bringing a water bottle. 'Well, it's just water,' they say. Well, I understand, but we have a policy we have to live by, just like they have a policy that they have to live by." *Ah yes. Rules are rules.* "People get furious at this policy," Skeet says, laughing. "And we're calm, just repeating 'I'm sorry. You can't do this. You can't bring this.' If they're getting upset, then we can give them options of what they can do, not just for the water, for anything," he notes, referring to the standard TSA options for nonthreatening contraband—take the item back to the car, put it in checked luggage, and so on.

"They may blurt out something that they may not have wanted to say at that moment," Skeet continues, euphemistically describing when grown-ass adults throw full temper tantrums over bottles of water and oversized shampoo. "We're calm, and they're completely irate. That infuriates them too!"

And here Skeet starts to get at the crux of my research—how do people express and control (or not) their emotions in security? Although I'm appalled at the idea of people throwing fits and verbally abusing TSOs over trivial toiletries, I also know the intense frustration of having personal property confiscated and feeling powerless in the face of seemingly nonsensical rules.

While Skeet snickers, I ask how he feels when passengers lose it.

"There are times I feel calm and act calm. I know they're yelling at me, but it's not me. Personally, *I* am not telling them they cannot have this particular thing. I'm there to enforce the rules, not to make the rules," he says. "They can yell at me all they want to. Normally, when somebody's yelling at me, that brings attention to where I am standing," Skeet remarks, explaining how his coworkers have his back. "If it escalates, the supervisor will come over or law enforcement will come."

In emphasizing the ability to keep calm during abuse, Skeet is describing *emotional labor*, a term coined by sociologist Arlie Hochschild in the 1980s to describe how service workers control the expression of their emotions at work. Hochschild studied how employees manage complex "feeling rules"— for example, flight attendants swallowing their annoyance and keeping a friendly attitude in front of rude passengers, and bill collectors remaining neutral when debtors cry or scream at them. Emotional labor—especially the kind that requires difficult emotional suppression or simulation, such as pretending to feel one way while actually feeling another—is associated with stress, burnout, and even negative health consequences such as increased blood pressure.[3]

Then Skeet's description of emotional labor starts to take a strange turn. Describing circumstances where passengers go off the rails, Skeet says, "I don't really have to say anything anymore. Now I'm completely calm, and they're still irate. I'm standing there, like, 'Ha ha!' Not really 'ha ha,' but I'm smiling. You've heard the phrase 'killing with kindness'? I'm smiling, being kind in a totally snotty way."

The passive-aggressive part of me appreciates this perspective. As later TSOs will tell me, they have to keep calm in the face of bad behavior— passengers yelling, throwing personal effects, criticizing them personally—so as not to lose their jobs. TSO "Jeff" recalled his experience of having a passenger flip out over the confiscation of his cologne. "They said it was too bad that my mom didn't abort me when she had a chance. She must be really pissed off about that today, because of what I do for a job." Jeff recounted this memory without emotion, like it was a run-of-the-mill experience. I struggle to imagine ever saying something so horrible to anyone, let alone a stranger just doing his job.

Skeet's "being kind in a totally snotty way" seems like a decent approach to keeping sane in the conditions that many TSOs face on a regular basis. And it fits with their training—to be "calm, cool, and collected" in all situations and to communicate "a commanding presence" so as to keep passengers in line.[4] But it also feels a touch sinister, especially when Skeet admits "messing with" passengers on occasion.

"I pass the time by joking around with people," Skeet says, describing playing innocent games of "Simon Says" with passengers as they finish screenings. "I'll stand there with my hands up, not saying a word." He mimes making an A-shape over his head. "And they'll stop in front of me and do the same thing."

I'm picturing what that must look like. A passenger and an officer in the middle of the checkpoint, facing each other with their arms in the iconic "YMCA" dance pose.

"I'm not saying a word. . . . At first, they think, 'What's going on? I must do this.' Once they figure out what's happening, it puts a smile on their face," Skeet says, inadvertently illustrating one of my great concerns: that in the face of authority, some people automatically comply with the guy in uniform, even if the directions seem goofy. "And there are even other times where I have to take something away from somebody. Somebody will say something [rude] . . . so I make it fun for myself." It sounds like Skeet wants to punish them. He clarifies, "When somebody is extremely rude or gives me an attitude, I'll take my time."

I ask Skeet for an example and he describes a time when a passenger got upset about being detained for a secondary screening.

"And so I started to do my screening and he continued to give me an attitude. [So I said,] 'Well, I'm sorry, I need to start over.' So now I started over with what I had to do," Skeet explains, in this case describing a pat-down. "And then he proceeded to give me an attitude again. [So I say,] 'Well, I need to . . . darn it. Short-term memory loss . . . I have to start over again.'

"After a little while of him realizing that, okay, I was going to do what I had to do, and it wasn't going to change—his attitude wasn't going to change what I had to do—he calmed down. He legitimately calmed down to where we had a short conversation on where he was going, how he was doing that day, why was he going there. His demeanor changed completely from a negative to a positive.

"Then, after we got done, I had to do a little more screening of his personal property—he forgot to take his laptop out of his bag. . . . And then he started to go negative again. I informed him of what he did wrong and he told me that there should be signs in place to tell him. I informed him that there were, but they were on the other side of the checkpoint. I asked him, 'Do you want me to show you?' For some reason, this guy said yes."

Smirking, Skeet goes on to explain how he waited for the passenger to pack up and put on shoes, and then he escorted the man outside of the checkpoint to see the signs that explain security rules. Afterward, the passenger tried to follow Skeet back into the checkpoint via the employee entrance.

"Then I inform him that he can't do that—he had to go back through [security]. Of course that didn't help his situation." Chortling, Skeet crows, "I removed myself from the situation so that he [couldn't] go through the screening with me. He was not happy, but I got a little laugh out of it."

As a researcher, I try to stay neutral, no matter what interviewees tell me, but I can hardly control my face in reaction to this story. And while I admit, the evil part of me finds the scenario pretty funny—jerks deserve to be punished!—this passenger didn't seem like a jerk. He seemed like any one of us who would be annoyed to be stopped and subjected to additional and then long, drawn-out, perhaps unnecessary screenings. The organizational researcher in me is completely appalled, and I feel so much empathy for the passenger. To get all the way through security, with a pat-down and bag search, only to be tricked into having to do it all again? And for what? A trivial mistake and poor attitude?

I'm immediately reminded of a conversation with "Robert," a passenger who harbored extreme skepticism toward the TSA. A frequent traveler, Robert discussed feeling tremendous discomfort with the seemingly arbitrary power of TSOs.

"These people don't want to be there. One of them could just not like the looks of me and really make my life complicated in a bad way. . . . It's a very unsettling situation," Robert said. With resignation, Robert described feeling constrained, like his only choice is to deal with the discomfort or not fly, which is not reasonable given his travel-loving lifestyle.

A TSO actively bullies a passenger, punishing him for showing "attitude" and making a very common mistake like not taking his laptop out of his bag? It's Robert's nightmare come to life.

Although we have a pleasant enough conversation and I learn a great deal, I leave Skeet's house feeling conflicted. Will future interviews confirm more TSO stereotypes? Do all TSOs devolve into messing with passengers after years of dealing with rude behavior? Why do some TSOs overreact to mild rudeness and others take horrendous abuse without complaint?

I continue the quest to talk with more TSOs.

And yet again I come up nearly empty. I speak with Skeet in early spring, and *months* go by with only a couple of interviews, even though I am flying around the country passing out business cards and pleading with acquaintances to share their TSA connections.

As I stare down the remaining months before my dissertation is due, my anxiety skyrockets. Will I spend hundreds of hours researching and thousands of dollars traveling, only to fail? Thankfully, no.

I get a wave of inspiration and start hunting online. I search for online TSO groups and discussion boards—there are a few, but no moderators respond to my requests to post messages about my study. So I take to LinkedIn, joining two TSA professional groups and posting my recruitment message to the forums: I'm a graduate student looking to speak with TSOs about their work.

Most of my messages get ignored, but one TSO responds, warning his fellow officers against talking to me. Like many (foolish) young people, I do not have a professional headshot for my LinkedIn profile. Rather, I've used a somewhat sultry black-and-white image from my engagement photoshoot, where I'm standing in a field looking over one shoulder, staring soulfully into the camera. The TSO calls bullshit and says no one with this kind of "glamour shot" could really be a researcher.

After immediately changing my profile picture, I reply, confirming my nerd identity. Then I start messaging TSOs directly. I'll end up spending hundreds of dollars for the privilege since LinkedIn only allows a few free direct messages per month. But since this expenditure will end up saving my dissertation, I don't complain too much.

Most of the more than one hundred people I message ignore me. Some reply back saying they are prohibited from participating without explicit permission from supervisors. Many express skepticism about my intentions. Like Sally, several seem scared of me and worried about how my project might impact their livelihood if they were to consent to an interview. I start to overemphasize the confidential aspect of the interview process.

Luckily, a few TSOs start talking. Most interviews take place over the phone, at all hours, at the TSOs' convenience. I speak with officers around the country, including "Rick," a screening manager from Chicago who seems both really into his job and really burned out; "Neecie," from the South, who appreciates helping "little old lady" passengers but gets fed up with management bossing TSOs around all day; "Ty," from the Southwest, who gives off distinct conspiracy theory vibes; "Alexa," a young mother from California, who confesses that she is tired of "putting up with passengers' shit" all day; and "Greg," a behavior detection officer, who will not disclose his specific location but tells me it's a large metropolitan area with one of the ten busiest airports in the world. My favorite interview takes places near home, at an ice cream parlor with "Roger," a TSO who will eventually start giving me gifts of homemade sweets.

In addition to many questions about emotions at work and what the job is like overall, I ask most TSOs variations of the question "How do you survive this job?"

"Jonathan," a Pacific Islander in his midthirties, doesn't paint a pretty picture. "Tens of thousands of people transit through my airport. I have to touch them and their stuff. A huge percentage of people are disgusting—dirty, smelly, with absolutely no concept of personal hygiene."

Yuck, I think. I regularly ruminate on the social aspects of the airport, but the physically dirty part? That's a whole other level of no-thank-you.

"It's also frustrating to watch proof time and time again of people's complete disregard for others' welfare . . . the total lack of simple courtesy and respect for other people," Jonathan adds.

Listening to Jonathan, I realize that the occupation of a TSO qualifies as *dirty work*—a scholarly term for work that society considers dirty or tainted. Work can become stigmatized in multiple ways—by being physically dirty, by involving contact with socially undesirable groups, by requiring morally questionable activities, or by entailing objectionable emotional labor.[5] In other words, most of what it means to be a TSO.

Why would you choose a job where you are surrounded by thousands of mostly rude and apparently gross people who don't like you, day in and day out? As many TSOs will tell me, the answer is: "To put food on the table." And, as unskilled work goes, the pay and benefits are great.[6]

"Cat," from Las Vegas, recalls how she got involved with the TSA: "Well, 9/11 happened and I was working in a casino that was going downhill. Some other coworkers at the casino were talking about [airport security]. It was a government job. At that time, it wasn't government, but they were going to roll it into a government job and were going to do massive hiring."[7]

Cat continues, "I really, really, really wanted the job. I was getting to be forty-five years old and I thought, 'Wow, this'll be a great opportunity for me.' I really didn't have much of an idea what it'd be like. I just thought, 'I'm just going to try to get the job, and try my best and do my best.' I was hoping, actually, to get into the government and be able to transfer, because up in Boulder City there's a lot of government jobs."

This is another familiar refrain. Many of the TSOs I meet say they hoped that the TSA would be a stepping stone to other types of government work or more advanced security positions.

"But I found out later it doesn't work like that," Cat says, with a gravelly resigned laugh. "So that was kind of a letdown."

"So, do you like it then?" I ask.

"I enjoy it because you see people from everywhere. I like that you do different things all day, you rotate from this job to that job," Cat explains, referencing how TSOs generally spend thirty minutes at a time at various checkpoint positions (see appendix for details about TSO roles). "It's an okay job. If you get irate people, then it's a little stressful," she continues before pausing. "Sometimes it can be boring. . . . It's a real monotonous job. It's real mundane. You know what I mean?"

I don't really know what she means, but I believe it. I think about the mind-numbing tasks in my life—grading, filing papers, meetings that should be emails—but I'm very lucky. Nothing comes close to the nonstop repetition of TSO work. Especially for positions without a high difficulty level like giving instructions about shoe removal or monitoring the exit, I can't even wrap my mind around the boredom quotient.

And while I've become empathetic as a researcher who's gotten to know several TSOs, many passengers are more than a little judgmental about TSA work: "When I think of a TSA agent, it's someone that's, like, hard. Like their exterior is hard. . . . There's only been, like, a handful of people that have been more happy," reflects "Rachel," a casual flier who travels regularly for vacations and to visit family. I spoke with Rachel during an early phase of my airport research, when I wanted to understand what going through the airport is like for passengers and how they contend with the pressure to manage their emotions.

"[They're] like emotionless, kind of [like] robots because they're always saying the same thing over and over again, like, 'Can I see your ID?' or, 'Please roll your bags on the conveyor belt,' 'Take off your jacket,' 'Take off your shoes.' So it's kind of like a robotic response to their workplace," Rachel says.

Many passengers I meet describe TSOs as machines, and make assumptions—not much different from my initial judgment of Sally—about the relationship between what TSOs express emotionally and their attitudes or abilities. Neutral apparently equals robotic to some people. And while TSOs are specifically trained to mask emotions, portray neutral expressions, and act intimidating, passengers criticize them for it.

"You hear stories all the time about TSA officers falling asleep while they're supposed to be on duty, of them letting people through that they're not supposed to let through, of them just not doing their job," says "Alice," a frequent business traveler. "You have these agents who probably aren't very well trained. They probably aren't getting paid very much. They probably don't necessarily believe in the mission of the TSA and are kind of just viewing it as a job. They don't really care."

"Some of them couldn't get a job at McDonald's," says "Dirk," an IT engineer who flies several times a year, usually for business. Comparing TSOs to security guards, Dirk adds, "Security guards are generally people that really want to be in positions of authority and cannot pass the psychological interviews and cannot pass the intellectual exams or cannot pass the physical to actually become a law enforcement officer."

But despite Dirk's derision, Alice's skepticism about competency, and Rachel's condemnation of robotic behavior, all of them discussed readily complying with TSO directives, tolerating TSO attitudes, and submitting to screening that made them uncomfortable, largely without questioning the protocols.

One of my quests was to understand why some people comply with security screenings and defer to authority automatically, while others comply but inflict abuse on TSOs or act entitled. What informs people's perceptions of the TSA and its officers?

One influence is characterizations of the TSA in the popular press. And the reviews aren't great. Much of the news coverage about TSOs aligns with Rachel's, Alice's, and Dirk's descriptions, or worse. In media portrayals, TSOs are often cast as incompetent, thieving, deviant, brutish oafs. Many vilifications represent officers as ludicrously controlling, depraved, and concerned with illogical procedures—patting down infants without parental consent, breaking ostomy bags, hassling people with disabilities, and confiscating cupcakes (apparently frosting counts as a gel in some airports).

TSO Jonathan referenced being aware of these representations, saying, "I do not like the public image we have." And while the negative media accounts did not really resonate with TSOs' personal experiences at work, they certainly framed the TSOs' interactions with passengers. In fact, many TSOs I spoke with presumed that passengers gave the TSA a "bad rap" in large part because of the media. But the situation is a little more complex.

In my observations, TSOs rarely lived up to the most outrageous or scathing media or passenger representations. But while TSOs complained about feeling limited in their power and constrained by rules they did not create, some, like Skeet, took liberties to exercise their control when possible. I watched TSOs try to coerce passengers into complying with advanced imaging or berate passengers who got security procedures wrong. TSO Alexa, for instance, described times when she enforced her authority with passengers she didn't like by saying, "My house, my rules." However, TSO "Carrie" lambasted this type of colleague for lording over their "little fiefdoms" and exerting undue control over passengers and subordinates.

All of these forms of discourse—personal depictions of TSOs messing with passengers or acting mean, organizational rules and training that limit TSOs' ability to show any emotion beyond neutrality or intimidation, and societal conversations that portray TSOs almost exclusively in a negative light—come together to construct the Stereotypical TSO, a prominent category in my research. I use the term *Stereotypical* to capture the descriptions of TSOs I heard from passengers, read in the media, and learned about in my travels and interviews. Stereotypical constructions don't represent the typical or average TSO, but rather how the average traveler or media story might represent TSOs.

In my research, I noticed two distinct types of Stereotypical TSO: the Apathetic robot type that Dirk, Rachel, and Alice described and the Tyrannical type, like Skeet messing with passengers and the TSOs who run "fiefdoms," as TSO Carrie claimed. But these Stereotypical images, especially if drawn from a single source such as disgruntled passengers or judgmental media, can be limiting and inaccurate. They also conflict greatly with how TSOs describe themselves, as I'll discuss throughout this book.

So where do these Stereotypical images originate? Many emerge from the interactions between TSOs and passengers, especially passengers who act in stereotypically inexperienced or hostile ways.

Pro Travel Tip #3:

"Robots" Have Feelings Too

Guilty of thinking about TSOs as robots or machines? Be careful not to treat them that way. Communication research shows that passengers, especially those without a lot of travel experience, "read" TSOs to know how to behave in security. If a TSO smiles and greets you, you're likely to smile and greet them back. If a TSO snaps at you or shows no emotion, it's easier to express negative or dismissive emotions back.

So what's the problem? Just because a TSO (or anyone!) does not show their feelings, it doesn't mean they aren't experiencing emotions. And treating TSOs like machines—dehumanizing them—can have negative consequences. For TSOs, dealing with passenger negativity can require simulating calm and suppressing negative emotions. And guess what? Suppressing negative emotions makes the experience of those feelings even more intense. Over the long term—for TSOs who deal with passengers all day long—emotional suppression can trigger a rise in stress hormones and generate adverse cardiovascular and immune functions.

What's more, emotions can be contagious. So while you might think "So what? It's the TSA's problem for training their workers to act like robots or jerks," negative emotions can create cycles in the airport that affect passengers too.[8] Have a tussle with a TSO in security? What's the first thing you'll do? Complain about it to travel companions or on social media, more than likely. You've just shared that negative experience with many others. And what about the folks who watched your negative interaction? They're linked into the cycle now too.

When these emotion cycles spin off, they can morph and escalate. It's not hard to imagine negative feelings starting in security and flying through the airport and onto your flight, making travel more exhausting and difficult than it is already.

3

Fear and Loathing in Airport Security

On Stereotypical Passengers

May 2, 2012.

I thought I knew frequent flying. During my first two years of doctoral study, I lived in Arizona and flew home to Sacramento every other week. The airport felt like home. I knew the staff on my routes. I could recite the in-flight safety briefing by heart. But now in my third year the situation has flip-flopped. I'm living at home and flying to Arizona every week to teach a night class.

For the last nine months, I've spent nearly every Wednesday waking in the ugly predawn hours to catch the first flight to Phoenix. Up at 3:30 or 4:00 a.m., through security by 5:00, and in the sky before the sun starts rising. I'd take the last flight home around 9:00 or 10:00 p.m. But today, my last official Wednesday of the school year, I'm taking it easy with a midmorning flight. As I'll catch the last flight plane in twelve hours, it makes for a relatively short travel day for me.

It's strange to arrive at the airport during daylight hours, and right away I recognize the benefit of my usual early-bird flying: parking. My favorite level of the garage is packed full and I have to scour the remaining floors until I find a space. Of course, I'm more than an hour early for my flight, so I stifle irrational flickers of anxiety from my past life as a nervous traveler.

Once in the terminal, I just miss the train to the security checkpoint. I wait for the next tram, standing in front of the farthest-most door—the one that opens closest to the security checkpoint. I stay slightly to the right of the white metal doors to make room for the passengers who inevitably get off on the wrong side of the tram.

As the train pulls up, a fruity-smelling woman with long, multicolored locks rushes up, cutting me off. Her scent suggests she's taken a bath in vanilla passion fruit body spritz. Her brightly patterned bags trail in her wake, blocking my access to the door. For a moment I feel irritation spike, but then I school myself: I am not in a hurry. It's fine. There's room for everyone. I still glower in her general direction, but she's not paying one bit of attention to me.

After the sixty-second train ride, I immediately head over to the Flyby priority security lane, for passengers like me who fly way too much. As I walk, I notice how different the light looks at this time of day. Typically, I see the predawn terminal brightened with harsh artificial rays. The natural light streaming through the overhead windows is soothing.

While I am wondering about the lighting, the cloyingly fragrant woman appears out of nowhere to cut me off *again*. A frisson of energy surrounds her as she shuffle-runs in fuzzy slippers, beating me to the priority lane. Her breath comes in ragged gasps as she guzzles from an icy bottle of Smartwater, the condensation a clue to its recent purchase. Her small eyes dart from side to side as she joins her husband in line.

I can't help but think that stopping for water when you're obviously late seems like poor form. I watch as the woman I've mentally named "Suzanne" spits orders at her husband "Ronny" as she rearranges her many belongings.

Poring through a leopard-and-pink Betsey Johnson travel bag, Suzanne pulls out an iPad in a Louis Vuitton case, a small can of luxury hairspray, and a bottle of fruit and floral lotion. She shoves the iPad toward Ronny and commands him to retrieve her boarding pass.

Meanwhile, the line barely moves.

Every couple of minutes Suzanne asks, "Do you think we're gonna make it?"

Ronny remarks, "I'm glad we chose this line since it's shorter."

They have no idea that it's a special lane for frequent fliers, and to my chagrin the TSA agents do not inform them.

No less than four times, Suzanne queries the TSOs nearest us.

"Are these liquids and gels okay?"

A blank-faced female TSO replies, "If they are less than 3.4 ounces."

Suzanne: "Does my iPad need to come out?"

A stony-faced thirty-something TSO: "No."

Suzanne: "My laptop?"

TSO, sighing: "Yes."

Suzanne: "I have to take my shoes off, right?"

TSO, in passing: "Yes."

Before they reach the ID checker, a male TSO walking along the line says, "You can't take that" in reference to the Smartwater.

Suzanne blurts "I know, we're drinking it!" before taking another giant gulp.

At the same time, a female voice whose owner I cannot see says, "You can drink it out there, though."

Suzanne keeps chugging.

The nervousness buzzing off of Suzanne is comical. Her squinty blue eyes, painted in shimmery pink eyeshadow and blue mascara, stretch wide as she continues to blink left and right, putting me in mind of a vintage Kit-Cat Klock. She bounces and hops to see around the line, as if that will make it move faster. Ronny must have told her to calm down because she snaps, "I *am* trying to relax!"

To be fair, the line is extra slow today, something I attribute to the infrequent fliers and the reduced number of open checkpoint lanes.

When Ronny walks ten steps away to toss the Smartwater before they get to the ID checker, Suzanne doesn't know where he's gone. She screams (yes, screams), "Ronny!! Ronny Where are you?!" as if they are lost in the wilderness. Before I can respond, a female TSO explains that he went to throw away the water. Suzanne heaves her ample chest as if her heart might thump right out of it.

Suzanne is covered in brightly colored tattoos across her arms, neck, hands, and chest. But when she speaks to the TSOs, she uses a small, quiet voice, which seems a stark contrast to her colorful persona and the way she snipes at Ronny. After they get their documents scanned, I watch her long, hot pink wave of hair swing as she walks into the checkpoint.

Meanwhile, the TSO checking IDs tells me to have a nice day, and I return the suggestion. A familiar manager walks past, surveying the line. I catch his eye and we both smile. I notice that across the security area, none of the TSOs are smiling. They wear worn looks, tight lips, blank eyes. Of course, at 9:30 a.m., they are now five or six hours into their shifts, and perhaps they are in their equivalent of a late afternoon slump.

The security lines move like molasses compared to the ones at 5:00 a.m. Every element of the journey slinks on at a sloth's pace, but passengers don't seem to be dragging. I do notice that most of the travelers seem casually dressed compared to the power travelers I usually run with.

Finally inside the security checkpoint, in my typical left-most line, I notice a usually pleasant, white-haired TSO whose face looks pinched and annoyed. When I see he is counseling Ronny and Suzanne before the screening, I think I know why.

As they load luggage for X-ray screening, Suzanne and Ronny keep looking at their boarding passes and craning to see through the security line into the terminal. As I get closer, I hear them discussing further whether they can "make it." The TSO admonishes them for being so late, asking Ronny repeatedly, "Why?"

Their flight must be imminent because Suzanne starts literally jumping up and down now. She runs long, acrylic-nailed hands through her hair, huffing, and runs toward the advanced imaging machine, even though it's only a few feet from where she was just standing. In contrast, although he is as late as Suzanne, Ronny remains outwardly calm.

When Suzanne gets into the scanner, she's carrying her boarding pass—a no-no. But the TSOs don't tell her to put it through the X-ray baggage scanner, so she shoves it into her cleavage before hoisting her bejeweled arms over her head. Of course, she is pulled to the side for additional screening, which amplifies her anxiety immediately. Ronny holds his hands straight up into the air as if cops have just yelled "Freeze!" as he passes through the scanner. When finally they are free, Ronny and Suzanne scuttle toward their gate and I can't help but chuckle.

Of course they don't make it.

With their every bounce, blink, huff, and sigh, Ronny and Suzanne exemplify the largest group of passengers at airports—Stereotypically Inexperienced travelers. While it may be hard to believe for those of us who travel regularly, only about half of the U.S. population flies in a given year. And on average they fly fewer than two round trips each. Because flying is not a frequent activity for most people, it tends to be an emotional experience—fraught with uncertainty and anxiety.

In my preliminary research about airports, I focused on the emotional experience of travel and what it feels like to be an airline passenger. The people I spoke with, from once-in-a-decade fliers to twice-weekly sky warriors, described the highs and lows of air travel. Everyone agreed: airport visits are almost always somewhat stressful. And depending on the reason for flying, they might be sad or demanding too. But folks also described the thrill of flight itself, the excitement of traveling to a new place, the anticipation of seeing loved ones, and the amusement of airport people watching.

It's no surprise, though, that feelings about airport security were almost exclusively negative, especially for folks who do not fly a lot and *because of* folks who do not fly a lot. For instance, passenger "Tex" reflected on the most taxing elements of air travel:

"I think one of the most challenging aspects is the fact that the travel itself is simple, but that the procedures and process add complexity, and often other travelers' feelings and opinions of that process further complicate things. But in the end, it's all about safety, and I personally haven't had any serious experiences with the TSA that have caused me to change my opinion of the process or to worry about it. But I know other passengers have these perceptions, which will cause them to try to hurry through and forget things, or to be frustrated when they are selected for additional screening, or whatever else might happen. And that usually equates to delays and increased frustration for everyone else in the line behind them."

By "perceptions," Tex means the complex mix of feelings passengers have about the TSA: that the TSA is a constitutional affront or security theater. That security is a race to get through as quickly as possible. That security is no big deal. That security is vitally important. That TSOs are scary beacons of authority with the power to bring pain. That TSOs are power-hungry peons with little actual influence.

"Then, on top of that, you have the human factor, where people just don't pay attention to how their actions impact others, and they cause further delays by not following instructions," Tex added. "To me, air travel by itself isn't necessarily challenging, but all of this added onto it complicates the process."

During my interviews, both TSOs and travelers like Tex described "typical passengers" as nervous, disorganized, unprepared, and emotional. TSOs were especially prone to generalizing broadly, constructing images of passengers who do not fly frequently or who seem to find the process of security nerve-wracking. In my observations, travelers embodying passenger stereotypes moved slowly (unless they were literally running, like Suzanne and Ronny), seemed oblivious to their surroundings, and took up extra time by making mistakes, sometimes trying to rush and fumbling.

Fellow travelers, while not always kind about passengers with the tendency to slow down lines, often attributed nerves and mistakes to inexperience. In contrast, TSOs described these same people as "stupid" and lacking in common sense for not listening to TSO directives, neglecting to read up on policies, and "checking their brains with their baggage," as TSO Alexa described. Pilot-turned-TSO "Peter" concurred, saying that people at the airport "just don't think."

These generalizations typecast passengers as a group but do not necessarily represent the average flier in an airport. Thus, in similar ways as TSOs, passengers are discursively constructed as stereotypical, although the stereotypes stem primarily from the discourse of personal experience rather than from various societal discourses. From my participants' descriptions and my own observations, I noted two major Stereotypical passenger identities—the Inexperienced and the Hostile.

The Inexperienced

Ronny and Suzanne demonstrated the ultimate in Stereotypical-Inexperienced traveling. Running late, they appeared unprepared for security, extraordinarily nervous, and terrified of TSOs. They attempted to manage their nervousness—recall Ronny telling Suzanne to relax and Suzanne trying to breathe deeply—and tried to swallow their feelings to get through the line and onto their flight. But research tells us that suppressing negative emotions usually amplifies them (and incidentally, over time, suppression brings lots of challenging consequences like anxiety, stress, and heart disease).[1] So it's no wonder that Suzanne in particular came across as an emotional hot mess.

Some Inexperienced passengers' actions appear to be shaped by compliance such as "following the rules" and "not questioning authority." These ideas are reinforced by commanding TSOs who enact organizational policies. Although an extreme example, Suzanne and Ronny's behavior exemplifies how Inexperienced passengers seem bent on controlling emotions and doing things "right." Even though the rules and rule enforcers intimidated them, Suzanne and Ronny tried to get through screening by doing everything correctly and asking questions to make sure they conformed to expectations. During these interactions, the procedures themselves were accepted unquestioningly.

Indeed, much of the security setting is specifically designed to provoke compliance. The attire of officers—royal blue uniforms, complete with insignia and brass badges —is intended to evoke law enforcement's clout. Borrowing from military regalia, TSO uniforms, while mostly alike, use understated cues, such as shoulder chevrons, to indicate rank.

The TSA transitioned from white to royal blue uniforms in 2008 in order to signal a distinction between the white-shirted private security guards of old and the new federal officers who should be treated with respect and deference.[2] As persuasion literature suggests, people often attribute credibility to those in uniform, even if their actual authority is illegitimate.[3] TSOs, though technically federal officers, are not trained in law enforcement, carry no weapons, and have no legitimate authority to arrest or subdue passengers. However, the uniforms connote authority and power, a societal discourse that passengers "click into" and "fall in line" around without thinking, according to passenger Kristine.

In fact, a hallmark of some Inexperienced fliers is that they appear to comply without thinking critically about the TSA.

Summer 2011.

Because the vast majority of my travel experience is related to work and research, I do my level best to be productive on planes. I joke that I get my best writing done at thirty thousand feet when I'm strapped into a chair, the internet doesn't work (because I'm too cheap to buy it), and nice people bring me drinks.

But I knew productivity wasn't going to be possible this trip when I realized I was sitting next to "Sir Talks" A Lot. A lovely Latino gentleman with piercing sky blue eyes, he smiled a lot, giggled occasionally, and never once stopped talking during our ninety-minute flight.

At first he yammered to the younger fellow next to him about his recent travels, the shape of the airplane's wing, and his tea-drinking habit. When the younger man (conveniently) fell asleep, Sir Talks A Lot explained that he takes two thermoses of tea wherever he goes. He lamented not being able to bring them through security and onto the plane.

While trying unsuccessfully to tune him out, I perked up when he said he hadn't flown since 1997, when he got out of the U.S. Air Force. Of course, fourteen years later, the whole experience of flying was different.

"I'm usually an Amtrak or bus kind of guy," he said. "Subconsciously I think all the new rules kept me from flying all these years. I don't wanna say fear, but um . . ."

Now nicknamed "Eddie" in my mind, he went on to describe calling the airline three times to check about rules and regulations: Could he carry his suit on board? Are wire hangers considered weapons? He told me that the employee said he would have to check his garment bag, to which I replied, "Really? I see them on board all the time."

"I knew it!" Eddie exclaimed with chagrin.

He made his second call to inquire about the three-inch pocket knife he carries with him at all times. Could he check it in his suitcase? (*Yep.*)

Eddie described lots of uncertainty about the process of flying. Would they feed him on his flight? (I mentioned that there is usually food for purchase on other airlines but not typically on Southwest.) Does he pick up his baggage during his connection? (I explained how baggage is forwarded unless you switch airlines.) At one point he praised the TSA because, compared to what he's seen on the news and heard from family and friends, his security experience was extremely fast and "excellent."

Despite the negative reputation of the TSA—the inconvenience, hassle, and inefficiency—he said he's happy to deal with security if it means safety.

"Better too much than too little," he said, before admitting he's the kind of guy who will "pound three nails when two will do." Laughing, he confessed, "Maybe that's because I haven't flown since 1997, though."

My cheerful, albeit involuntary, conversation with Eddie made me wonder anew about how much nervousness factors into people's emotional reactions during security, particularly for people who don't fly that often.

In one very colorful conversation, "Patrice," a passenger with an extreme fear of flying, talked about her mental preparations for the airport.

"I get all stressed out about making sure I get there on time," she said. "And I want to make sure I get into a good boarding group so I can sit with my husband, Grayson. Because that also feeds into the dying aspect. I don't want to have to hold the hand of a stranger if the plane goes down."

Although she laughs, her mirth is barbed. Throughout our conversation, it's clear that Patrice feels utterly terrified of flying, and that anxiety tinges every part of her travel.

Patrice goes on to tell me about the security screening process. "Typically it's easy. You just go through, put your bags here, walk through that thing, no problem," she says, referencing the metal detector. "Now if they try to frisk you or if some idiot like Grayson is trying to take three bottles of Two-Buck Chuck through and they have to search his bags, and I have to sit there going, 'Oh my god, I'm married to an [idiot],' then it's different."

Gasping from laughter, she tells me about the TSA reaction before her last flight when her husband indeed tried to smuggle three bottles of Charles Shaw's finest in his carry-on. "They pulled out the wine and said, 'You can't take this through. You can check your bag or we can escort . you to your car.' I was livid! I'm like, 'We'll abandon it. We need to catch our flight.'"

Apparently Grayson started to put up a fight, so Patrice snapped, "'Honey, it's six dollars. We need to move on.' But of course, like an idiot, he's like, 'Next time, I want to take my wine. I'm going to check my bag.' And I'm like, 'Honey, you sound like an alcoholic,'" she recounted, chuckling.

When describing how the TSO reacted, she discussed bantering with him as he patted down Grayson. "I was just talking to him and joking around, and he kept laughing."

Patrice explained how she purposefully chats with TSA officers because she thinks that "talking to them and being a real person disarms them. And I think they're likely to treat me kindly if I'm nice."

While she's probably generally correct, I can't help but think about how TSOs frame passengers, especially the Inexperienced ones.

In all of my conversations with TSOs, they related "dumb passenger stories." While they definitely evidenced compassion and humor here and there, most referred to travelers who demonstrated Inexperienced passenger behaviors in demeaning ways—rolling their eyes when they recalled passengers' "stupid" and yet amusing behavior.

Other, more seasoned travelers recognized and in some cases ridiculed inexpert passengers as well, making fun of those who seem nervous or anxious about the security process. As passenger "Mac" asked, rhetorically, "What's the big deal?"

Likewise, passenger "Jaycee" said, "Some people are really stressed out. I do this quite a bit and I'm just like, 'Alriiiight,'" giving the impression of a verbal eye-roll. "When you're calm, people don't give you grief, I guess."

Passenger "Evan" admitted that while he finds travel an exciting process and enjoys observing people, he finds "unreasonable behavior to be stressful." He cited as examples "the obnoxious passenger who is berating the gate agent about flight delays, or the traveler whose luggage clearly exceeds the number and dimensions of the carry-on requirement, yet expects to be allowed on board anyway."

As passengers and TSOs derided and distanced themselves from Inexperienced travelers, they often reinforced their own more expert status. For instance, Evan explained, "I witnessed a gentleman have to take out his laptop and power it on back when laptops were first being screened separately. He made a big fuss about the inconvenience of it, complaining and giving the officer grief. The screener was patient enough and explained in a clear voice what needed to be done. I wasn't surprised, but it's not behavior I would condone. When my turn came to go through security, I cheerfully acknowledged the screener's commands and shot a smirk over to where the gentleman was standing. Others more or less kept to themselves and didn't engage the gentleman or make any comments."

Later in the interview, Evan emphasized how he acts friendly and helpful to other passengers, but he made a point to differentiate himself from this blundering man and join others in ignoring him. "Portlander," a more-than-weekly flyer, also described how he routinely helps others, but he laughingly admitted not getting impatient with infrequent travelers only because it's in his own best interest. Acting impatient "just scares people and makes them move slower," he said.

Like many other experienced travelers I met, Jaycee, Evan, and Portlander each emphasized a key difference between Inexperienced passengers and others: Inexperienced passengers exhibit high levels of anxiety and emotion. And part of the trouble stems from their not knowing how to act in airport security, at least emotionally.

Officers have training mandates for expressing their emotions. They're specifically taught to be "calm, cool, and collected" in the face of rudeness and to exert a "commanding presence" to keep passengers in line. But passengers don't receive such guidance. There are rules for quantities of liquids, types of appropriate electronics, and proper forms of identification—along with a hundred other things—but no specific directions for displaying emotions. Consequently, passengers fill in the gaps by reacting to the scene and gauging how others are behaving. Many describe trying to suppress their emotions and act calm, worried that *any* display of emotion will trigger security officers.

Of course, it doesn't help that security checkpoints are *designed* to provoke emotions like fear and anxiety. The winding long lines. The imposing structures. The officers with symbols of authority like crisp uniforms, heavy boots, brass badges, and epaulettes. These features are specifically devised to prompt obedience and what philosopher Michel Foucault would call *docility*. The default customer service–type emotions that passengers might fall back on—friendliness or even a customer-is-always-right entitlement—don't generally work in airport security. As an example, passenger Evan expressed surprise when a security officer "wasn't responsive" to his attempts at pleasant conversation.

The only emotions that are clearly inappropriate—although tolerated to a degree—are those of anger and hostility. And those adverse emotions are part and parcel of the second type of Stereotypical traveler: the Hostile passenger.

The Hostile

Whereas Inexperienced passengers come across as naive in their behaviors and in depictions by others, Hostile passengers act aggressively and in some cases egregiously, especially when interacting with TSOs. Portraying the Hostile role involves reacting to the stress of the security environment and being triggered by TSOs' actions.

"Nate," a regular traveler, described how passengers demonstrating hostility react nonverbally in security: "The [TSO] will be like, 'You'll need to remove your belt, sir.' They'll sigh, shuffle over, and they'll slap it on the thing and then walk back, rolling their eyes or slamming their suitcase down on the conveyor belt."

While the Inexperienced passenger manages emotions in a way that may inadvertently reveal emotions such anxiety or fear, the Hostile passenger communicates irritation and anger clearly, although not always directly.

For instance, Patrice, who described being "nice to all," admitted acting irate in security once. She was pulled out of the metal detector line after being "randomly" selected for advanced imaging during the pilot testing of the screening machines, which take images of passengers through their clothes. "When I had to go through that body scanner, I was so pissed! I said to them, 'You have got to be kidding me.'"

Much of Patrice's anger stemmed from feeling like she was singled out for the controversial screening by virtue of being an attractive woman. "There was seriously a line of these old men," she said, "and there was Grayson right behind me. Really? This was 'random'? I don't think so. I was so pissed and I let them know it! I called them perverts as I walked off. Everyone was like looking at me, too, as I was going off about what a bunch of perverts they are. I'm surprised they didn't pull me off and try to fine me."

When I asked how the TSA officers reacted, Patrice said, "They decided to ignore me. Because they wanted my naked pictures. I expect to see them on the internet!" she added, with a giggle.

I didn't have the heart to tell Patrice she was nowhere near detention or fining levels, especially since she complied with the TSO directives and only expressed anger as she was leaving security. But her experiences reveal that people can exemplify all sorts of identity characteristics and emotions in security.

In contrast to Patrice's sassy theatrics, some passengers stand out—to TSOs and other travelers—because of their antagonistic behavior and reactions to organizational policy. For TSO officers, the Hostile tend to be the subject of memorable stories.

For example, TSO Jeff described rude passengers who often react to having their belongings confiscated: "They will call you ... anything from fuckers to assholes to ... all kinds of stuff. They'll just blabber something off to you. It's amazing what people will say to you, which they would never say at someone in the grocery store or anything like that. It's not a normal thing to say to someone, but they will say it to you, because you work for the government. You're a TSA agent."

As Jeff, unfazed, mentioned that dealing with rude, hateful behavior is just part of the job, I wondered how much of the animosity he sees is associated with any government position and how much is unique to the TSA role. Do DMV and postal workers share the same abuse stories?

Likewise, "Amber," a TSO in the Southwest, described passengers who had just the day before called her a Nazi and screamed that she had assaulted their daughter by giving her a pat-down. Unlike travelers (and interviewers) who find Hostile behaviors somewhat shocking, most TSOs I spoke with, including Amber, referenced antagonism as par for the course, routine enough to be ignored or compartmentalized.

Abuse seems especially clear in interactions where passengers sexualized encounters with TSOs for no reason. For instance, in early November in 2012, I was catching a predawn flight to Phoenix to watch my best friend defend her dissertation. I'd just left the security checkpoint after a mundane pat-down.

Walking into the terminal, I beelined to Starbucks. In line, the man ahead of me—forty-something, wearing a slate gray shirt with dark jeans, a blue backpack slung over his shoulder—turned back in my direction.

"What a way to start your day," he said.

Quizzically, I replied something about it being so early. (I'll never get used to a 4:30 a.m. wake-up call.)

"With a pat-down," he clarified.

"Do you opt out too?" I asked, to see if he was trying to commiserate about his own pat-down or admitting he observed mine.

He was referring to mine but said that he had a metal bar in his leg so often had pat-downs. (It's no wonder I feel watched all the time. I *am* being watched.)

"I start messing with them . . . 'Ooooh, ahhhh, right there,'" he mimicked, scrunching up his face into an "O-face" I did *not* need to see.

I blinked, unsmiling, and remarked, "My lady was really sweet today."

Taken aback, he stammered, "By and large they're good. They're just doing their jobs."

If they're "just doing their jobs," why do you have to make it hard on them? I wondered as we both bought our coffees and headed in separate directions. *Then again*, I thought, *why did I feel defensive on behalf of TSOs?*

Despite feeling very critical of TSA policies and procedures, and generally supportive of those expressing resistance, I realize my defensiveness comes from understanding the human element of TSA work—something that Stereotypical passengers, especially Hostile passengers, don't often recognize.

For instance, in talking with TSO Alexa, I learned about the types and scale of belligerent behavior TSOs manage.

"Can you give me an example of an outburst you've seen? Or abnormal activity?" I asked.

"Nothing abnormal," Alexa replied, inscrutably, before sharing several examples that seem completely strange to me. "Sometimes there are people that are like . . . I don't know . . . I think it's being touched, or pat-downs. I've just had a few old ladies that are like, 'Okay, well don't fondle me,' or, 'Don't grope me' [during the security process]. I'm just like, 'Look, I'm going to pat you down because I have to. Either because you don't want to go through the machine, or because you went through the machine and they saw something. . . . The machine tells me where I have to pat you down. I don't know what the reason is.'"

Alexa continued, describing passengers who strip down in protest, yell, complain loudly before, during, and after screening, swear vociferously, or melt into hysterics. "People have to understand, I don't want to touch you, just as much as you don't want to be touched," she said, her newly emphatic tone making me chuckle. "I'm not coming onto you or whatever. People just take it like so much further than what it really needs to be. I'm just patting you down to make sure you don't have any knives or weapons or stuff that you're not supposed to have."

"How many of those pat-downs do you do every day?" I asked.

"Oh wow, honestly, I don't even know. Let's say, maybe, I probably do at least sixty to seventy-five pat-downs a day. It could be even more. I have never kept count on the daily."

While Alexa mentioned plans to track the pat-down numbers during her next shift, I was struck that so much of what makes her job challenging is not the job itself—the checking, screening, searching, talking, touching. Rather, it's the reactions from passengers—especially those who act in stereotypically terrible ways.

Passenger outbursts often stem from travelers not being familiar with policies and from arriving at the airport unprepared. When they react negatively, passengers respond to and reinforce the societal discourses that portray airport security as a hostile, conflict-ridden space. Although aggressive behavior was uncommon in my observations, every TSO I spoke with had myriad passenger stories about irate or outrageous travelers shouting, hitting, or throwing things. And many, like TSO "Lucky," expressed resignation about it.

When asked how he feels when people make mistakes in security, whether intentional or not, Lucky said, "I wouldn't say I get irritated, but it gets me to wonder. You've been traveling before; I *know* you've traveled before. You know the rules. If you couldn't take it before, why would you bring it in again and get it taken away again and try to argue? It doesn't make sense to me why people would make the same mistake again after they were told the last time they flew that they couldn't do that."

I could explain that rules that are so familiar to him because he works with them all day long are likely *not* foremost for many passengers.

"It's a little irritating, but not to the point that I'm mad at them," Lucky said. "Disappointed. It makes me feel disappointed."

Also sounding disillusioned, TSO Alexa, shared how a recent passenger had cracked a joke when she checked his ticket, making her smile. "Then after I've done a bag check, and I've been completely nice about everything, he's mad that I touched his shaving cream. . . . He stomped off and called me a bitch," she said. "It's hard sometimes to keep your composure. We're all just regular people underneath the uniform. . . . We do have feelings."

Lucky and Alexa's forlorn commentary about Stereotypical behavior—remarks that likely resonate with others who've worked customer-facing jobs—beg the question: Where do these disappointing and difficult Stereotypical passenger identities originate? As the next chapters show, many emerge in response to TSA policies that limit personal freedom and require passengers to make themselves vulnerable.

Pro Travel Tip #4:
Don't Succumb to a Racing Mentality

One of the things that unites us as human beings—across cultures and creeds—is a seemingly universal hatred of waiting in line. (Seriously, there's a whole body of social science research about queue theory and our social behavior and attitudes in lines.)

In one especially long and slow security line, I overheard a passenger mutter, "I try to think Disneyland . . . but it's more like the post office." Another passenger chimed in, "No, the DMV," making all of us laugh. In the airport, lines don't just mean a wait, they can mean stress from detailed security screenings, anxiety about getting through fast enough, and fear of invasive pat-downs. And a lot of these feelings are intensified by the pressure of time.

Throughout my research, passengers overwhelmingly described the business of travel in terms of time and, in many ways, competition.[4] In the opening to this chapter I admit that even during a leisurely, no-pressure travel day, I'm compelled to beat other passengers to parking spaces, trams, and lines, and feel utterly foiled by Suzanne and Ronny. And I'm not alone.

When viewing travel in this way—as a race—people subconsciously mark their co-travelers as competitors, the TSA agents as referees, and lines as hurdles or hoops to get through before they reach their final destination. So it's not surprising that airport travel and security lines can be so challenging. If travelers view fellow passengers as competitors, they might be more likely to avoid interaction, even the friendly and helpful kind.

And it's no wonder, then, that they feel negatively toward rule enforcers, especially if the "refs" seem unfair.

So if you feel yourself getting sucked into a race mentality, which can exacerbate stress and negativity, try cognitive reappraisal or reframing. Like the passenger who tried to think about the security lines as like Disneyland, you can reappraise the situation by actively looking for the good in stressful situations or thinking about stressful situations in a positive light. For instance, it might mean viewing fellow travelers not as competitors but as collaborators, with a "we're all in this together" mentality.

4

Is That a Salami in Your Purse?
(Or Are You Happy to See Me?)

On Contraband Confiscation

September 7, 2011.

"It that . . . is that a . . . salami?"

It's 6:09 a.m. and I'm in line at airport security. The queue is progressing briskly. but I hear newbies wondering aloud if they will "make it through" before their flight. I smile benevolently, assuring them with veteran calm that the process at this regional airport is quite quick.

I pass the ID checker, collect gray plastic bins, deposit my shoes and laptop in said bins, and shuffle through the metal detector. Same old, same old. That is, until the baggage scanner lady removes my purse from the conveyor belt, asking wordlessly with her raised eyebrows if it's mine before sending it through the X-ray a second time.

Watching the officer scrutinize the image on her computer screen, I'm guessing it's my lotion or lip gloss that's given her pause. (Thankfully, I've remembered to remove my mace after forgetting to take it out before my two previous flights.) After a moment she sheepishly asks about the salami.

I laugh and reply, "It's a banana."

She giggles, leaning in. "Okay, I just had to know."

I walk away, bemused. Why didn't she open the bag and inspect it herself?

It's not until I'm on the plane and fully caffeinated that I realize what she must have suspected about the mysterious cylindrical item in my purse.

She likely wanted to avoid a dirty visual before dawn. The exchange got me thinking about what passengers are allowed to bring through security checkpoints and what common items are now considered contraband.

In the months immediately following 9/11, the list of prohibited carry-on items ballooned. The TSA deemed scissors, razors, tweezers—just about anything sharp—forbidden, along with any type of weapon or firearm.[1] In 2002 the restriction included toy weapons and anything that could be shaped to look like a weapon such as a Transformer robot action figure. The policy changed in 2013 to focus on items that looked like reasonable facsimiles of actual weapons. However, in 2016 TSOs seized metallic stiletto shoes with bullet trim and heels that vaguely resembled gun barrels from a carry-on.[2] (The TSA says they would have been allowed in a checked bag.) And as of 2018 foam toy swords and snow globes larger than a tennis ball were still banned.

Constantly changing, the carry-on rules have long seemed capricious, banning toy weapons and sporting equipment like hockey sticks but allowing other sharp items like ice skates. Fishing poles? Allowed. Hooks? Not.

In the early days of the TSA, officers confiscated toiletry items by the hundreds of thousands, painstakingly hand-searching bags. However, by the end of 2002 the TSA again allowed tweezers, razors, and eyelash curlers, among other little personal items, in order to make lines move faster. Small scissors (with blades four inches long or less) and certain tools that are seven inches long or less became acceptable a few years after that. In early 2013 the TSA even flirted with allowing small pocket knives—one of the most frequently confiscated items besides large liquids and gels—as long as the blades remained shorter than 2.36 inches. But in April 2013 the TSA suspended implementation of the policy amid vociferous complaints by flight crews and unions.

While some things like weapons are obviously prohibited, some innocuous items fall into a gray area. Airports and individual TSOs implement national policies differently or even develop their own local practices, leading to much passenger confusion. Many veteran fliers I interviewed described how different airports cultivate reputations for how easy or strict they are about contraband and even about screening allowable items.

For instance, in late 2017 I flew from Dallas to Sacramento with a plane change in San Diego. Since my connecting flight was in a different terminal, I got to experience security screening twice that day. The gallon-sized bag of snacks that didn't get a second glance in Dallas got dumped out in San Diego. Every individual item—four salted caramel Kind bars, a wrinkly bag of Goldfish crackers, jerky dust, seven packets of Emergen-C, and a nearly empty carton of Reese's Pieces—was wiped down and tested for explosives. The value pack of Mentos buried in my suitcase? Extricated and scanned.

With raised eyebrows (that I pretended were not about my stellar nutritional choices), the TSO suggested that maybe, next time, I leave my snacks at home. Yet there was no policy preventing foodstuff. Since then, the TSA has said no formal policy is forthcoming, but that individual airports may implement extra screening, as I experienced.

Of course, individual airports can also decide to prohibit any particular carry-on item they want. Since 2002, airports have variously (and sometimes temporarily) banned ink cartridges, cupcakes, gaming systems, sharp fidget spinners, snow globes, and all liquids and gels, depending on the locale.

But not, apparently, computers.

March 11, 2011.

The security line winds through snaking cloth ropes, as passengers move like overburdened snails toward the checkpoint. I'm surprised the line proceeds so slowly considering the number of open X-ray lines and the multiple blue shirts running around. At every turn around the stanchions, I worry about my bag.

Will I have to justify myself? Argue? Defend the size of my suitcase? Will they try to send me back to check the bag? I formulate responses as I mush forward with my fellow passengers. It occurs to me that the lanes seem narrower than usual. My suitcase wheels keep catching the base of the dividers.

Around me, no one smiles, per usual. We gaze at each other with pensive faces, eyes shifting one to another. No one chats, outside of couples, friends, or families traveling together. It's spring break season and college students are obviously making their escape. Technically that includes me. But spring break in grad school just means more time to procrastinate on term papers.

A woman carrying a bruised banana asks me if she can take her water through. When I reply "no," she blushes, admitting that she forgot it in her bag. She walks in front of me, not turning to speak, only angling her curly head back when she replies to my questions. She's keeping her eyes on the ID checkers. I try to involve her in conversation, relating how I've taken things through accidentally. She laughs but doesn't engage.

A petite woman with ruddy coloring and freckles, she's wearing a flouncy yellow and red outfit with a country look. I'm trying to decide if she's from Phoenix when I spy a Texas driver's license. She seems nervous. I wonder if she came from a small airport to Sky Harbor International and is over-whelmed by the airport that I now take for granted.

As we get closer, I scope out the ID checkers. They seem pleasant enough while talking to passengers but do not show much emotion. The players shift a couple times during my eleven minutes in line. Two TSOs saunter around, gazing at the rows of passengers squished together, murmuring into walkie-talkies and gabbing to each other. Not doing anything. Not looking menacing necessarily. Just peering around.

After showing my documents, I enter the checkpoint area, approaching an older white TSO with bushy gray hair. As I draw close, he barks into his radio: "We need some more bodies down here!"

When I mention that I have a computer in my suitcase, he orders me to put it in a gray bin.

"But it won't fit," I say. "It's a *desktop* computer."

Brows furrowed, he looks askance and doesn't reply right away. With a resigned grunt, he tells me to just put my suitcase through the X-ray. I can't tell if he's irritated at me for existing or annoyed generally at not knowing what to do. Although I fly weekly, I feel unequipped to deal with this situation and worry about getting detained.

It's been one of those weeks. I completely spaced out on a meeting with a senior administrator at the university. I misread reimbursement forms, losing hundreds of dollars. And then my computer started dying—intermittently crashing and holding my midterm papers hostage. With husbandly tech support seven hundred miles away and long-distance fixes unfruitful, I was instructed to haul the whole box home for repairs. But not before sloshing a twenty-ounce tumbler of water on the keyboard of my work laptop. With the way my luck was going, I would be locked in a TSA prison and strip-searched.

The situation turns out to be anticlimactic, of course. The lines thin out significantly once I'm inside the checkpoint. I walk to an X-ray line and choose a metal detector lane, being careful to avoid the backscatter scanners. I strategically place my items in bins so that my purse and laptop are not left unattended if I get searched. Finally, I hoist my desktop up. It's encased in a crimson roller bag slightly larger than a typical carry-on but still within my airline's size rules. All things considered, I'm feeling relaxed now.

I collect my small items and wait. I see my computer show up on the scanner, and then the TSO screener, in her forties maybe, exclaims, "What is *that*?" She squints at the monitor, trying to make sense of the ghostly image of my Dell's innards.

"It's a computer," I blurt.

"Oh, okay," she sighs, her shoulders deflating some.

And that's it. She's off to another bag.

Before I walk away though, I hear, "Bag check on 12!"

"Do you need to see it?" I ask, reaching for the zipper as I pull the suitcase down the metal rollers.

"Nope."

Okay. I'd expected a little more interest than *that*.

Ten days later I'm back at the airport, this time in my hometown. As I pile my things onto the X-ray conveyor belt, a jolly officer beckons me through the metal detector and asks how my day is going.

I answer offhandedly, watching my suitcase going through the scanner. The alarm sounds and now the TSO glances at me sideways.

Responding to the X-ray screener's alarmed expression, a manager comes over to help, asking to no one in particular, "What do we have here?"

I explain that it's a computer and he carries my bag over to a screening table at the edge of security. He tells me I must stand behind the metal partition.

When he unzips the bag and spies the big Dell logo, he quips, "You know they make laptops now, right?"

"Really?" I reply sincerely, face straight.

We both laugh. He feels underneath the computer and then allows me to retrieve my bag.

I walk away feeling grateful for the humor and surprised later when I have a second mellow interaction with security. Night-and-day different from the time I had a corkscrew in my suitcase.

So I got to thinking: How do people with more dangerous contraband get treated by the TSA? The corkscrew netted me some sass and a quick pat-down. But what about those with weapons, for instance?

I get part of the answer when, on a predawn flight to Phoenix, I meet a veteran flier, "Sam" (pseudonym assigned for his resemblance to Taye Diggs's character Sam Bennett from the show *Private Practice*). With Bose noise-canceling cans around his neck, Sam tells me about his frequent travels.

I can't quite keep my face neutral when he recounts the time in Seattle when he accidentally brought magazines of ammo in his carry-on. He says he bought the bullets on his trip and didn't have time to ship them home. So he took them out of their original packaging and wrapped them in a ski mask. A ski mask. Because *that's* not suspicious.

When he went through security at the airport, the TSOs found the magazines and launched into an interrogation. Sam describes one of the managers as "foaming at the mouth" about the infraction, posturing and "acting hard." I can only imagine! I've seen TSOs act like folks were trying to smuggle state secrets because they forgot a water bottle. I can't quite fathom the reaction for ammo in a ski mask.

Sam remembers wondering, "Am I going to lose my job? Am I going to be arrested?" He expected, at the very least, to miss his early morning flight.

The TSOs called the Port Authority police and made Sam watch as they tore through his neatly packed bag. When the police officer came over, he led Sam away.

"Where are we going?" Sam asked, terrified. The officer explained that there was a shipping place around the corner where he could mail the ammo home.

The officer said, "We'll get this mailed and I'll have you back at the front of the security line."

Sam recalls being escorted back through security in front of TSOs, who clearly wanted his head, and offering them a "Nyah nyah nyah nyah nyah" attitude.

My mind is blown. Not only did he *not* get arrested, he got through without even a pat-down?! Although Sam shared this experience with war story bravado, I couldn't help but wonder what he left out and what his fears were at the time. To be a Black man interacting with law enforcement isn't easy on a good day, but to be a Black man with bullets in a ski mask at the airport?

I glimpse a bit more of Sam's emotional experience when he shares a story about a minor infraction at a regional airport.

"Security in smaller airports is tougher," he admits, describing an interaction in Eugene, Oregon, in 2007. The security officers must have had the sensitivity jacked way up on the metal detector because his belt sounded the alarm. (This was before mandatory belt and shoe removal.)

"The officer pulled me out of line and had me remove this, that, and the other," Sam recalls, remembering his annoyance. "So I finally said, 'Do you just want me to take off all of my clothes?'"

The officer replied in a steely tone, "Are you making a *threat*?"

"He was obviously on a power trip," Sam says, eyes wide with remembered shock. "I said no, and apologized, and got through."

While TSOs themselves do not have the power to make arrests, they maintain license to escalate situations to law enforcement, even offhand jokes.

I tell Sam my desktop computer and salami stories, and he laughs in disbelief. As we trade tales, I keep ruminating on the absurdity and angst riddled through our experiences. But I also can't imagine being on the other side, as a TSO trying to find contraband.

"It is scary, the X-ray is," shared Cat, a fifty-five-year-old TSO at McCarran International Airport in Las Vegas, one of the busiest airports in the United States.

Peter, a fifty-year-old TSO, concurred. "My first inkling of not knowing what to do was in the interview when I had to do the X-ray. They show you big X-rays and say, 'You're gonna look for contraband.'"

A former pilot who was laid off during the recession and then turned to the TSA for employment, Peter continued, "The X-ray's very difficult because people have those bags stuffed to the gills."

The worst offenders? Flight crew. "Because they live out of those bags," according to Peter.

Thinking back to the images I've seen of my own luggage passing through the X-ray, where makeup and curling irons appear sinister, I can imagine it's a challenge to ferret out problem items accurately.

"After I got done with my X-ray training, I had a new respect for the TSA, quite frankly," Peter added, sharing how as former flight crew, he did not think much of the TSA. Now he usually gets volunteered to work with airline personnel coming through security.

Rick, a thirty-something TSA manager at Chicago O'Hare, said he found the X-ray an exciting challenge. "My favorite task on the checkpoint was always working the X-ray," Rick said, sharing that he'd worked for the TSA almost since its inception. "I was good at it, and I was quick. I was also incredibly accurate. . . . I was so good at one point, I could identify the brand and model of laptop just by looking at it on the X-ray. I was almost to the point where I could identify the model [of] car based on seeing the car keys on the [screen]. . . . I never failed an X-ray test."

In fact, TSOs face regular assessments of their contraband-catching abilities, which can lead to on-the-job paranoia, according to Cat.

Recalling a time when she was off duty and traveling through her home airport, Cat described being stuck in an excruciatingly sluggish security line. Watching the X-ray screener, "I thought, 'My god, this TSA agent is slow.'"

I interjected, "I can tell when the person doing the X-ray screening is new, because they call over a supervisor for every bag."

"That's what this kid was doing!" Cat said, describing how she watched the new TSO scan and rescan the same item. "I thought, 'Boy, this kid is new.' Because I could see it, it was a movie camera type [thing], a big [professional] one . . . but it was by itself in a bin. Now why would you have to rerun that?"

We both laughed again and I asked, "So, why would he do that?"

"Because he's not sure what he's seeing," Cat explained. "It is scary. It's your interpretation of the image, and if you've got all these thoughts in your head that there's something in there, you're going to see it. You're going to *think* you see it. He was just being cautious, but just new. Not really knowing. Like for me, I've seen a million of them."

"Is that a really stressful position when you're first starting?" I asked.

"It's stressful. It's stressful even if you're not just beginning because they run tests. If you miss them, it's a check off. . . . It's on your record."

Cat described the ongoing assessment process that TSOs endure—secret shopper-style tests designed to trip them up at every facet of their jobs, from taking tickets and checking IDs to viewing the X-ray images or patting down passengers. The best TSOs at her airport win "Top Gun Awards," although she grumbled that usually there is no money or incentive involved, just bragging rights.

Peter lamented all of the surprise exams. "We're always being tested," he said. "I think test bags are put together by people who are evil in so many ways. . . . But they make us better."

The most frequent tests, though, come from the regular flying public who bring dangerous materials to the airport. According to their annual report of carry-on "finds," the TSA discovered an average of 12 guns per day in 2019—a record 4,432 firearms in total for the year—almost 90 percent of them loaded.

And the excuse that most people with guns in their carry-ons give? They "just forgot."

"I can't tell you the number of times we have found hunting knives, bullets, even guns in bags and people claim that they forgot it was there," Rick complained. "How do you forget there is a five-pound pistol in your bag? Wasn't it a bit heavy when you picked it up to pack your stuff?! Forgetting about a pocket knife, I can believe that. Forgetting about a gun or a hunting knife? Not likely."

But it happens. Often, apparently.

Peter described a number of times when passengers "forgot" weapons. "I'm doing a bag check and I ask, 'Anything sharp, fragile, or dangerous in your bag?' [The passenger] says no . . . and then I pull out a six-inch knife." I could hear Peter's sarcasm dripping. "So I say, 'This doesn't fit in any of the categories of sharp, fragile, or dangerous? Why do you have it?'"

Previously jokey, Peter now sounded like a frustrated school teacher dealing with unruly students as he described the guy shrugging and admitting stupidity. He recalled another passenger, who shouted, "Oh geez!" when Peter reminded him to take everything out of his pockets before the advanced imaging screening.

Still amused years later, Peter recounted asking, "What did you forget?"

"He pulls out a six-inch hunting knife that he'd obviously had for thirty years because it was worn in all the right spots. So I said to him, 'Oh, isn't that special? I'll give you some ideas of what you can do with it.' And he said, 'Oh, it's not gonna matter.'"

When Peter started to lay out the passenger's options—taking the knife out to his car or checking the bag—the passenger mentioned that he was past the airline's timeframe for checking luggage.

Sensing the passenger's dejection, Peter asked, "Would you like to kiss it goodbye?"

I remembered how angry I felt at having a cheap souvenir corkscrew from my honeymoon confiscated. I couldn't imagine parting with such a keepsake. Of course, I also couldn't fathom forgetting a knife big enough to disembowel a deer.

"Or you can give it to me," Peter said, recalling teasing the man as he fake-cried while crooning to his "beautiful knife." Laughing, Peter said, "Look at the interaction. Humor. He's not a criminal, he made a mistake."

Peter added, "The answer is aqua threat," meaning that the item in question is comparable to the harmless water bottles he confiscates on a daily basis—not really a "threat" at all. "People just don't think. They check their brains at the door."

In fact, "dumb passenger stories" were a hallmark of my conversations with TSOs. Carrie, a fifty-eight-year-old TSO from an international airport in the Midwest, sniggered, "I've seen a woman get arrested with three little kids for trying to smuggle a can of Coke in between her breasts. She didn't want to buy a can on the other side. How ridiculous is that?"

Hearing these stories, it didn't surprise me that people in bureaucratic occupations like the TSA use negative emotional displays like sarcasm and irritation to keep sane during repetitive service interactions.[3]

Peter remembered, "We had another person come through with a scale model of a broadsword, five feet long, made out of wood."

Apparently, the owner of the sword, which was modeled after a medieval knight's thick, double-edged blade, asked naively, "You mean I can't take this through the checkpoint?"

"No!" Peter sneered. "That's a five-foot-long broadsword!"

I imagined someone trying to shove that giant wooden spear in the overhead bins and shuddered.

Despite his disbelief at passenger antics, Peter confessed, "If they didn't shut their brains off, we wouldn't be entertained."

I had to agree. Thinking back through my travels, I recalled watching a woman weep when her Civil War–era bullets—a gift from her husband—were seized from the cigarette holder/coin purse combo she kept stowed in her daughter's diaper bag. And later I observed a man in his midfifties, with closely cropped gray hair, traveling alone, staring impassively as a young TSO searched his suitcase. Gingerly holding a large, soiled-looking diaper, the TSO pried open the nappy, which seemed to be pulled tightly around something square. As other TSOs started to nervously converge, I'm pretty sure I witnessed my first live drug bust. Definitely entertaining.

Along the same lines, TSO Jeff recounted his favorite memory as a TSO. He described working in a small regional airport in Washington State when a young woman went to the ticket counter and inquired about assistance getting through security.

"It was weird because she wasn't in a wheelchair. She was about twenty years old. Really, no reason for anybody to help her." By comparison, elderly people and people who require mobility assistance can get help, typically from airline or airport personnel.

Jeff recalled that the young woman was turned away by one ticket agent so she left the terminal, returning half an hour later to talk to someone else.

"But this time she came back in and she was pregnant," Jeff recalled.

I was confused for a second, but Jeff explained that the woman came in to speak with a different ticket agent, this time with a distended-looking belly. She claimed to be pregnant and in need of help getting through security. But when the ticket agent referred her to the TSA, she left again.

"The reason why she was suddenly 'pregnant' was that she was trying to smuggle five pounds of marijuana through security," Jeff said.

"What?!" I exclaimed.

"Yeah, totally," Jeff chuckled. "She tried to make it *look* like she was pregnant by putting the pot under her shirt in such a way . . . but she eventually came through security thin."

Changing her mind about trying the maternity route, the woman had split the marijuana between her checked bag and her car, so the TSOs didn't actually catch anything in the checkpoint.

"So, she gets on the plane and goes on her way," Jeff continued. A little later two guys came into the airport asking about the nonpregnant woman in question. Jeff explained how she had hopped on a flight to Denver a couple of hours earlier. "Then [the younger man says], 'Oh man, she stole my car and all our stuff!' Come to find out, this kid is pretty stupid," Jeff went on. "He called the police. When the cop opened the front [car] door . . . there was about a pound or two of weed sitting on the front seat. And the car had actually been stolen from a Hertz lot. The kid ended up going to jail."

"Wow!" I replied.

"Later I heard the lady was arrested in Denver for smuggling," Jeff said, sniggering. Apparently the TSOs in Washington had phoned ahead to Colorado to report the woman's suspicious activity and made sure law enforcement was waiting when her plane landed.

"That is drama" I said, and we both laughed again.

Jeff continued on, describing someone who had robbed an elderly man and stolen his credit cards. The thief showed up at the airport and purchased two last-minute, one-way tickets.

"The counter [staff] thought it was weird, so they let us know," he recalled. "When he came through security, he was doing all the signs. He was shaking slightly. He was looking around a lot; he was very nervous."

Jeff described how the passenger and his girlfriend's nervous behavior was a "pretty obvious" tip-off that they had something to hide. After detaining the pair, the TSOs called the onsite sheriff.

Jeff recounted the moment the passenger realized he would likely be going to jail for credit card fraud and theft. "He runs out of the sheriff's office just a few feet away from me. Just takes off! So the cops go running and they tell me to watch his girlfriend. There was a big stack of cash on the table. [So that] was interesting."

My mind somewhat spinning—I'd never considered the TSA useful in a theft detection way before—I asked, "How did those two experiences make you feel?"

Jeff replied, "It makes me feel good. . . . I think the public need[s] to hear those stories. . . . People in the TSA get a bad reputation. [There are] all these little things that the TSA, that people that work there are catching. They're catching the drugs. They're catching the people who are coming through who robbed someone. They're catching those types of people."

He was right. I told him I didn't remember ever hearing stories like that in the media.

"And that's one thing that I think people need to hear," Jeff emphasized. "They don't put stories like that on the news. They only put it on the news if the TSA finds a bomb in someone's crotch!"

I was chuckling again as Jeff said, "That's all you hear about. . . . [TSOs] have actually stopped hundreds of pounds of coke, they have stopped all kinds of people trying to smuggle knives, trying to smuggle gold. . . . In Yakima, a little while ago, a guy was trying to bring through an unmarked gold block . . . and [TSOs] caught that.[4] They're catching drugs, they're catching criminals, they're catching all kinds of people. If it was just a typical security thing, these people would not have been caught. People only hear the horror stories about how grandma got patted down or something."

"They don't share those [good] stories," agreed Alice, a twenty-nine-year-old frequent business traveler. "They don't talk about how [threats] were caught. . . . They probably have saved us millions of times, but we don't know that."

Despite anecdotal evidence, however, the TSA maintains an uneven reputation for capturing dangerous content. For instance, they repeatedly fail to discover the vast majority of contraband in secret tests set up by the Department of Homeland Security. TSOs were unsuccessful nearly 95 percent of the time in 2015 and upward of 80 percent in 2017. In response, TSA administrator David Pekoske released a statement describing the steps the TSA would take to improve security, including increasing training and considering CT scan imaging systems to replace X-ray screening.

However, the concerted focus on dangerous *items* has drawn criticism from security specialists, media, and passengers alike. Bruce Schneier, a renowned security technologist, best-selling author, and fellow at the Berkman Klein Center for Internet and Society at Harvard University, has long criticized the TSA. Schneier's main complaints? The TSA's expense, inefficiency, and ineptitude—in large part a result of focusing on dangerous items rather than dangerous people or plots. Lambasting the TSA for its $7 billion security expenditures in 2015 while missing 95 percent of guns and bombs, Schneier argued that security should be "ratcheted" back down to pre-9/11 levels.[5]

While many passengers I spoke with, including Alice and twice-weekly flier Portlander, said they didn't always agree with or like the TSA, they nevertheless appreciated the focus on safety. Others couldn't disagree more.

Robert, a frequent traveler, described going through security: "I roll my eyes at the theater of it, because I don't feel like it's really made us any safer. It's just making travel a lot less convenient."

When I asked about the purpose of the TSA, Robert said, "The mission as I understand it is . . . to keep dangerous things or possibly dangerous people off of airplanes."

I replied that the stated mission is "to protect the nation's transportation systems to ensure freedom of movement for people and commerce."

"Right."

"Now how do you feel about that?" I inquired.

"I feel like, yes, as a stated mission, that makes sense," Robert admitted, pausing. "Actually, I want to change my answer. I think that the purpose of the TSA is to help stupid people feel safe."

We both chuckled.

"Tell me more about that," I said.

"As we've seen over and over again, people who want to be up to nefarious things—if they are not stupid—are going to find [a way]," Robert continued. "I think that airplane-related terrorist things are kind of like school shootings in that every once in a while, something's going to happen. Yes, we need to take reasonable steps to attempt to prevent [those events]. But I don't think the TSA really does that. Instead, post-9/11, the TSA is a great big organized game of charades that people can look at it and go, 'Well, at least the government is doing something.'"

Indeed, polls by Gallup and travel organizations report that in the early years of the TSA, the average traveler would describe the TSA as doing a "good" job, with nearly half of Americans surveyed indicating positive feelings toward airport security generally. However, as more time elapses since 9/11, impressions of the TSA have diminished, especially among the majority of frequent fliers.

The TSA continues to emphasize its focus on dangerous items through its Instagram and other social media accounts run by "Blogger Bob," the TSA's friendly social media mouthpiece. The Instagram account, ranked by *Rolling Stone* as one of the hundred best (beating out Beyoncé and NASA in popularity), showcases some of the dangerous, funny, and strange items the TSA finds every day. The feed features lots of hidden weapons—knives concealed in the handles of canes or in belt buckles—as well as the utterly bizarre, such as a life-size, zombie-like, fake dead body. Apparently it was a prop from the movie *Texas Chainsaw Massacre* that was taken through security in Atlanta.

"I don't think [the TSA] really makes us that much safer," Robert continued. "I don't think it makes us safe enough to justify most of the giant pain in the ass that flying has turned into. Yeah, I think that its actual mission is to give the impression of safety to people who haven't really thought about it."

I asked Robert if he knows anyone who buys into it.

"I don't know of anybody who thinks that, 'Oh yeah, it's a good thing the TSA is there, because otherwise flying would be so much more dangerous.' I don't know anybody who thinks that way. Yes, it is, I guess, probably, technically safer to check too much than to not check at all, because you would inevitably have somebody walk onto an airplane with something destructive," Robert said. "But locking up the cockpit does a lot toward taking care of that kind of thing."

And so do intelligence activities outside of the airport, handled by various law enforcement and intelligence agencies around the world, as Schneier frequently argues.

Robert recounted hearing stories about plots being broken up before they ever got to the airport, and how the TSA operates a "look and see" model. "It is so systematic, and it seems to be staffed by people who can execute that system, and not people who are employed for their judgment, nor are they given the power to have common-sense judgment," he said.

I thought about the requirements to become a TSA officer. While the hiring process is arduous and lengthy, the conditions for employment are minimal. Candidates must be U.S. citizens with a high school diploma or the equivalent, speak English proficiently, and have no felony convictions.[6]

"So you have babies being searched, and old women," Robert said. "It just seems like it is this big, one-size-fits-all, really poorly executed solution to a problem that is so much more complex. It is won, very much, I think, in other arenas than how much mouthwash I'm able to take on the plane. It also seems to be really, really very [reactive]. Nobody had to take their shoes off until some jackass put a really, really shitty bomb that wouldn't have actually done any damage into one of his shoes. Now all of a sudden, instead of trying to keep an eye out for that guy, everybody now has to take their shoes off—ninety-year-old women, toddlers, everybody in between."

Robert's comments illustrate some of the main gripes of passengers and TSOs alike: constraining policies that don't make much common sense; officers who can't use their discretionary powers for good; and security protocols that seem mostly for show.

But Robert inadvertently hit upon the most surprisingly consistent complaint, the one featured in chapter 5: shoe removal.

Pro Travel Tip #5:
Don't Check Your Brains in Your Baggage

While desktop computers and corkscrews might get you some TSA side-eye, be aware that prohibited items carry stiff fines. The TSA is authorized to impose civil penalties for contraband of up to $13,066 per violation per person, along with criminal referrals to law enforcement. Forgetting your mace (like I have accidentally done several times) might set you back somewhere between $330 and $1,960, as will lighter fluid, hatchets, cattle prods, meat cleavers, stun guns, and throwing stars. Loaded firearm fines start at $3,920, and if you're hauling gunpowder (more than ten ounces) or grenades? Bring your checkbook. Those fines start at $7,840.[7]

Ever wonder where all those confiscated items go? Or the change you emptied out of your pockets and forgot?

It's easy to imagine, given the news stories about TSO theft that pop up from time to time, that security officers leave work with their pockets lined with our confiscated pocket knives and oversized toiletries. However, once items are taken by the TSA, they become property of the federal government, under the purview of the General Services Administration (GSA). (And for the record, the TSA claims that they maintain a zero tolerance policy, with immediate termination for thievery.)

Following strict GSA guidelines, individual states decide how to dispose of materials taken by the TSA or left behind by passengers. Some states donate items like scissors and sports equipment to schools. Other states sell seized property—all but the illegal goods—to raise money. If you're in the market, some states sell their stuff on sites like eBay and others have annual auctions in major cities.

Unclaimed cash is a slightly different story. Since 2005 the TSA has pocketed all money left behind at security checkpoints. And not just a few pennies. U.S. travelers forgot $960,105 in coins and currency in 2019, for instance. However, not everyone is happy that the TSA keeps the cash. In 2013 the U.S. House of Representatives passed a bill aptly named the TSA Loose Change Act. The act required the TSA to direct all unclaimed money to nonprofit organizations that provide services for armed services members and their families. The bill eventually died in the Senate, but individual airports have taken up the charge to avoid inadvertently lining the TSA's pockets. Many large airports have kiosks where passengers can donate their change to worthy causes.

5

"One Shoe, Two Shoes, Red Shoes, Blue Shoes"

On Shoe Removal

My professional career started in health care marketing and corporate communication. I don't know if it was the exposure to portrayals of disease processes and the importance of handwashing, my obsession with the then-new *Grey's Anatomy* medical drama, or my germaphobe cubicle neighbor, but I regularly had bacteria on the brain. It didn't help that said neighbor harbored hypochondriac tendencies. A bad headache? Brain tumor. Dizziness? Early signs of MS. Earache? Definitely the Big C (er, cancer). During those few years I joked that I earned my Google MD searching every one of our symptoms.

October 1, 2010.

Years later, out of health care and into studying airport security, I find myself regularly touching some of the germiest surfaces on earth. Ticket counters, tray tables, toilet flush buttons, airplane armrests all burst with thousands of germs and are rife with norovirus, fecal matter, and bacteria like *E. coli* and MRSA. Yes, I am that passenger who wet-wipes armrests, tray tables, and any hard surface I might touch on a plane, with absolutely no shame.[1]

About a year into my time as a frequent flier, I've kicked off my sandals and deposited them in a bin for scanning, the bins being one of the dirtiest surfaces in the airport. The line is slow. I fixate on all of the germs my toes must be touching and rise onto the balls of my feet. I don't even consider how dorky I must look on tiptoe. I think about the grit, dust, and hair down below and want to have as little of my skin in contact with it as possible.[2] And no, I'm not wearing socks. I'm flying in the Arizona heat!

I send my luggage through the X-ray machine and tiptoe toward the metal detector. The TSA screener is someone I've seen often and we have always maintained a friendly rapport. A few months before this interaction, he teased me for having a "smiley mug" and I've always pegged him as one of the good ones.

Out of nowhere he says, "What, what, what?" and motions me—hand waving down as if he's patting a child on the head or playing "Duck, Duck, Goose"—to stand flat-footed.

Immediately, I drop my feet to the floor, stunned.

As I wait to walk through the metal detector, he asks me why I'm walking on my toes, and I say, "The floor creeps me out."

He laughs, and I giggle nervously. I'm embarrassed, not for my goofy walking—I always do that—but to be called out so directly.

No one has noticed or cared before. Was it because I looked "deviant" compared to other flat-footed walkers, or was he trying to be funny? I've seen this particular officer in other security positions but never at the metal detector. Is he new to this position and being vigilant? What does it matter if I prance through the checkpoint?

I drag my laptop, purse, suitcase, bag, and shoes over to a nearby bench, and wet-wipe the soles of my feet before slipping my sandals back on.

As a frequent flier, I find that the shoes-off policy is second nature now. Somehow it seems almost normal to arrive at the airport, strip off outerwear, and slip out of shoes. It's easy to forget that this policy, one of the most irksome, derived directly from a bomb threat early in the TSA's history.

Just a few months after 9/11, Richard Reid, a British passenger flying from Paris to Miami, attempted to blow up American Airlines Flight 63 using a homemade "shoe bomb."[3] Reid, who was radicalized by al-Qaeda in Afghanistan, had plastic explosives lodged in the lining of his thick-soled black high-tops. When a flight attendant noticed Reid attempting to light a fuse, nearby passengers helped subdue him with a combination of plastic handcuffs, seatbelt extenders, belts, and headphone cords. Speculation suggests that the fuse wouldn't light due either to the damp weather or Reid's own perspiration. But thanks to the near-dozen passengers and crew, along with onboard doctors who tranquilized the would-be mass murderer, 197 lives were saved.

Following this failed terrorist attempt, the TSA implemented rules regarding the screening of footwear. Passengers fumed at this security change, complaining stridently and causing some airports to react by providing complimentary socks for a time, for those needing to get completely barefoot.[4]

Like the ever-changing carry-on restriction list, early shoe removal rules caused great confusion. Initially, not all shoes needed to be doffed, just those with thick soles or metal inserts that might trigger the metal detector and prompt further screening. Frequent and savvy fliers took to wearing sneakers or flimsy sandals to avoid triggering alarms but otherwise stayed shod.[5] Further confounding passengers, shoe-removal practices differed by airport or at the whims of individual TSOs, despite TSA insistence that bare feet were not absolutely required.[6]

In a conversation about being reprimanded by TSA officers, frequent-flier Dirk described his small protests in the early days of shoe removal.

"Before their policy came out where you had to take your shoes off, it was an *unwritten* rule," Dirk said. "I had hiking boots with metal eyes all over them and everything else, but I could still pass through the scanners and not have the alarms go off. So I would look at the officers who would ask me to take them off and say, 'Why? I passed through your scanner. I must be fine.' They'd say, 'Well those boots have steel plates in the bottom of them,' and I'd say, 'Well, I guess they don't' when the alarm didn't sound. Or they'd say, 'Well, your sole is too big.' And I'd say, 'No it's not.'"

Dirk's memories and residual frustration strike a chord with me as I remember several not-so-fond encounters with TSOs who made me remove my Old Navy flip-flops "in case" the flimsy rubber somehow concealed metal.

"I used to be very . . . I would poke the badger with a spoon," Dirk said, mischievously. "I would make them earn their inconveniencing me a little bit. At the time I was traveling for work a lot. I would do things like leave my belt on. I still will. My belt doesn't need to come off—it doesn't set any alarms off. They just don't like it. They get upset. They really want you to take it off. They want you to take all sorts of stuff off."

As someone who flaunts a few rules on occasion, I understood the impulse completely.

"But if I'm passing all of their scans [with my belt on], then either they need to make their scans tighter or they need to change their policies," Dirk said.

To put an end to the ambiguity, the TSA did eventually change their policy. In response to a raised "threat level for the aviation sector," on August 10, 2006, the TSA ruled that *all* shoes must be removed during security screening and passed through the X-ray scanner, ending four years of confusion, for a time.[7]

October 7, 2010.

Four years after this policy change, I'm spending part of my evening in a stopped-dead security line. The lane winds around and around, and I try to keep my cool. I'm not stressed about being late—I'm early as usual—but I *am* worried about my head exploding.

Behind me, a woman in a dark skirt and frilly scarf is popping her gum. POP, smack, smack. POP, smack, smack. Not even the dinging of security alarms, the rolling of bags, the chatter in line, the whining of toddlers, or the smash of a young boy's race car into the stanchion can distract me.

POP, smack, smack. POP, smack, smack. I'm completely sensitive to mouth sounds. I realize with every POP, smack, smack that I am growing more anxious and irritated by the second.[8] I wonder what contextual cues instill stressful feelings for other line-goers. I have plenty of time to ponder because the line is so sluggish.

As I approach the ID checker, TSO "Jane" motions with a flat palm for me to stay put. The lines are backed up at the X-ray machine and I presume they are making room for us. Almost instantly, Jane says to a neighboring colleague, "They think I'm making room, but I'm not," and she laughs. Is she messing with us? The only thing worse than a long security line is a long security line that doesn't move.

For five long minutes we stand and wait. It's probably just turned 6:00 p.m., and I wonder if there is a shift change or another cue she is following. No managers are nearby. What could have signaled the pause?

After an age, she motions me forward, looks at my ID, and says, "There you go," without any pleasantries. I look behind me and notice the line grinding on.

Passengers bear furrowed brows, tight mouths, taught postures. I notice their demeanor contrasts with TSOs who appear more relaxed, postures sunken. During a chat with passengers a few minutes before, the TSOs mentioned how the area slopes downward.

"You walk down toward us," Jane explains to the passenger ahead of me. "We work on a slant eight hours a day."

I notice she balances over her stool and I wonder what the angle is like. The awkward body mechanics must add an extra exhaustion factor, I think, and consider what support their thick-soled boots provide.

Now in the checkpoint, I walk to the X-ray machine. Behind me, "Madame Gum Popper" asks me about protocol.

"So we just put our shoes in the bins?" she asks.

"Yep," I reply curtly, still annoyed at her symphony of mouth sounds.

When she explains that she hasn't flown in a while, I soften. I tell her she'll want to put her shoes and purse in a bin and her bag on the conveyor belt. It's rote for me, but she seems grateful for the advice.

"When did you fly last?" I ask.

"1997," she says with a sheepish smile.

"Wow! That's been quite a while," I exclaim, wondering how someone can go without flying for almost fourteen years.

"The last time I flew, we didn't do . . . all this," she says, gesturing to the security area.

I admit that with all of my flying, I can barely remember the "before times." We go through security without fanfare, and we both sit to put on our shoes, still chatting. Apparently, her husband bought surprise plane tickets for her birthday so she could visit a cousin in Southern California. She admits to getting to the airport two hours early.

I ask if she was nervous during security.

Nodding, she says, "Only because I wasn't sure how it worked."

It seems like she was expecting more drama from the security experience—spending longer waiting around at the airport than actually flying—because she adds, "That wasn't so bad!" with a big relieved sigh.

April 25, 2012.

A couple of years after this exchange, I'm reminded that while security protocol like shoe removal is second nature to me, policy reminders are still important for infrequent fliers and a key part of the TSO job. I'm in the airport in Sacramento. It's 5:15 a.m. The sun won't rise for an hour, but it feels like the birds are already chirping. When I get to the terminal, two male TSOs are holding court near the coffee shop, smiling and chatting. They greet me, wish me a good flight, and turn to the next passenger. No caffeine has yet passed my lips and I cannot comprehend why they are so damned cheerful already, just hanging out by the coffee shop.

As I drag myself to the tram, barely staying awake for the short ride to the main security checkpoint, I notice that other passengers seem wearier than normal.

Security looks different than last week—more crowded and congested. I realize that the center lane is blocked off so that we passengers stream like ants around to the remaining two checkpoints.

When I get closer to the screening line, I hear the TSO in the center stating reminders. He declares a litany of things that should not be in our pockets—boarding passes, IDs, wallets, lint, paper, vitamins, very small rocks. . . . He does this rapid-fire, but nonchalantly. I meet his eyes and catch a feisty gleam, and we both smile. This is a performance!

The TSO looks from right to left to see who's watching. Then he continues. He starts rhyming about shoes: "One shoe, two shoes, red shoes, blue shoes . . . laptops, flip-flops . . . they all must come off."

I'm tickled! The TSO has adapted Dr. Seuss's *One Fish, Two Fish, Red Fish, Blue Fish* into a dramatic reading of security procedures. It's so unusual to be this pleasantly amused in security. Passengers all around us smile and laugh.

The man in front of me comments, "Your wife must tell you you do this in your sleep."

The TSO chuckles and says, "No, when I hit that tram, it turns off."

After a beat, he clarifies, "I have a fifteen-minute window to talk about work, and then I shut it off." He says he has more in life to focus on than work. He mentions this pleasantly, not sounding bitter about his job, which surprises me because so much of his day consists of hollering banal reminders to frequently oblivious passengers.

In an interview later, TSO Roger also seemed laidback about the need to remind passengers about things like shoes. He emphasized the importance of providing detailed information for travelers. "I say, 'Basically, anything below your feet, except for the ground you are walking on, has to come off.' That pretty much covers everything below your feet, not around your feet. Some people ask me about socks. I say, 'Below your feet, not around your feet.'"

I don't point out that socks are both under and around.

Roger's comments about questions and detailed information put me in mind of earlier travel experiences where I realized that TSO tone and demeanor definitely influenced how comfortable travelers feel asking questions. Unlike Roger and the Dr. Seuss impressionist, some TSOs are not kind about shoe issues.

Passenger "Sunny" recalled a time when she opted out of advanced imaging and requested a pat-down. She remembered the officers grumbling and trying to pass off the task because they didn't want to be bothered.

When someone finally came to administer the pat-down, Sunny panicked. "I had to take my shoes off and noticed the mat was wet. I didn't want to step on it. The lady was like, 'Put your feet here.' And I interrupted, 'But it's wet. I don't want to be standing here on a wet mat while you pat me down.'"

I really don't blame her here. Fungal infections like athlete's foot thrive in moist environments like a damp mat that hundreds of others have stood on in bare feet.

Sunny recalled, "I didn't say it meanly. I said it gingerly. When I first stepped on it, it was wet, so of course I stepped off. Then she seemed a little frustrated." Sunny explained that she didn't want to escalate the conflict, so she stepped back on the damp mat.

"I told myself to focus on my breathing. I had to breathe it out. I just felt like in that moment she wasn't having a good day and I wasn't having a good moment. After it was over, I just went off to the side and tried not to pay attention to everyone staring at me. I was like, 'Whatever.'"

I would've been more concerned about just why that mat was wet in the first place!

Four years after making mandatory shoe removal official, the TSA announced a new policy for kids old and young. Among other things like not having to remove light jackets or belts, people age seventy-five and older and kids twelve and younger are now able to keep their shoes on in security checkpoints.

Passenger Ramona talked about how her stepfather was eagerly awaiting his upcoming seventy-fifth birthday. "Once he's seventy-five, he doesn't have to take off his shoes. . . . He's very excited about that!"

Our conversation covered a lot of ground, including vulnerability, sexuality, and fear. She mentioned how revealing it is to strip down, even one layer.

I added, "Well, even just the practice of taking our shoes off, that's a vulnerable feeling. Because by and large adults are not barefoot unless we're at the beach or at the park or something. Shoes are a layer of protection, and if you take it away, it's a very strange thing."

"It's interesting you mention that," Ramona said. "Whenever I'm in that line waiting to get through, I always look at people's feet."

"You do?!" I was now retroactively mortified, wondering how many other people have peeped at my peeling pedicures.

"It's more to see if they're wearing socks or stuff like that," she explained, referencing a similar germ consciousness as me. "But almost everyone is kind of fidgety with their feet. You should check it out next time you're flying." I most definitely will!

"It's like what you just said," Ramona continued. "It's a nervousness or vulnerability to have your shoes just stripped off you. And especially, I think that connects more to age, like [for] older folks that tend to be less stable, it would be even more of an issue. It just seems to be more like a, more of a vulnerability when it comes to older folks."

Ramona hinted at what probably prompted the new policy . . . fall prevention. Seniors are much more stable in their shoes, and keeping an elderly person from landing on the concrete is an important benefit of the policy. Likewise, those with diabetes or nerve damage are advised to always wear shoes to avoid accidentally cutting themselves and not being able to feel it. It was at this point that I realized why there is sometimes a chair is in the middle of the checkpoint. It's not for TSO lounging. It's probably for people needing help removing their shoes.

Despite attempts to improve travel for the elderly, the age-related shoe rules still prompt confusion for passengers. TSO Alexa recalled an experience while working as the divestiture officer who gives reminders to passengers before screening.

"I had this passenger, older man, maybe like sixty, sixty-five, and I told him to take his shoes off," Alexa explained. "He said, 'Well, I'm not taking off my shoes, because I'm older than sixty-five.' I'm like, 'That is a new rule. Passengers who are seventy-five do not need to take off their shoes or light jacket.' He completely ignored all the signs. He just didn't want to go through the advanced imaging machine. I said, 'Someone will be here to pat you down in a minute, once we get everyone through,' and he completely snapped! He threw off his shoes and then he started to get mean."

Alexa described how the man started yelling and hollering at her, explaining loudly that he had a medical condition and couldn't take his shoes off. But he kept repeating "I'm over sixty-five," to which Alexa replied, "Over sixty-five is not an acceptable reason."

Like many policies, the age restriction seems arbitrary and comes with no rationale. Why is seventy-five the magic number? And it's not universally supported in the TSO community.

For instance, TSO Carrie admitted, "I do not believe that people over the age of seventy-five should be allowed to go through with their shoes on."

When I asked why, she said, "Because people that are seventy-five years and older have nothing to live for."

When listening to our recorded conversation, I audibly gasped here.

"If you look at it through my eyes, what if somebody came up to them and said, 'We've got your family. If you don't try to smuggle this through, we're going to kill them.'"

I replied, "Yeah," having no idea what to say to this paranoia that doesn't seem related to shoes.

"You have to look up the Chechnya bombing. The two Russian planes were blown up by two Chechnya women who portrayed themselves as pregnant. They detonated at almost the exact same time on two different planes."

"Oh my god," I commented.

"This was in the eighties, '86, I think. They were not young women. Somebody paid them money to get on that plane too."

"Wow, that's awful," I remarked. Later I would search to find evidence of these bombings. While there were numerous news references to Chechen bombers, I could not find the story she referenced.

Carrie continued, "It's not that I'm being unkind to older people. It's just that you have to look at the way a terrorist would look at things."

I wondered if "thinking like a terrorist" was part of TSO school, but somehow I doubted it. I started wondering how much of her opinion was based in personal suspiciousness or trained in by her supervisors through constant reminding of bombings past.

"What if somebody said to you, 'I have your family,'" she said. "And they call and you hear your family say, 'Please do whatever they say; they're going to kill us.' Wouldn't you do whatever they said?"

"Yeah, that would be really hard," I agreed, somewhat noncommittally.

Carrie continued. At this point, I heard ice clinking in a glass as she adjusted her phone.

"It would be very hard to decide what to do, wouldn't it? I tell you one thing, if they said to me, 'You've got to smuggle this or we're going to kill your family,' I'd smuggle it through."

"Yeah, I mean, that's an impossible position," I commented.

"But I would," she admitted. "My family is more important than my job. Do I want them to kill my family? How do you make that kind of decision? But it happens all the time. You wouldn't believe how many times."

Here Carrie veered off into discussing how some TSOs have a reputation for looking the other way on certain rules, and I was so curious how a discussion of shoe policy led us to Chechen bombers and TSOs being bribed. I was also curious how policies like the age-related shoe protocol are framed for officers and how they make meaning of them. Are TSOs an especially skeptical bunch, prone to thinking the elderly have nothing to live for and so are susceptible to terrorists' coercions?

"It's just important that we treat everybody the same way," Carrie commented. "That means from babies. Now you think of this. This is ridiculous. If a circus monkey comes through and they have a diaper on, the owner of that monkey has to take that diaper off and show us that there's nothing in there."

Okay, sure. Because there are so many diapered monkeys traveling through security checkpoints? And as it turns out, there are some. Monkeys regularly traverse airports and occasionally get free. In 2018 a monkey escaped from its crate at the San Antonio airport, but alas, it did not go through a security checkpoint.

"But do we do that to humans?" she asked. "No. Why? They can't smuggle an explosive through in a diaper of a child? A diapered baby, they don't get their hands checked. It's only when they're an adult coming through. If they put explosives in that baby's diaper, we would never know it and it would never show up in the body scanner either. So everybody, from babies through a hundred years, should be screened the same way."

I didn't know if I quite agreed with her. It seems like common sense to allow different rules for differently abled people who are likely less risky. But in thinking about the size and scale of some airports, I realized why TSOs like Carrie might be worried.

TSO Cat admitted the scope of her airport is overwhelming. "I think like sixty thousand people a day on an average day go through my airport."

"Sixty thousand?" I asked.

"Flying out!" Cat exclaimed. "That's not even the ones coming in."

"That's a city!" I shouted.

"Amazing, I know," Cat said, continuing on about how many of those sixty thousand are people who have an attitude about the rules. "Well, yeah, I'm sorry, you have to take off your shoes," she said, in an "excuse the heck out of me" tone. We both laughed.

"Then you get the ones, they take off their shoes and they act like they can't walk on the carpet," she said, dismissively, and I immediately felt called out. "It's like, if you have that much of a . . . if that grosses you out that much, wear socks! Put a pair of socks in your pocket or something. I don't know!"

We were both laughing and I admitted how gross I find airport carpeting.

"I agree, it is gross," said Cat. "But I bring socks."

While the divestiture officer position can be challenging, some folks, like the "red shoes, blue shoes" TSO, purposefully instill humor into their work. Peter described how he frames the shoe policy for passengers: "'Enjoy our hospitality,' I say. 'We spent a lot of time making sure you have a sandy beach to walk on . . . you take your shoes off so when you walk across this floor, you feel all the dust and dirt on your bare feet.'"

"I do a little joke," Peter said, continuing. "'Children under twelve and people over seventy-five, you can keep your shoes on, the rest of you here are toast.'"

I chuckled.

"You get them to laugh," Peter added.

And it is appreciated. I recall a past trip where a TSO giving instructions reminded us to take our shoes off. He joked that the floor was cleaned at least once a year, but the socked people would sweep it clean for everyone. I watched him interact with waiting passengers, including an elderly woman who explained her age. With a cheeky grin, he remarked that she would have to keep her shoes on because "You can't possibly be seventy-five."

The passenger, with closely cropped white hair, giggled, her eyes beaming through thin blue wire frames. "You made my day," she said.

The shoe policy remains a continual source of passenger frustration, and the TSA has spent millions of dollars testing shoe scanners that would allow passengers to stay shod in security. Unfortunately, none of the machines have met muster.

Pro Travel Tip #6:

Straight from a TSO—the Airport Is Not a Fashion Show

When asked for advice for new travelers, one TSO was crystal clear.

"For new travelers, old travelers—everyone—the advice is the same," TSO manager Rick said. "The airport is not a fashion show. Be smart and travel in something comfortable. Please don't dress like you're going to a club; most of those outfits are not conducive to moving around in an airport. Shoes should be easily removed and comfortable for walking a good distance. High heels, twenty-eyed Doc Martens, and the really tall boots are inconvenient to be getting in and out of. Use a little common sense about what you wear. If you have a pair of metal-studded jeans, those will likely alarm something called a metal detector. If you don't want to be patted down, don't wear those jeans. I always suggest regular denim or sweats and a T-shirt, personally."

Referencing the behind-the-scenes complexity of airport operations, Rick said, "Also, airports are dynamic places. There is much more going on than what you see. Many of those things can cause a delay to your flight, so plan on being comfortable."

As someone who has unfortunately spent eighteen hours waiting out tornadoes in the Dallas airport, I completely concur.

6

No Crying over Stolen Shampoo

On Liquids and Gels

Labor Day Weekend 2007, West Yellowstone, Montana.

We've come to the end of a mini family reunion at Yellowstone. I haven't been to the home of Old Faithful since I was twelve. Back then I was held hostage in the farthest corner of my grandfather's blue Aerostar minivan. I remember routinely scowling at my little sister, nine at the time, and breathing shallowly in a futile effort to minimize the damage from the chain smoking happening up front.

Though the majesty of the Grand Tetons eventually broke through even my dark middle school malaise (I was just approaching my goth-esque, all-black-wearing, terrible-poetry-writing phase of life), I soon grew tired of counting the ever-present bison and elk, and oohing and aahing over sulfurous steam traps.

Thirteen years later, I've arrived in much grander style, cutting dozens of hours off the trip and descending through the sky to land at the Yellowstone Airport in my not-yet fiancé Tim's 1963 V-tailed Bonanza. He's part of a flying group and borrowed the plane for the weekend. It's really the best way to facilitate a three-day weekend at Yellowstone when you live in Sacramento and don't want to spend thirty hours in the car.

After a lovely few days visiting my great aunts, uncles, and cousins from Idaho at their cabin at the edge of Montana, I marvel at how different a voluntary adult visit to Yellowstone feels. Those oohs and aahs were a lot more genuine this time around.

On Monday we find our way back to the Bonanza. Yellowstone Airport sits in the western portion of the great park, at a corner where Idaho, Montana, and Wyoming come together. The facility itself is small—a modestly sized terminal that services mainly private aviation traffic—the way we've come in. Delta, its one commercial carrier, offers limited and pricey service.

Dragging our bags in from the car, we walk to the general aviation service counter where we pay our fuel bill and overnight fee, a nominal charge to park at the airport. While waiting for Tim to complete planning for the flight home, I notice a large sign tacked up behind the counter, showcasing Ben Franklin's famous quote: "Those who would give up essential Liberty, to purchase a little temporary Safety, deserve neither Liberty nor Safety."

I find the quote all the more poignant as its bold letters face toward the TSA security area behind us. It's still a few years until I will start studying the TSA professionally and sharpening my skills as an ethnographer, but as a lifelong journaler, I can't help but observe and record my surroundings.

The TSA checkpoint is nothing more than a partition and a red line taped on the floor that extends outside onto the ramp. On one side of the red line is the private "general aviation" business, with no security procedures to speak of, only hospitality in the form of cozy leather armchairs and free snacks, water, and coffee. On the other is the checkpoint for commercial travelers, with shoe removal, limits on liquids, and the whole security shebang. Literally the only thing separating them is this red line—no fencing, no guards—a host of rules and regulations, and people's willingness to respect them.

Once our preflight business is concluded, we heft our baggage and head toward the plane. Feeling feisty, we salute the commercial passengers, joking about carrying sharp objects and extra liquids. It's a personal joke for us as I've just made labels for an upcoming trip to Las Vegas. We're shuttling our friends via "AirRedden," piloted by my beloved, Tim Redden. In charge of in-flight entertainment and refreshments, I outfit the plane with water bottles and air sick bags, featuring labels with slogans like "All the Liquids and Gels You Can Carry."

Outside, the red line breaks off a few yards onto the ramp, where planes wait, commercial and private alike. Commercial and general aviation traffic mix at many airports in small locales like this, and I can't help but think how arbitrary and meaningless the division seems. One side of the line is "safe" and "clear" and TSA approved. And the other is what? To me the divide is merely the difference between a leisurely trip with an unmolested body and bottle after bottle of water, and a fundamental curbing of freedom in the experience of travel.

In 2007 the TSA's ban on liquids and gels is not even a year old. It arrived on the heels of the shoe rules becoming mandatory, and for a short time the TSA banned *all* liquids and gels from commercial aircraft cabins.[1] This meant no toiletries in carry-ons, no overpriced water bottles purchased after security, no beverage service from flight attendants. The reactive provision came in response to a foiled terrorist plot out of the United Kingdom, in which twenty-four British citizens of Pakistani origin planned to smuggle liquid explosives in their carry-on luggage to blow up ten planes bound for the United States.[2]

Of course, completely banning liquids wasn't feasible, so a month later the TSA's 3-1-1 rule was born.[3] The new measure curtailed each passenger's carry-on liquids to one quart-sized plastic bag filled with containers of liquids, gels, and aerosols of no more than 3.4 ounces each.

The 3-1-1 regulation sparked considerable debate among consumers and pundits who questioned the veracity of the measure.[4] There is no public information from the TSA that explains, for instance, why 3.4 ounces is safe, but 3.5 is not. Neither does public messaging address concerns that miniscule amounts of some materials would be enough to cause serious damage to public safety. Furthermore, the rules seem to privilege the prevention of explosives coming through security (an acknowledged priority of the TSA), but they say nothing about chemical or biological weapons.

When the rule was implemented, TSA director Kip Hawley suggested that the regulations were scientifically valid and too complex to describe in a sound bite.[5] Yet, from other historical examples—like the mailing of anthrax spores or the attempted distribution of ricin powder—we know that certain toxic substances could easily get past strict airport security rules and cause significant damage. In fact, security professionals regularly assess the risk of terrorists using chemical, biological, radiological, and nuclear weapons—especially highly contagious biohazards like smallpox or viral hemorrhagic fever—in civil aviation contexts.[6]

Although the 3-1-1 rule is still in full effect for most passengers, certain liquids are permissible in larger quantities, including medication, contact solution, and breast milk, although these liquids must be declared and possibly pass special screening before they can be carried through security. Likewise, icepacks can travel through—if still frozen—as can gel-filled bras and prosthetics.

One key thing to note, however, is that TSA policy states that "the final decision rests with the TSA officer on whether an item is allowed through the checkpoint." This opens up a lot of unfortunate ambiguity for passengers who must convince random TSOs that their items are medically necessary.

And passengers aren't always compliant with extra screening. For instance, TSO Roger shared how a mother traveling through the checkpoint with breast milk was angry when Roger scanned the liquid. "We usually do some checking to make sure that the liquid is safe, and for some reason she dislikes people touching the milk for her baby, so she rambles on about the freedom of something, that 'you cannot do that to my kid's milk. It's for him, not for you to touch it because you might contaminate the milk.'"

Shaking his head, Roger continued, "She goes on and on and on, and we have to control that outburst and inform her that we are not putting anything inside the milk. It's not being contaminated. We do searches in a way that we can verify it's safe without opening it."

The woman finally calmed down and Roger explained how many passengers with medically necessary liquids are afraid that officers are adding something to test the liquid.

"She was angry because she thought that we would put something inside the milk to test it. I guess she was not well informed," Roger said. "That or she hadn't been to the airport. Usually people who haven't been traveling a lot don't know what is going on, so anything out of the ordinary and they are panicking. They are afraid that they are being violated, in terms of their rights."

Roger described this interaction as particularly difficult because he prides himself on being a service-oriented officer who goes the extra mile to take care of passengers.

I asked all of the TSOs I interviewed what policies they would change if they could, and many officers mentioned the liquids and gels rule. TSO Peter said, "I know why we can't take fluids. . . . I went through the checkpoint the day after 9/11.[7] Richmond had five thirty-gallon trash cans lined up full of shampoos and conditioners, including from the crew. About a week later they said the crew could keep their water."

I think about the signage I've seen in airports since then, such as the "pour your water here" signs at Portland International, which point passengers to bottle refilling stations at various locations in the terminal.

Peter explained how many of his conflicts with passengers involve water bottles. "We can test for water, and we don't," he complained. "It would take too long to test." He was referring to a scheme the TSA was trying to work up to visually assess water bottles and allow them if they fit into a quart-sized bag, but nothing has yet materialized from that idea.

The TSA does technically allow baby bottles of booze to be carried on, as long as they "fit comfortably" in one quart-sized zip-top bag. The only limitation besides 3.4-ounce (or smaller) servings? The booze must be less than 140 proof or 70 percent alcohol by volume. However, the TSA's "airline partners" and the FAA request that passengers not transport their own cocktails. A recent blog post states: "Be sure to check your airline's website to make sure they are cool with being a designated flyer for your hooch."[8]

Despite being fairly familiar by now, the liquids and gels rules are among the most contentious of TSA policies.

Ty, a TSO in the southwestern United States, discussed how difficult it is to remind people of the rules, especially travelers who should know better. "People who could probably go out and buy their own G-V [Gulfstream

Corporate Jet] choose to fly on this [small, regional] carrier. They act like, 'Well, I fly all over the world with my five gallons of liquid.'"

We laughed, and I commented, "No, you definitely don't."

"I'm thinking, 'Honey, the TSA has existed now for eleven years and you're trying to tell me you've never heard of this before?'" Ty said, the "puh-lease" evident in his tone. "I use that as an example," he continued, referring to my original question about security procedures he would change. "But what I could say is: every single thing that you know TSA requires," meaning he would change just about everything. "Right now, because of the shoe bomber, we have to remove footwear. But they've lightened up on seniors and children now. It's just a work in progress. It's going to be an eternal work in progress," he said.

Ty observed, "But I have noticed the money issues," and I expected him to bring up the cost of security or the TSA wanting to reduce costs. But he was referring to socioeconomics. "It's usually the higher the income, the more they feel a right to skirt any type of security at all. They feel like we should just escort them straight out to their plane and carry their things for them."

While Ty bristled against the entitlement vibes from affluent travelers, the TSOs' consternation with passengers' flouting the liquids and gels rule is about security and the fear that another terrorist attack could happen under their watch. And they see that some passengers just don't get it, despite the attempted terrorism incident that spawned the 3-1-1 rule.

For example, TSO Alexa said, "People think I'm stupid sometimes. They're like, 'It's only water.' I *know* that it's water, lady. But at the same time, I can't really take your word for it that it's water and not liquid explosives. There are so many different things that people have tried in order to endanger others . . . just to cause harm to others on the plane or in an airport." Alexa intimated that every policy is there for a reason.

"I mean, we're pretty smart. You can easily take out a liquid and put it with something else that's harmful. And [passengers] don't seem to understand that."

"Do you try to explain that to them?" I asked.

"I do and I don't," Alexa answered. "Just because certain things we're not supposed to say or whatever. We're not supposed to overexplain and make [passengers] scared or worried. I'm just like, 'Look, we're here for a reason.' I don't tell them that people have tried to blow up stuff before. You don't want to say 'blow up a bomb' because there are certain words you're not supposed to say at the checkpoint. Like you don't want someone to overhear and yell 'BOMB!' And then it's crazy and chaos." Alexa chuckled. "I just explain there's a reason why for everything."

Trying to stay friendly, I did not probe Alexa's reasoning or clarify her historical errors about the advent of the 3-1-1 policy. But I wondered why she and the TSA are surprised that adults remain unsatisfied by their "because I said so . . . just trust me" explanation of one of the more annoying and challenging policies on their books. In fact, many passengers I interviewed were extremely critical of it, including "Leroy," who said, "I hate [security] checkpoints, largely because I know that they're all for show. I know that anyone who really wanted to harm me or their fellow travelers would need very little in the way of 'contraband.'"

Leroy continued, "I know that three ounces of most noxious or poisonous liquids is plenty. And I have zero faith in the TSA employees—who typically range from vaguely incompetent to actively malevolent—to actually do much to preserve my safety. My overall impression is that the plastic bags of liquids, the pat-downs, the whole production is just that—a production staged before me so I'll feel safe from the *terrorists*."

Then again, a lot of the concern TSOs feel about the liquids and gels policy is that it seriously slows down their workflow. Whether it's because they have to rescan a bag because the passenger didn't remove their liquids and gels or because someone is carrying errant contraband like a large tube of toothpaste or because they have to do extra screening on medically necessary liquid, the 3-1-1 policy means regularly wasting time.

My field notes are littered with quotes from TSOs harping on liquids and gels in carry-ons. Some "advisements" at the security checkpoints I observed sounded like threats, as officers shouted variations of these warnings: "You *will* get a bag check if you don't put your liquids and gels where we can see them!" "To avoid a bag check, you *must* bring out your liquids and gels!" "We will shut down the *whole* X-ray just to search your bag!"

Confrontations over the liquids and gels policy illustrate clearly the conflict between organizational and societal discourses. On one hand, TSOs describe an enormous responsibility to protect the public and prevent terrorist attacks, with screening for liquids and gels as a key part of security. But on the other hand, a more rational and pragmatic view of liquids and gels would dramatically improve their daily working conditions.

During a flight through Phoenix, as I'm waiting to have my baggage screened, the TSO harps on the liquids and gels: "If you have any liquids or gels, any lotion, water, spray, anything, it needs to be out of your bag and in a bin."

The rules have been repeated so many times, I want to shout, "We know, okay?!"

Then the officer changes tack, "It's doesn't matter what happened last time or what happened at another airport, they need to be out of your bag and in a separate plastic bag."

Interesting, the reference to other airports. I smile inwardly, knowing I'm full-up on liquids and gels but not planning to remove any of them, including the mace that I forgot to remove, *again.*

I'm still waiting as I notice a young male Latino officer addressing the now growing line.

"Get everything out yah pockets. Cellphones, billfolds, paper, even lint. Get the lint out yah pockets," he says.

The X-ray screener looking at luggage seems meticulous, scrutinizing every picture on his monitors. We stand for a full five minutes without moving and the crowd behind me starts to get restless.

The TSO with his dark, slicked-back hair, perfectly manicured sideburns, and easy smile paces energetically around the spaces between the X-ray machine rows, performing to a captive audience. He keeps a constant banter with his coworkers while commenting blankly to passengers. Noticing that the women behind me are annoyed, he says, "We want to get a good look at yah." He doesn't seem menacing, though, because his thick Brooklyn accent lends a comedic air to his performance. A few minutes pass.

"The good news? This new line is opening up. The bad news? If you have liquids in your bags, I'm gonna kill yah!" He whispers the last part theatrically.

At this point, smiling broadly, I ask, "What's your obsession with lint?" He's mentioned it three times already. He beams back but stumbles in his spiel, ignoring my question.

I let it go, just as the TSO scrutinizing my bags doesn't notice or at least doesn't mention that my luggage is riddled with liquids and gels.

TSO Jeff admitted that bag checks due to liquids are "irritating because it [the liquid] was in *your* baggage," implying that we passengers presumably packed the bags and should know better what's inside.

"It goes through the X-ray machine—now unless you don't know what an X-ray machine does—well, then okay." The heretofore easygoing Jeff now sounds scornful. "Or you get some people . . . ," Jeff says, pausing to laugh. "You tell them, 'You can't take any liquids through.' And after you've already pulled [the liquids] out of their bag, they say, 'It's not a liquid! It's soda or it's Gatorade. It's not a liquid, it's water.' It's like, 'Oh my gosh!'" he says, mimicking the dopey passengers.

I do not mention to Jeff that I'm one of those jerks who never removes her baggie of liquids and gels from her carry-on. But then again, I'm a meticulous packer who's not smuggling a six-pack and pretending I don't know that soda is a liquid.

"That always gets irritating, when you have to deal with people that are stupid, I guess," Jeff adds.

I don't want to even imagine. It seems like a variation on the *Saturday Night Live* liquids and gels skit come to life.

In the 2007 sketch, two instructor characters provide a refresher course to TSOs. The course is about liquids and gels in response to TSA rule changes again allowing liquids on planes after they had been temporarily banned following a terrorism attempt. When asked for examples of liquids and gels, the classroom goes silent and the TSOs shift uncomfortably. The instructors beg for examples.

Finally, someone says "water." Then another officer says "toothpaste," as another says "shampoo." Then a TSO adds "a turkey sandwich!" on account of the fact that "turkey is wet sometimes." The characters go on to debate when a turkey sandwich might be considered a liquid—for example, when it's blended or has 3.4 ounces of mustard on it.

The next segment involves the instructor explaining the new 3-1-1 rule and how liquids need to be three ounces or less because "three ounces can't blow up an airplane," to which one TSO replies, "But four ounces can?"

Before the instructor can reply, another character pipes up, "What's to stop two people from each having three ounces and meeting on the plane to combine them?"

The instructor stammers and immediately changes the subject back to listing examples of liquids. The skit ends when someone shouts, "Meatballs!"

While satirical, the sketch outlines questions that the TSA still hasn't answered nearly twenty years later.

Five years after that *Saturday Night Live* sketch airs, I'm heading to an evening flight. At security I walk purposefully flat-footed on the prickly Astroturf-like carpeting and happen upon a funny version of the liquids and gels call-and-response.

As I go through the metal detector, one of the TSOs is telling incoming passengers to remove liquids and gels from their carry-ons. He starts giving examples of liquids, and when he says "no water," the baggage screener looking at my luggage on the X-ray mumbles, "What about vodka?"

I smile. He doesn't realize he has an audience.

He follows up with "Gin and juice?" He's talking mostly to his coworker, who doesn't appear to be listening.

I laugh at that one and he smiles, caught.

"Maybe on the plane," I say.

I hear him laughing as I walk away.

Pro Travel Tip #7:

Bring the Bottle, Skip the Water

If you are interested in staying hydrated without paying airport prices for bottled water, bring an empty bottle with you. Many airport drinking fountains include bottle-filler attachments with filtered water. And if you're me, you'll also include a baby bottle of Baileys in your quart-sized ziplock bag.

7

Naked Scanners Are for Perverts

On Advanced Imaging Technology

November 7, 2012.

With confidence, I tell the TSO giving directions in the middle of the checkpoint that I want to opt out of advanced imaging. For once, there's no cajoling or attempts to convince me otherwise. He quickly speaks into his ear piece, "Female assist on B, female assist on B."

Waiting for my pat-down, I stand near the backscatter machine, observing the line and my belongings slowly sliding into the X-ray. Soon I am collected by a petite woman with short curly hair who reminds me of a ginger version of "Carla" from the 1980s television show *Cheers*. She's wiry and explosive in her movements. Why just reach when a full lunge will do? I can almost feel the energy bouncing off of her as she asks, "What side are your things on, sweetie?"

I gesture, and we walk to the opposite side of the conveyor belt. I notice other passengers watching me as we walk toward the secondary screening area. Carla gathers my things, placing them on the steel table. Meanwhile, we chat about life. She describes her daughters and her grandson who is "so cute, I could just eat him with a spoon." Unlike most TSOs who pat me down, she doesn't seem even vaguely annoyed at the interruption my pat-down brings to her workflow.

While changing gloves, she leans in toward me. Standing close enough that I can smell her minty breath, she asks if I've been through a pat-down before and I confirm. Leaning in even closer, she confesses, "I could get fired for saying this."

Holding my breath, I wait. Her heavily penciled blue eyes stare directly into mine as she admits, "I won't ever go through the X-ray and I won't let any of my five daughters either."

Eyes wide, I remark, "I never go through them."

She seems to breathe easier. She doesn't explain really, but she intimates that the advanced imaging scanners aren't safe, especially for women.

We gab—me about my doctoral work, she about her daughter in medical school. She proceeds to tell me, leaning in as if I am about to learn trade secrets (and apparently I am), about ways to guarantee a trip through the metal detector, as opposed to the advanced imaging scanner. Among other things, which can't be revealed for the sake of confidentiality, she mentions signing up for TSA PreCheck.

With a brisk pace and firm pressure, she pats me down, omitting some of the instructions as she likely (and rightly) assumes I know them all. I laugh when she says, "There's more than one way to do this," evoking the adage that there's more than one way to skin a cat and referring to ways to get around the system. We both chuckle.

She tells me to "stay put" while she tests her gloves. When she comes back, we chat amiably for a while longer before she resumes work and I put on my shoes. As I pack up my laptop, she walks back over, again standing less than a foot away. She pulls a business card out of her breast pocket, pressing it into my palm. She admonishes me to call the 1-800 number and complain about the backscatter scanner, to say that I don't like it, that I don't appreciate it, and so on.

I agree that I will. And for the first time, I shake hands with a TSO.

Bewildered, I walk toward my gate. It's not every day (or ever) that I meet a TSO willing to share concerns so openly and to encourage resistance among passengers. Up until that point—and up until the writing of this book, in fact—I'd never had my fears and skepticism about the safety of advanced imaging machines validated by a TSA staff member. I'm a staunch opt-outer, meaning I avoid being screened by advanced imaging at all costs. It's partly a political statement and a tiny way to express resistance about the invasion of privacy. And it's partly a concern for health—mine and others'—as I'll discuss below.

But where did this advanced imaging come from? When did good old-fashioned metal detectors stop being enough?

Perhaps the most significant recent changes to airport security procedures—advanced imaging and enhanced pat-downs—came in the wake of the unsuccessful "underwear bomber" of 2009, three years before my interactions with Carla.

Under the direction of American-born cleric and al-Qaeda leader Anwar al-Awlaki, Umar Farouk Abdulmutallab smuggled a bomb in his undergarments onto Northwest Airlines Flight 253.[1] Abdulmutallab, then a twenty-three-year-old Nigerian citizen and son of a wealthy banker, flew from Nigeria to Amsterdam to Detroit on December 25, 2009. The Christmas date and Detroit destination were chosen somewhat randomly to fit Abdulmutallab's schedule and budget. His main mission from al-Awlaki? To bring the plane down over American soil.

While Abdulmutallab considered detonating the sophisticated plastic explosive bomb in the restroom—indeed, he visited the facilities to make final preparations—he wanted to be sure the plane had actually crossed the U.S. border from its route over Canada. He returned to his seat to check the moving map one more time before depressing the plunger under his clothes that would mix the chemicals and create an explosion.[2] Thankfully, the bomb malfunctioned, saving the lives of the 290 people on board.

Whether due to excess moisture in Abdulmutallab's nether region or some technical issue, the bomb did not explode but instead set the bomber's pants ablaze. When he jumped up to tear off his flaming clothes, passengers clobbered him and at least one crew member threatened to throw him out of the plane. After pleading guilty to eight criminal counts, Abdulmutallab was sentenced to life in prison, and he remains one of the few attempted suicide bombers to provide insights into his decisions to law enforcement.

In response to the underwear bombing attempt, the TSA ramped up their planned implementation of new screening techniques. After nearly four decades of relying on metal detectors, the TSA announced it would use advanced imaging technology (AIT) in the form of backscatter and, later, millimeter wave scanners, as the default screening technique. Along with AIT, the TSA announced a new "enhanced pat-down" procedure, discussed in the next chapter.

Advanced imaging machines—nearly a thousand of which are now deployed at approximately 340 airports throughout the country—take images of passengers through their clothing to reveal their naked forms and other "metallic and non-metallic threats" that metal detectors might miss.[3] Pilot tests of whole body imaging (WBI) began at select airports in 2008 and, after a series of delays, were deployed broadly in 2010.

Almost immediately, advanced imaging—especially backscatter technology, which emits potentially harmful ionizing radiation—embroiled the TSA in controversy over passenger privacy and safety.[4] Dubbed "naked scanners" in the popular imagination, AIT machines first came under fire for producing detailed images of passengers that TSA officers viewed in the security checkpoint to assess for danger. Privacy advocates and passengers complained loudly enough that eventually the employee viewing the images was moved to a separate room, away from the passenger receiving the scan. This shift seemed to come in the wake of allegations that during testing, attractive passengers, especially young women, were chosen more often for "random" advanced screening.[5]

Complaints also stemmed from the durability of privacy invasions. Despite protestations from the TSA that the machines were calibrated to not store images, one hundred nude pictures from a Florida courthouse millimeter wave machine were leaked online in 2010.[6] Editors at *Gizmodo*, a technology weblog, released one hundred of the thirty-five thousand images they obtained via the Freedom of Information Act to demonstrate the security limitations of AIT in the public sphere, especially airports.[7]

The release of these images was particularly startling considering the TSA's claims in its 2008 Homeland Security Privacy Impact Assessment that "the images created by the WBI technologies are not equivalent to photography and do not present sufficient details that the image could be used for personal identification."[8] Except that, as you can see in the image gallery, the images can be extraordinarily detailed and personal. Just ask Roland Negrin, a former TSO at Miami International Airport. In 2010 Negrin was arrested for assaulting a coworker who had repeatedly ridiculed him about the size of his genitals after they were displayed on an AIT image during a training exercise. When the coworker wouldn't stop the abuse, Negrin confronted him in the employee parking lot, hitting him with a police-style baton and forcing him onto his knees to apologize.

At the same time, health advocates mounted protests on safety grounds, questioning the amount of and exposure to radiation in the backscatter machines. The TSA has continually asserted that advanced imaging is "safe for all passengers and the technology meets national health and safety standards," including, specifically, those for pregnant women and children.[9] The TSA reports suggest that backscatter technology gives an X-ray dose of radiation equivalent to two minutes of airplane flight at altitude, and that the millimeter wave technology gives off energy that is a hundred thousand times less than cell phone transmission. Yet medical professionals concede that the health risks of this type of technology are still unknown and that there is really no safe level of radiation exposure, especially for officers who work around the machines every day.[10]

The controversy stemmed partly from uncertainty about the health and safety testing conducted prior to deploying the machines and the lack of peer-reviewed studies of the technology.[11] Because the machines are used for security assessment and not medical testing, they are not classified as medical devices and are therefore not subject to the strenuous testing or oversight normally required by the Food and Drug Administration. As such, the machines fall into a problematic gray area and they are not monitored in the same manner as medical devices.[12] So when the TSA says the machines "meet national health and safety standards," they are really leveraging a loophole to encourage passengers to accept them. There are no health and safety standards applied to the scanners.

To put this into perspective, there do not appear to be procedures in place for reporting equipment malfunctions—such as backscatter machines releasing too much radiation—or mechanisms for contacting passengers who may have been exposed. Furthermore, the research upon which the TSA bases its claims of safety suggests that the machines pose a negligible risk, not that they are safe per se.[13] Medical researchers and politicians have called for independent review and regulation, as well as "publicly accessible, and preferably peer-reviewed evidence," on deployed scanners, rather than just factory prototypes.[14] It bears mentioning that the medical arguments suggesting humans should limit their exposure to radiation that doesn't have a medical benefit prompted the European Union to ban backscatter machines in 2011 due to health and safety concerns.[15]

Since the installation of AIT and enhanced pat-downs in 2010, the TSA and the Department of Homeland Security (DHS) have fielded numerous lawsuits regarding safety, privacy, and inappropriate behaviors during screening. For instance, taking issue with invasion of privacy and potential health risks, the Electronic Privacy Information Center (EPIC) launched several lawsuits against the DHS, the first of which called for a halt on the use of scanners until appropriate health testing could be done.[16]

The TSA made no policy changes except to ease restrictions on children and the elderly.[17] In what seemed to be a reaction to public outcry regarding upsetting screenings of young children and the elderly, the TSA developed screening exemptions for children under twelve and adults seventy-five and older. People who meet the age criteria are allowed to proceed through the metal detector rather than through advanced imaging.[18]

In 2012 the TSA started quietly moving backscatter machines out of many major airports and into smaller regional facilities.[19] At the time, officials suggested that the move was to speed up security screenings at busier airports. However, in early 2013 the TSA announced that it would remove all backscatter scanners as the machine manufacturers were unable to meet congressional mandates for increased passenger privacy in the form of a software upgrade. The new software would not show not a passenger's unique image, but rather a generic figure with either a green "pass" light indicating that the passenger may proceed or a red "fail" light signaling a need for further screening.

The machines currently in use are millimeter wave scanners that have the privacy software enabled and do not emit ionizing radiation. Millimeter wave scanners use electromagnetic waves to generate high-resolution images of passengers to identify threats—the idea being that the underwear bomb, for instance, would have been revealed by technology. However, the TSA will not say how effective these machines are or what they can and cannot actually detect, claiming the information is classified.

A former TSO, Jason Edward Harrington, went on record with *Time* magazine to condemn the TSA for its ineffective and unnecessary screening. In an editorial, he claimed that the millimeter wave scanners generate "outrageous false-positive rates" resulting in unnecessary pat-downs.[20] Indeed, according to ProPublica, the millimeter wave scanner generates so many false alarms—some of them at innocuous things like perspiration— that countries such as France and Germany have banned them.[21]

Despite research showing that no terrorist plots since 9/11 have been foiled by AIT, the TSA stands by their multimillion-dollar investment and continues to try out other new forms of technology.[22] And passengers remain unhappy.

Frequent business traveler Alice described feeling annoyed about airport security generally and screening technology specifically. She said, "Like on the one hand, you understand TSOs are there to do their job, and their job is to keep you safe. On the other hand, though, a lot of people, including me, feel that a lot of the stuff is unnecessary. There has to be a better way of doing things."

"What type of steps do you think are unnecessary?" I asked.

"The whole idea of putting in the body scanners and then realizing that they weren't working. They've stopped using them in a lot of airports," Alice said, reflecting on the initial deployment and then retraction of backscatter scanners in 2010, and then the swapping to millimeter wave machines years later. "It's a little frustrating that you would spend so much money to put in a body scanner and then realize that either it doesn't work or it's harmful to your health, and then start removing them. So stuff like that. You learn a new process and then they're constantly changing the rules."

Alice touched on a key criticism of the TSA—mass confusion about rules and what seems like constant change. For instance, when AIT was deployed in airports across the country, passengers were offered the choice to opt out of the scanners and receive an invasive pat-down instead. Some people like me opt out for health and political reasons, or because they have metal implants or medical devices that exclude them from AIT. However, it seems that TSA officers were initially trained (or possibly incentivized) to encourage passengers to submit to the automated screening.

"The TSA [officers] are a little more aggressive about trying to coerce people to use it [AIT]," passenger Sue complained.

During our conversation in 2011, Sue said she had recently started opting out as she learned more about the scanners. But she felt stressed out by officers trying to compel her into compliance, and she often had to wait a long time for a female agent to be available to perform a pat-down.

"Each time I have been fairly accommodating," Sue said of rapid security changes. "But I really felt when they implemented the scanners—the full body image scanners—I thought they just crossed a line. I honestly believe, and I have read studies that [have] shown, that if somebody wants to get something past TSA, they're going to regardless of these ridiculous measures."

As we learned in the discussion of contraband, Sue was not wrong here. Security experts say that weapons routinely make it through AIT screening.

"I feel like it really crossed the line with those scanners impinging upon the rights of people. . . . I don't think that those things help," Sue said. "Although the machines probably make TSO work easier."

The TSA jury is out on that one, at least among the officers I spoke with. In fact, the technology seems to represent even more work and more opportunities for conflict with passengers. TSO Alexa, for instance, complained about AIT protocol adjustments.

"We have the body scan machines now that are automated and I personally don't like that," Alexa explained. "I don't know that they're as efficient, just because we have an operator running the machine from upstairs. They're in a whole different room, and they can't see the passengers.

"If I'm upstairs running the machine, I don't know what that person looks like, who they are . . . I just know that it's a male or a female. So passengers were just making a big uproar about, you know, 'It's invasive! You can see my naked body!' and this and that," she said, mimicking a whiney passenger voice.

"Okay, I'm sorry," Alexa continued, her voice tinged with exasperation, suggesting she hears passengers complain *a lot*. "We're all adults. Women have breasts and vaginas and butts, and you know, men, whatever. It's a body. It's not a big deal and I don't know who you are, and I never will," she stated, suggesting that passenger complaints about privacy were immature.

Indeed, Alexa's clinical, matter-of-fact discussion of body parts contradicts the view of TSOs as fiends who want to use AIT for sexual purposes.

"The point is," she explained, "I can tell if someone has a knife in their pocket, and I can tell if there's something maybe attached to the person's back. I feel like the body scan machine now just detects more obvious things—if there's a belt on or a key in their pocket. . . . When we did have an officer upstairs running the machines, we could go a little bit deeper. We're able to rotate the screen and really scan the person head to toe and front to back, and really, really make sure that they're clear."

Alexa continued, "Now the new machine is automated." If there is an alarm, she said, "I can pat down somebody for their front torso, but then when I get to the waistline I can feel that there's a belt, or I can feel if there is something in the pocket. But the machine didn't show me that. I found that on my own."

"Right," I said.

"I would go back to having the body scan machine run by live officers instead of having it automated."

Alexa's comments illustrate a key tension with AIT. On one hand, the scanners operated by a live person were able to see, in vivid detail, what passengers looked like under their clothes. But while AIT made it easier to identify false alarms and limit the number of unnecessary pat-downs, it also caused legitimate privacy concerns. The compromise of machines producing generic images means officers then have to pat people down to clear the anomalies, which include things like bulky clothing and items in pockets. This is why divestiture officers constantly shout at people that they must remove everything from their pockets.

TSO "Elizabeth" described how sometimes the passengers' clothes, particularly undergarments, set off alarms. "People, women especially, will wear those waist trainers, which is essentially a corset . . . those will always alarm at the groin," she said. "I hate the amount of groin pat-downs I do for those."

But the automated process, while meant to ensure some measure of privacy for passengers, also inadvertently created uncomfortable complexity related to gender identity. Namely, TSOs have to guess people's anatomical sex so that the scanner functions properly—literally hitting a button if they think a passenger is a man or woman. But the officer's guess might not agree with the anatomy that the machine sees, and the disagreement will cause an alarm to sound.

Elizabeth described how TSOs try to guess someone's sex by the tone of their voice if they do not seem typically male or female in terms of their outward appearance.

"We'll try to talk to you," Elizabeth said. "Just, 'Hey, how's your day going?' And wait for [your] response. Sometimes it's hard. Prepuberty, boys and girls sound the same. So then you have to do the guessing game, and then if you get it wrong, it's 'Oh I hit the wrong button, let me send you back in.' A lot of the times you can get it off the voice alone. 'Oh, you're a woman. Oh, you're a man. Let me hit the proper button. Let me hit blue or let me hit pink.'"

"I never realized that you had to guess," I commented.

"That's the hardest thing because we have certain criteria for rescanning and one of them is [selecting the] wrong gender for scans," Elizabeth said. She explained how she covers any confusion on her part by pretending she accidentally pushed the wrong button rather than that she guessed the wrong gender.

"I'll say, 'Oh, I hit the wrong button. That's all. Let me send you back in.' No problem. Right? Usually, 99 percent of them don't know why we're doing that. They really, honest to god, think we've hit the wrong button," Elizabeth said, sounding relieved. "I don't want to offend you. I don't want to embarrass you at all." (I didn't mention to Elizabeth that many passengers probably know *exactly* what's going on.)

For instance, passenger "Sammy" described her struggles with TSA officers correctly guessing her anatomy. "TSA agents just always have trouble trying to figure out what I am," she said, especially in smaller or more conservative towns like Salt Lake City, where she was living at the time of our interview.

"When I lived in Denver, this was never a problem because there are a lot of people who look like me and the TSA agents were like, 'Yes, that is a female person who has short hair and you know, dresses a little more androgynous.' But that's very typical there. . . . In Utah, everyone just thinks that I'm a fifteen-year-old boy," Sammy said, laughing. "Build-wise . . . I'm a relatively skinny person and I have like super small boobs and no curves, and I have short hair. But I also have like a deeper voice and broader shoulders and it's very confusing, I think, for some of them. So they often push the wrong button, which then, you know, alarm bells go off or they're like, 'You don't have a penis.' I'm like, 'Sure enough.'"

We both laughed.

"But then someone has to come over and frisk you, or a person has to awkwardly be like, 'Oh, well go back in there,' and then they push the other button. So it's almost enjoyable for me to watch them, like watch the gears crank and the person's head as they're trying to figure out what button to push," Sammy said.

Continuing, she explained that TSOs will sometimes ask her questions that seem irrelevant to the scan in order to hear her voice. "They're trying to figure out, am I a boy who just hasn't really gone through puberty yet 'cause I have kind of a baby face? Or am I a girl who, like, wants to be a boy, or whatever their little personal script says?"

Sammy described an experience at the airport in Charleston, North Carolina, where the TSO working the scanner asked how old she was.

"I could see the wheels turning," she said, explaining how the TSO was sizing her up. After she answered "twenty-five," he hit the "female" button and she went on her way. "I knew he was trying to ask without asking, but I thought it was kind of creative on his end. . . . I did appreciate that at least he was putting some effort forth to not have an embarrassing situation."

I agreed and shared how in a conversation with TSO Elizabeth, she explained that it's very awkward for TSOs and they regularly try to make encounters less embarrassing for all involved, if possible.

Elizabeth continued, describing how screenings can be especially challenging for transgender people. Indeed, the TSA has struggled for years to accommodate the needs of trans people.

Early on in the age of post-9/11 passenger screening, if passengers could not go through the metal detector or advanced imaging, they had to be screened by an officer of their same sex. For trans passengers who presented differently than their legal identification, this posed significant problems and undue humiliation. However, thanks to the protests of trans people and activist groups such as the ACLU, the TSA changed their policies to enable passengers to be screened by officers of the same gender presentation. So a trans woman with male genitalia could request a pat-down from another woman, and a trans man with female genitalia could be screened by a male TSO.

But Elizabeth explained that it can be tricky to accommodate passengers' needs. If a trans person needs to request a different-than-assumed officer to pat them down, they have to out themselves or leave it to TSOs to guess. Although TSO training recently changed to better serve trans people, it still isn't ideal.

"They changed it to the most horrifically offensive phrasing ever. . . . So our training now is [to say] . . . ," Elizabeth continued in a robot voice, "'I present myself as she and her. What do you present yourself as?' Honestly it's so offensive, so freaking offensive. You know what we do?" she said, looking at me. "We look at you and guess. Which one? Male, female? Pink, blue? Pink, blue? Pink, blue? I'm gonna hit pink."

If you guess wrong, she said, "you're going to alarm in the groin. Some place you wouldn't normally." So, she said, she sends the passenger through again and apologizes for hitting the wrong button.

Emphasizing that she wants to minimize personal embarrassment, Elizabeth said, "They don't need to know I guessed the wrong gender. They don't need to know that."

But guessing and apologizing sometimes isn't the best choice. Elizabeth described one passenger encounter where a woman came through for AIT screening.

"She's got the boobies, thin frame, you know. The long hair, makeup on. I'm going to scan her as a woman."

But the alarm goes off with an indication of something hidden in the groin area.

"This was probably the first week I've been certified on my own without a trainer behind me anymore," Elizabeth said. "Looked like a woman in a sun dress. . . . Scanned again, dumb alarm in the groin again." She then had to conduct a pat-down. "I'm patting [her] down and something's in the groin. Like, what? What's this on the legs? You know, I keep going over the groin and couldn't figure out what it was. So finally I asked, 'Do you have something in your pockets?' She motioned for me to stand up and talk to her real quick so I did. And she leaned in and went [in a big stage whisper], 'That's my penis.'"

"Then I went, '*Oh*, okay! Thank you for telling me. Alright!'" Elizabeth continued, laughing as she recalled her bumbling surprised reaction.

I asked how the passenger responded, and Elizabeth assured me, "She took it well. She thought it was hilarious." Explaining how it was her first pat-down of a trans person, Elizabeth said she told the passenger, "I've never had to pat that down before," referencing the contraband penis, and they both laughed.

Of course, it happened to be one of Elizabeth's first-ever pat-downs. "It was embarrassing, more than anything. Now, it gets to the point that after your fifth or sixth pat-down, like, in general, you don't care anymore. You don't care what you're touching. Like whatever. It's like nurses, I've seen it all, I've patted it all down," she said, echoing Alexa's clinical description of anatomy.

But one of the first? And with an unexpected penis? Although she didn't say so, I can imagine that Elizabeth was grateful for the passenger's grace and humor.

Since then, Elizabeth said, she has assisted numerous trans people and nonbinary folks. "They're usually pretty calm about it. There was one passenger who was kind of ambiguous, they were [gender] fluid, so I had to ask them, 'Who do you prefer to pat you down? Do you want me to pat you down or him to pat you down?'" indicating a male coworker.

The passenger requested her. "I'm like, 'Okay, cool, let's do this. Let's get you through here,'" Elizabeth recalled. "It gets to the point where you're calm about it and you don't care anymore."

Elizabeth expressed appreciation for passengers who reduce ambiguity for officers and help them avoid guessing or creating embarrassing situations.

While a lighthearted example—and not at all typical of trans people's experiences in airports—Elizabeth's interactions and training showcase the unintended social consequences of advanced imaging that are hard to quantify, especially when technology signals the need for physical screening in the form of pat-downs.

Pro Travel Tip #8:

Keep Your Eyes Peeled for New Technology

While the TSA is testing new technologies that may improve travel experiences for passengers—namely CT scanners for carry-on luggage that would potentially eliminate the need for passengers to remove liquids and gels from their bags—they might try to trick you into submitting to privacy-invading scans without your consent. In 2015 the TSA started testing biometric testing for passenger identification screening. Since then, they've been piloting facial recognition software in large airports such as McCarran International in Las Vegas. This type of scanning is optional, so if you don't want your face in a database, you can request to be screened manually.

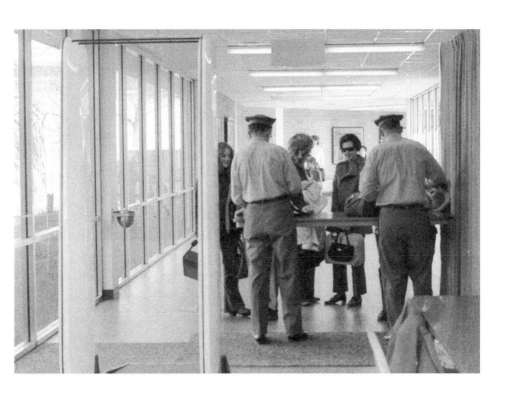

1. The early days of airport security. Flickr, "Airport Security (1973)." Photograph by Hunter Desportes. https://www.flickr.com/photos/hdport/3536539276.

2. The September 11, 2001, terrorist attacks in New York, as seen from Liberty Island. Flickr, "9/11 WTC Photo." Photograph by 9/11 Photos. https://creativecommons.org /licenses/by/2.0/.

3. Jets flew into the World Trade Center in New York on September 11, 2001, in a series of coordinated attacks, with targeted crashes in Pennsylvania and at the Pentagon. Flickr, "9/11 WTC Photo." Photograph by 9/11 Photos. https://creativecommons.org /licenses/by/2.0/.

4. Many societal discourses showcase TSA missteps such as officers falling asleep or looking bored, as in this photo from Chicago's Midway Airport on September 28, 2007. The image also shows TSOs in their original white uniform, before they switched to the royal blue law-enforcement-esque shirts. Flickr, "TSA Preparedness," September 28, 2007. Photograph by Erin Nekervis. https://creativecommons.org/licenses/by-nd/2.0/.

5. Much of the TSA's job involves enforcing rules and confiscating contraband, much to the chagrin of passengers. Transportation Security Administration, Wikimedia Commons.

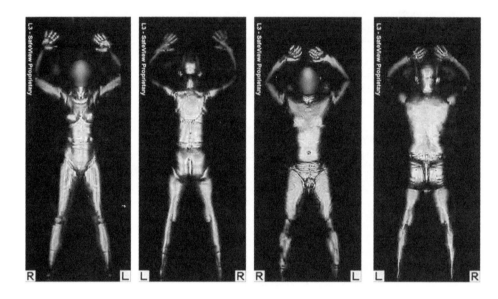

6. Despite the TSA's assurance that advanced imaging machines could not take detailed, personally identifiable images, nor store said images, Gizmodo found that similar machines in a Florida courthouse absolutely stored images. This image was obtained via the Freedom of Information Act from a GEN2 millimeter wave scanner. Transportation Security Administration, Wikimedia Commons.

7. Far from the early days of a table and metal detector, modern airport security is now complex, cumbersome, and technology-driven. Denver International Airport. Photograph by Dan Paluska, Wikimedia Commons.

8

Meeting Resistance

On Enhanced Pat-Downs

September 2010.

When I open the email from my husband, I think he's sent me an article from the satirical website the *Onion*. Surely TSA naked scanners are a joke? But no. The TSA actually plans to start offering passengers two screening choices: step into a machine that uses radiation to see through clothing and skin, or have a head-to-toe groping of your body. Just to get on an airplane. I'm dumbfounded.

November 2010.

The TSA timed the debut of enhanced screening measures for the holiday travel season, starting with Thanksgiving 2010, the fabled "busiest travel day of the year." Privacy advocates stated concerns (and later brought lawsuits) on grounds that both the imaging and the pat-downs constituted illegal searches. The Fourth Amendment to the U.S. Constitution says that citizens are protected from illegal searches and seizure of property without probable cause. And the TSA was treating *all* passengers as potential terrorists. The only cause? Wanting to fly. (The TSA continues to work around this constitutional snafu by claiming the right to search via civil code rather than penal code.)

Activist groups such as the American Civil Liberties Union and Pennsylvania Coalition Against Rape claimed the searches constituted an invasion of privacy and could potentially traumatize victims of a past sexual assault.[1] In fact, Claire Hirschkind, a rape survivor who could not go through advanced imaging because of a pacemaker, refused to allow a TSO to touch her breasts or groin, although she did consent to the pat-down initially. Hirschkind was presented with two options—consent to the screening or leave the airport. When Hirschkind declined to leave the security area (and miss her flight), she was arrested, and later she was found guilty of "knowingly failing to obey a lawful order from airport security."[2]

In the same vein, a San Diego passenger's recorded interactions with the TSA turned into a rallying cry of sorts for those opposed to the TSA's new practices. After opting out of advanced imaging, John Tyner consented to a pat-down but did not want his groin touched. His comment—"If you touch my junk, I'm going to have you arrested"—turned into the slogan "Don't touch my junk," and his recording of the conversation went viral online.[3]

At the same time, civil protesters questioned the TSA's ability to search without probable cause and the use of what some called a legal loophole—the argument that pat-downs, baggage searching, and advanced imaging procedures constitute administrative searches and not criminal ones. It bears mentioning that the liberties taken by TSOs are not legal for police officers to take.

As the machines rolled out across the country in the fall of 2010, a grassroots campaign to protest got under way. The campaign declared Thanksgiving "National Opt-Out Day" and encouraged travelers to reject advanced imaging and request an enhanced pat-down to demonstrate their dissatisfaction and slow down security lines.[4]

I resolved to join the fight.

Thanksgiving 2010.

I barely sleep the night before. With National Opt-Out Day hours away, I wonder what it will be like to stand in line with hundreds of people trying to get home for Thanksgiving and to declare, "I opt out." Opt out of the backscatter scanner screening technology that captures a full-body naked picture. Opt out of the potentially harmful and definitely unmonitored radiation. Opt out of mindlessly letting the government conduct a search of my person and property without cause. And opt in to having my body groped by a stranger, all in the name of national security.

I actually practice saying "I opt out" on the way to the airport. Later I stand with hundreds of other early morning travelers, sleep deprived and shuffling carry-ons, waiting to say my one line.

April 13, 2011.

As it turned out, I escaped that moment for another five months because the scanners were slow to start in my home airports. But the possibility of opting out never left my flying frame of reference. With every flight out—a biweekly event for me, at the time—I wondered if my next trip would be "the one" where I would face a gropey pat-down. Would it be like the horror stories I'd read in the news and heard from passengers? Would I, like so many others in the public sphere, feel humiliated, violated, and angry?

It was a Southern California TSO who first molested me. I say "molested" in terms of Merriam's second "somewhat old-fashioned" definition: "to annoy, disturb or persecute." I called my husband immediately afterward and told him it wasn't that bad. I reported how the woman officer acted professionally, used humor, worked quickly, communicated well, and did not "meet resistance," a vague term that the TSA uses to refer to making contact with genitalia. It wasn't fun, but it wasn't the horrific experience I had envisioned for almost half a year.

It did get me thinking about the processes of security—the idea that we give up basic freedoms and allow invasive searches largely without question. That we must choose between molestation and naked scanning as a condition of travel. That the hassles—the time, money, emotional energy—don't appear worth the reward of potentially, perhaps finding a terrorist. The hassles seem like a *production* of security, a performance that we all—passengers and employees—willingly take part in while knowing it is just a charade.

Months later I'm in a practically deserted security area in Phoenix. Blue shirts outnumber travelers five to one. After completing the gray-bin, shoes-off performance, the baby-faced agent blocking the regular metal detector directs me to the nearest backscatter scanner. In the firm voice I've been practicing, I say, "I'd like to opt out."

Babyface rolls her eyes. "Female assist!"

"She opts out?"

"Female assist!!"

"It's a female? I thought you said male."

"Yeah, it's a female."

Yeah, it's a female.

Soon, nitrile-covered fingers grope my body, pressing firmer into my flesh than my first two experiences with the "enhanced" pat-down, as the TSA was still calling it in early 2011. I'm not exactly upset, but I'm interested in the fervor with which this young woman searches me. She describes and follows protocol to a tee, acting as if touching the breasts of a stranger is all in a day's work, no big deal. For her it is, I suppose. I learn that she conducts a disproportionate share of pat-downs compared to her male colleagues because there are far fewer female agents at this airport. *Well, It's-a-Female sure appreciates you being here.*

Unbeknownst to this TSO, I'm a communication researcher, gathering data, one pat-down at a time.

Spring 2011, sitting on a TSO's couch.

"So have you ever had to give anyone one of those advanced pat-downs?" I ask Skeet, referencing the new protocol that's been all over the media for months.

I'm sitting on the couch in his dimly lit living room where children's toys, clothes, and artwork litter every surface. I met Skeet through a friend who worked at his daughter's preschool. Every so often, the little artist pokes her head downstairs or zips through our interview, angling for a snack.

"Advanced pat-down?" Skeet says, screwing up his eyebrows.

I'll realize later it's *enhanced* pat-down, not *advanced*.

"I've had to give quite a few pat-downs," Skeet continues. "Are you referring to the new pat-downs where we have to touch the groin area?"

"Mm-hmm."

"Yes. That's actually standard procedure now."

Touching groins is now standard procedure. Fantastic. Indeed, it's around this time that the TSA stops using the word "enhanced" and just calls them plain pat-downs.

"What's that like?" I wonder.

"As uncomfortable as it is for you, you [only] have to do it once. I have to do it numerous times during the day." He lets that sink in. "Believe me. Like I said, as uncomfortable as it is for you, it's [more] uncomfortable for me. I don't really want to do it, but I know I have to. I'm going to touch you, and you're going to be done. I'm now done with you. Now the next person comes in, and I have to do the same procedure, same speech, same everything."

I consider his words, thinking about what it must be like to touch strangers all day long and how much it must suck to be the last passenger of the day, the tenth or twelfth or twentieth groin he's groped during a shift when his patience has run out.

"What does that make you feel like?"

He looks at me, seconds ticking by until nearly a minute has passed in silence.

"When I first got there, we didn't have this procedure. I mean, we did. When I first got there, it was not as in-depth." He references the first ten years of TSA history, when pat-downs were strictly reserved for people who set off metal detector alarms and when TSOs used the backs of their hands only. "But then as security evolved, then we had to change what we did to evolve with the time."

I find his rationalizing interesting. To think that touching "sensitive areas," to use the TSA euphemism for breasts, buttocks, and groins, is a natural evolution of security. The argument is basically that sexual assault—which, according to the California penal code, is unwanted touching of another person's intimate parts —is necessary for safe travel. My mind boggles.

"I heard about it like a lot of people do at work. Like, 'Oh, this is coming,'" Skeet explains.

I stare back, and he clarifies. "You might have your job and you would hear something was coming through the grapevine? So I heard about it. And I was like, No. That can't be right. We're not going to do that. And then when I was sitting down in the class, they taught us this [enhanced pat-down]. And I was like, wow. This is reality. This is really happening. And then we have to do it to ourselves first because we have to know what we're doing. It's the same way when you first start the training. This is the simulation part. Okay, so we're going to do it to ourselves. And we're going to do it to ourselves until we get it comfortable. And then they send us out there."

I'm now imagining a bunch of TSOs groping each other on repeat, and I strain to stay focused.

"So I'm in the class and I'm going 'This is pretty uncomfortable.' And now I have to go do it to somebody else. I kind of just clicked it in my brain: This is what I have to do. So I'm not like, 'Eww. I have to . . .' It's just something I have to do."

I listen and, for the first time, start to develop deep empathy for TSOs. I begin to imagine that as much as the security experience is difficult for passengers, it's also incredibly challenging for employees. I had started my research project wondering why passengers put up with such invasions of privacy, and now I can't help but think about what it must be like to work for the TSA.

June 2012, flying to nowhere.

I'm waiting for what will be my fifth pat-down of the day. Lately, my research has taken the form of flying to nowhere. While I typically collect data during actual travel, this summer I have booked eight daytrips to airports on the West Coast, specifically for the purpose of visiting security numerous times before returning home. I learn quickly that while flights to Burbank and Long Beach are cheap, their tiny security areas do not afford good data collection. I find way more interesting experiences up in the Pacific Northwest.

I've again opted out of advanced imaging and stand to the side of the scanner, confusing other passengers, who keep asking if I'm in line to be scanned and seem afraid of cutting in front of me. Soon, a diminutive woman with salt-and-pepper hair, parted in the middle and pulled back into a tight tail, comes to collect me.

We walk through a side gate that circumvents the metal detector. Languidly, she gestures for me to point out my belongings on the conveyor belt.

My three bags in her arms, she walks with me to a table adjacent to the AIT, where she says she needs to change her gloves. She inquires if I've had a pat-down before. *Yes, just twenty minutes ago, actually*, I think to myself.

Underneath the standard blue nitrile, she wears fuzzy white gloves, seemingly made of cotton. Having never seen a TSO wear them, I'm curious. She explains that they enable her to change nitrile gloves more quickly and also to avoid sweaty hands. Out of the blue she says, "I'm going to test my gloves."

I ask why, as in all my trips so far, TSOs have never *started* a pat-down with glove testing. In addition to checking for hidden contraband under clothes, TSOs test their gloves after pat-downs to identify any chemicals that might signal contact with explosives. If you've ever had your hands swabbed in security, it's the same idea.

She says, "It's just my habit," apparently due to false positive alarms.

After testing the gloves, which—fresh out of the box—are predictably negative, she turns theatrical, saying: "Pat-down commencing in 3, 2, 1 . . ."

"How long have you worked here?" I ask.

"Ten years." She sighs deeply.

"How on earth??" I exclaim, surprised and impressed. A tenure of ten years means she's been employed with the TSA almost since its inception.

"Well, it keeps me in my house. It keeps my bills paid. And it provides entertainment, sometimes," she quips, laughing.

Turning back to the business at hand, she inquires if I'm ticklish.

Never having been asked this by a TSO before, I reply, "A bit, but I promise to keep it in." We chuckle.

She sets to work after posing the usual questions: Do I have any sore or sensitive areas? Do I have any medical devices she should be aware of? Do I want a private screening? No, no, no. She confirms that when she gets to "sensitive areas" (read: breasts, butt, and groin), she will use the back of her hands.

I am fairly well shocked a minute later. Standing spread-eagle, I feel her double-gloved fingers brush hair from my collar before trailing down my spine, pressing into flesh, which takes no effort as I am wearing filmy pink rayon. She "clears" the waistband of my trousers, fingers sweeping deftly against the skin of my lower back before brushing my buttocks intently with the back of her hand. (The term *clear* is TSO lingo for checking and most officers use the term as they describe their actions during pat-downs.) Downwards, she strokes my legs firmly, before gliding up to "meet resistance." I startle. Did she just touch my lady parts from the back? An accident, surely.

Coming around to face me, she clears the collar of my blouse, her hands following the line of my draping cowl neck. I feel her finger*tips* trace the contours of my breasts and I grit my teeth. Only then does she use the back of her hands to sweep assertively around each breast, blue-gloved hands crashing through cleavage and cramming my bra into my breastbone.

Her fingers continue to probe my torso carefully, clearing my waistband from the front before sliding down my legs and coming up once again to "meet resistance." Without a doubt, this woman has just touched my clitoris, a body part not even my gynecologist has ever attended to. I want to scream.

Instead, I wait for her slow work to conclude. She walks away to test her gloves again. I stand in disbelief, seething, using all of my self-control to keep from shrieking. The memory of her groping hands makes me feel like my private parts are somehow burning. Standing stock-still, I take no notice of anyone or anything around me.

A minute later, when the beep confirms I am not smuggling explosives, she wishes me a nice day. For the first time in more than one hundred security experiences, I want to yell, complain, find a manager, make a scene. But I don't. Why not?

She smiles and tells me to have a nice flight, her grin now seeming malicious. I say nothing. Would it matter if I did?

I leave the security area mortified. Cheeks red, heart pounding, I walk across the green-and-blue carpet to sit in chairs aligned on what seem like longitude and latitude lines. Despite being so specifically located, I feel lost.

As I scribble field notes in a haze of anger, I don't yet realize that more than two years and probably sixty pat-downs into my research journey, I've finally experienced the type of pat-down that caused people to protest. The type of pat-down that people equate with sexual assault and that advocates for victims of sexual assault lambast in the news. Frankly, before that moment, I thought people might be exaggerating, even after one of my own passenger interviewees broke down in tears describing her experience.

But no. Right now I can relate to the feeling of being absolutely out of control and in the presence of perverted power. With someone who very clearly felt joy at controlling me and using her position to touch me in inappropriate ways.

So I sit, security to my right, a large hangar-sized window to my left. Seething, I pound laptop keys in a fury, of course stopping at the end to post an outraged and explicit version of events on social media. I feel myself getting worked up to the point of tears. Then suddenly I see a Facebook notification that a friend is nearby. While I have been getting groped and flailing about it on Facebook, a dear friend has been sitting in the bar behind me, oblivious.

We meet up, not having seen each other in a couple of years. After calming down and enjoying a drink, I skip off to catch my flight home with a much different attitude. Having my mortification so quickly interrupted, I get to thinking about the experience with a more level head.

I don't realize that my visceral repulsion will turn to abject humiliation, however. I'm not embarrassed about being touched, not really. That made me angry. No, I mostly feel ashamed because I did nothing.

I didn't question it.

I didn't try to stop it.

I didn't note the officer's badge number.

I didn't ask for a supervisor.

I didn't even complain later, despite the fact that I'd seen airport comment cards throughout the terminal.

No, I let the interaction go unchallenged.

At first, I console myself that it probably wouldn't have mattered if I had complained. Appearances from a security camera would show a standard enhanced pat-down with a pleasant-looking officer, not the overly intimate touch that had me questioning everything I knew about airport security procedures and my own agency. But when I consider how broad social discourses shape behavior and ideas, I begin to think differently.[5]

Societal discourses, including TSA rules as an extension of the social institution of security, can seem like an overwhelming force that manifests in passenger apathy. As passenger Portlander lamented, "I know I can't change it, so why bother?" The power of this discourse and enacted authority can overshadow opportunities for passengers to assert agency. Although passengers confess to feeling constrained by and impotent to influence airport security protocols that make them uncomfortable, evidence suggests that passenger voices *do* matter.

Even though bureaucratic systems like the TSA seem immovable, policies and practices change frequently. In airport security, changes arguably are most often prompted by security threats, but they also come after news coverage, customer demand, and legal action. For instance, after several high-profile media exposés on pat-downs involving children, the TSA debuted modified screening procedures for kids.[6]

Passengers should understand their rights so they know when TSO behavior is unacceptable and can take action against experiences that make them uncomfortable or upset. Get a badge number. Ask for a supervisor. File a formal complaint.

It might also help to consider that most TSOs aren't thrilled by their role as gropers.

TSO Jonathan said, "There's nothing like the tension in a situation where a person who chooses to receive a pat-down proceeds to inform you every step of the way of how you are now sexually abusing them. Not fun, and you really can't do or say anything but try to finish the job and get away. It makes me want to exclaim just how much we, the screeners, hate having to do the pat-downs."

November 10, 2017.

It's 5:24 a.m. and a TSO has her fingers pressed into my chest.

"Do you have anything in there?" she asks, pushing down on my left breast.

"Besides boobs?" I wonder aloud. I haven't had enough coffee to laugh with my joke. As she looks unconvinced, I pull down my sweater to give her a peek at the contraband-free goods.

As she walks away, I think she is going to test her gloves and let me go, but she comes back with a supervisor who says *she* now needs to conduct a second, private screening. As we walk into the closet of a screening room, I explain my frustration as an experienced business traveler. The supervisor ignores me and conducts the second screening.

Fingers now smashing my left breast, she queries, "Are you sure there's nothing there?"

"Besides a bra and boobs?" I snap, struggling to keep my voice even. Wrenching up the hem of my sweater, I ask, "Would you like me to take my shirt off?"

We stare at each other.

"You're cleared to go," she finally says.

Unlike previous uncomfortable interactions, this time I remember to look at both women's badges, and before I've even gotten through the line at Starbucks, I've lodged a complaint on the TSA's website and shared the experience publicly on social media.

The TSA should be prepared to meet more resistance from here on out.

Pro Travel Tip #9:
Know Your Rights and Stand Your Ground

It is your right to opt out of advanced imaging and request a pat-down. However, TSOs often try to convince passengers to just go through the advanced imaging; it's a lot faster and less disruptive for their workflow. You might hear them say that "you'll be exposed to more radiation in the airplane than you will in this scanner" or that the radiation risk is minimal because it's non-ionizing. Stand your ground. Politely, of course.

Deferring to authority is a strong social discourse. We're conditioned starting in childhood to respect authority figures—parents, teachers, doctors, police officers. Even though we might not normally consider TSOs in the same sphere of influence, in the security context—while wearing their crisp uniforms, thick boots, brass badges, and big attitudes—they communicate authority. And our default is to defer. But that doesn't mean you have to comply with a screening that makes you uncomfortable just to make their work more convenient. Politely and firmly repeat that you would like to opt out.

9

Risk-Based Security

On Things That Are Good in Theory

October 10, 2010.

It's a Thursday evening and I'm heading home for the weekend. In the plodding security line, crisp Dockers, plaid button-ups, and starched collars contrast with jeans, T-shirts, sweatpants, and sun dresses.

I notice a wiry woman in her late thirties. She wears clacking high heels and painted-on blue jeans with a star emblazoned on the back pocket. Her white linen shirt fits snugly across her chest, a complicated corset cinching up the back. Agitated, she is clearly in a hurry and is trying to get a TSO's attention.

Meanwhile, three female TSOs check in passengers. There are actually six female agents at the gate, which seems unusual, as men usually dominate this scene. One young brunette in her early twenties, hair pulled back in a stubby pony tail, screens IDs. I notice her shirt is untucked over a rounded belly. She meekly mouths pleasantries but does not smile. Across from her, a plain-faced brunette in her thirties welcomes people with a pleasant air. She doesn't smile either, but occasionally makes small talk with passengers, causing them to laugh.

Most prominent, though, is the hulking blond TSO at the front of the security line, who is scrutinizing passengers and pacing. I've never noticed TSOs simply moving around the check-in area at this time of the evening without a specific task. I wonder if it's a general security concern or perhaps the heightened alert in Europe.[1]

The TSO stands maybe five feet nine. Imposing, with a heavy frame and light blond hair in a messy ponytail. Although she is wearing makeup, she does not seem particularly feminine. She struts around the checkpoint, arms folded across her chest. She hawks the crowd, grimacing occasionally, as if she is looking for something. Her pacing and peering remind me of proctoring exams and keeping my eyes peeled for student malfeasance.

At some point the officer who I've now mentally dubbed "the Hulk" tells a ticketless man and woman to leave the security area. They put up a fight, arguing that they are waiting with someone who is going through the line, but she makes them leave quickly. I think back to my long-ago journey to college, when my mom and sister accompanied me through airport security and waited with me at the gate. I understand the impulse to stay with loved ones until the last possible second, but it does seem strange in the current security climate.

Four Latina women approach a TSO at a table across the checkpoint. I hear the agent say, "No English?" and see the women nod.

The agent seems flustered and calls back behind her for help, but no one is around. The Hulk comes over, but she doesn't speak Spanish either. The seated agent attempts to communicate, and finally a nearby passenger comes over to translate. It appears the women have passes to get through security, but no photo IDs. After five minutes, the agent lets them into the checkpoint with the promise of extra security measures.[2]

Meanwhile, the antsy passenger, "Tammy," is practically bouncing out of her Candies. She must be late for her flight. She seems to want the TSO's attention, but she doesn't call out. Finally, the woman next to her—a matronly fifty-something—yells "Excuse me!! Excuse me!!" in a resonant teacher voice.

But the TSOs are absorbed with helping the four women with identity verification and do not respond.

"Should I just go ask?" Tammy implores her new friend.

Timid but motivated, Tammy is waiting for someone to give her permission to leave the line. She ponders the situation a few seconds more and then crawls under the security tape.

I hold my breath, hoping for a scene. I've never seen anyone go under the tape so close to the security checkpoint, and definitely not with the intention of getting through the line faster.

Tammy tiptoes up to the Hulk and I watch, excited.

Nothing happens. The Hulk doesn't bat an eye. Tammy plaintively explains her situation, asking what her options are. The Hulk gestures vaguely to the express line with an "I don't care" air.

With that, Tammy walks to the front of the shorter line, cutting off two suits who don't seem bothered. They share departure times as she passes—with hers just ten minutes away, she'll never make it—and the men tease her. (Would they have been so jovial and accommodating if she was unattractive? Somehow I doubt it.)

Tammy clack-jogs through security and the Hulk goes back to pacing the line. It's early in my study of the TSA and I don't realize yet that the Hulk is a behavior detection officer. Her whole job is to observe and assess passengers, and apparently to intimidate them into compliance.

A few weeks later, as I'm walking through the terminal food court on the way to security, I see the Hulk chatting with a friend and laughing, waiting in line for dinner. I remember her as churlish and vaguely threatening, but she's smiling and jovial here. I wonder if it's exhausting to maintain two such different personas? I'll keep this question in mind as I investigate the TSA's forays into risk-based security.

A heated criticism of the TSA, heard most profoundly from security experts, is that airport security programs focus too heavily on finding dangerous *items* and not dangerous *people*.[3] Although the TSA seems to reinforce this image by advertising the plentiful and often outrageous items they seize during screenings of carry-on luggage, they've launched several initiatives focused on observing and assessing risk among various groups.

Their programs include passenger surveillance and differentiated screening programs for passengers and airline crew.

In regard to surveillance, the TSA quietly introduced its Behavior Detection and Analysis Program in July 2007 after a period of pilot testing. The program draws on behavioral analysis training designed by psychologist Paul Ekman. A pioneer in the study of emotions and facial expressions, Ekman was the inspiration for a character on *Lie to Me*, the TV show about detecting deception.

Behavior detection officers (BDOs) look for "suspicious facial expressions of tension, fear or deception."[4] These specially trained officers stand near lines and watch crowds, occasionally interacting with people they deem suspicious in order to refer them for extra screening or, potentially, to law enforcement.

"Our job is to find people that are not necessarily right in their mentality," said "Steve," a TSO and behavior detection officer. "Like a Secret Service person."

(At this point, dear reader, it's critical to mention that I did not laugh out loud.)

"The Secret Service's job is to protect the president. They are literally scanning the crowd for unacceptable behavior or triggers that require them to act," Steve continued.

Steve described how he was prepared for this work via SPOT training—Screening of Passengers by Observation Techniques—a program developed from Ekman's research.[5] SPOT training teaches officers to look for behavioral clues that signal nefarious intent, ranging from exaggerated yawning, arriving late, wearing improper attire, repetitive gestures, excessive clock watching, and wide-open staring eyes, among more than eighty other things.

If you're thinking "Hey, that sounds like every Stereotypical passenger mentioned in this book!" you're right.

"Our goal is to find the bad guys by using the training, by looking for differences," Steve mentioned. "A change in behavior from the rest of the group. That's the important piece of the puzzle. You may not be a terrorist, but if your behavior is different than the rest of the line, [expect to be stopped]."

Steve gave examples like laughing and joking when others are not, or acting sullen and put-out when others are neutral.

"It's common for ladies to fidget . . . playing with their jewelry, running their fingers through their hair," he said, confirming "exaggerated or repetitive grooming gestures" from the SPOT checklist. "Those are the things we see as behavior detection officers. Cues. Cues of stress, fear, deception that pertain to a person's psychological and mental state."

Of course, some signals are completely innocent. He gave an example of traveling home to care for a sick relative. "You're upset. You're kinda freaked out. Those kinds of behavior cues [are] something that we pick up on."

I asked how common it is to perceive such differences in crowds, and Steve said it depends on the day and the terminal.

"Today I was in United's terminal. There were probably close to three thousand people coming through on a given shift. Maybe a hundred that are acting out in an eight-hour shift. Then there's times when people are totally fine."

"So what happens if you do spot something out of the ordinary?" I asked, pun unintended.

Steve commented that odd behavior would invite a conversation. "For the most part, we ask, 'Hey, how's it going?' 'Hey, where yah going to?'"

He clarified that BDOs will initiate a conversation to see if the behavior is just typical travel stress or something more sinister. "It would be [figuring out], okay, is this person gonna snap or what? There are some people who are going to back down [when confronted]. There are other people who aren't going to back down no matter what you tell them. . . . Every person has their own particular cues. The bottom line is people just want to be heard. Maybe they're having a crap day. Maybe their boss rolled into 'em and they're getting frustrated, getting really loud in the checkpoint and taking it out on officers."

Despite having guidelines from the SPOT training, Steve confided that "in reality, there's not really a set threshold . . . of behaviors that would trigger a certain inquiry or further investigation by myself or a colleague. It's more along the lines of assessing 'hey, is this person going to be okay?' And that's why we work in pairs."

Steve indicated that the buddy system works for safety as well as for confirming threat assessment. "Your partner's gotta back you up one hundred percent or it's not gonna happen."

Waiting for anomalies can be nerve-wracking for some TSOs.

"They teach you behavior detection stuff, so you have to look not only at what passengers are putting through, but you have to look at the person, look them up and down," said Jeff, a TSO with some BDO training, describing running the X-ray machine and looking at passengers.

"And you're doing that over and over and over and over, and you have to do it very quickly and have to assess. . . . Basically, you're assessing risk. Now when it's busy, you're doing that not just to the person that immediately comes up to you, it's fifteen people behind them," Jeff continued. "You've already assessed all those people and now you're going further and further and further back, and so it gets very busy. It gets me very on edge, I guess."

Trying to spot the danger in a rolling sea of hundreds would stress me out too, I think. Then again, from a full-time BDO, the picture is a little more mundane.

"Sometimes our job can get really boring," Steve confessed. "You're literally standing there for hours on end, constantly on a hard concrete floor. Occupational hazard in my opinion. It's tough on your legs. Sometimes you get a little frustrated because, it's like, you can't sit down," he complained. "If you sit down, maybe it's that one little time that somebody is gonna walk by and cause a scene or get upset."

I asked him to explain.

"I would be annoyed if I was passenger and then all of a sudden . . . you're literally seeing two officers on the side who appear—*appear*—to be doing nothing. Officers standing talking about football or what's for dinner, really loud," Steve speculated, explaining how some officers give the

BDOs a bad reputation with management, and consequently management becomes more stringent.

"They don't want you to carry bottles of water with you," Steve offered, as an example. "Management says it's a hot topic. The passengers are going to get upset because *they* can't have bottles of water."

I rolled my eyes to myself here, thinking about how petty passengers can be. Yes, I personally think the 3-1-1 rule is BS, but I also don't begrudge TSOs proper hydration!

Rick, a former BDO and supervisor of the BDO program at his airport, supported Steve's assessments.

"Because BDOs work . . . in front of the checkpoint, they get a lot of flak from passengers when the lines are long, because they aren't inside working on a lane," Rick explained. "Not everyone in a TSA uniform is able to operate checkpoint equipment, and passengers do not understand the BDO role, and get upset at what they view as idleness on the part of officers."

Indeed, many passengers I spoke with mentioned feeling annoyed at TSOs "standing around and not doing anything." But the BDOs insisted that maintaining vigilance is effortful work, contrary to how it might look from the outside. Just like the Secret Service, as Steve emphasized. And that alertness might come at a cost. As in law enforcement, a job that involves constant vigilance can induce stress and spark mistrust in and out of work.

TSO Elizabeth discussed the consequences to her work and personal life of being certified for a special TSA program.

"So I got behavioral detection training to do this [program]. I was already paranoid. Let me tell you, that made it so much worse! I never used to be claustrophobic about crowds until I got that training and now all of a sudden it's like, 'You're acting weird. Are you a suicide bomber?'"

"Can you say more about that?" I asked. "And if you can't, no problem at all." *I'm always careful in interviews not to probe topics that might ask officers to reveal Sensitive Security Information.*[6]

"You don't want crowds. To be in crowds, you're a target. You see all the mass shootings or where they drive trucks [into crowds]. . . . Crowds now make me so nervous," Elizabeth explained. "Since I got behavioral training, I can look at a person and go, 'Okay, this is a normal baseline. This is how in this situation this person's supposed to be reacting.' And then you see, you know, person B over here who's sweating and twitchy and generally not reacting to the public around them. And you're going, 'What's wrong with you? You're either on drugs or you've got a bomb.' And I'm hoping it's drugs. I mean it's usually drugs. Yeah. It's almost always drugs."

We chuckled a bit. But then Elizabeth explained how her work-sponsored paranoia training had seeped into her personal life.

"So a couple months ago, I texted my sister, 'Hey, there's somebody outside and they've got like an ammunitions box, like the kind that you see in the military. . . . And he's got a shovel.' So I creep up to the window and open the blinds just enough, and took a picture of this guy and sent it to her," Elizabeth offered, admitting how she called their apartment complex's management office.

"Yeah, he was fixing one of our sprinkler lines. I was so convinced he was burying like drug money or something," Elizabeth chortled. "All my jobs ruined me. Like I'm not a normal person anymore."

I shared how my grad school mentor studied correctional facilities for her dissertation project. She analyzed how correctional officers also demonstrated severe paranoia in and out of work, even suspecting random people in public of being escaped convicts. Elizabeth said she understood and described how her training had changed her behavior.

"You stay where you can see doors so you can make quick exits. My brother who works for the police department, he does the same thing," Elizabeth stated. "You sit where you can see the exit. You stay to the side in elevators. You don't want to be directly in front of the doors in case somebody is going to try and hit you."

I thought about the defensive behaviors I demonstrate in life, things like walking opposite of traffic so no one can pull up alongside me and swoop me into their serial killer van, or carrying my keys between my fingers while walking to my car at night. I can't imagine keeping up that level of attentiveness during all facets of life. It sounds utterly exhausting.

In late 2011 behavior detection efforts became more formalized in two pilot airports, Boston Logan and Detroit International. The new program featured more focused interaction between BDOs and passengers. Dubbed "TSA chat-downs" in the media, the program experimented with short interviews between TSOs and *all* passengers, not just those found to be acting suspiciously. Modeled after the lauded Israeli model of behavioral profiling, the chat-downs involved asking passengers simple questions to probe for hostility or deception that might warrant further investigation.[7] However, the program was scrapped in a flurry of critiques about feasibility, hits to line efficiency, and racial profiling.

The whole behavior detection program has faced skepticism from security professionals, who question whether the level of training is sufficient for BDOs to master behavioral profiling, which demands a sophisticated understanding of emotional management and micro facial expressions.[8] Furthermore, critics point out that a program that works well in Israel— with its seven primary airports and eleven million annual fliers—is not scalable to the United States, where hundreds of millions fly through four hundred primary airports.[9]

Skepticism comes from inside the TSA as well. TSO Carrie said BDOs are trained by Israeli intelligence officers. But, she said, "basically, the Israeli security said that 'Our people who cleaned toilets know more about behavior detection than your behavior detection officers.' That's kind of scary, don't you think?"

"That's a little bit scary, yes," I agreed, knowing that reports in 2013 by the U.S. Government Accountability Office showed that the ability to identify behavioral threats using the SPOT approach is little better than chance.

"They've never caught anybody," Carrie said, referring to BDOs who scan crowds. "We've caught people." As Carrie is based in the Midwest, *I'm assuming a royal "we" here to indicate the TSA broadly.* "We caught somebody in Midland, Texas, with two pounds of C-4," she said. "That made the national news, so I can tell you that."

"My goodness!" I chirped, promising to look the story up later.

Carrie continued, "The reason the BDOs didn't catch it is because he didn't act suspicious. . . . If you know anything about [behavioral profiling], you know that most psychopaths don't show any signs [of] their business or odd behavior."

"Sure," I commented, although the entirety of my behavioral profiling training comes from watching the CBS drama *Criminal Minds*.

While Carrie was right about the confiscation of the C-4, the perpetrator in question did not turn out to be a psychopath. Sergeant Trey Atwater was indeed arrested after TSOs in Midland, Texas, discovered two and a half pounds of C-4 in his backpack on New Year's Eve in 2011.[10] Atwater, a Green Beret and demolitions expert, had traveled from North Carolina to visit family over the holidays. The FBI dropped the felony charges against him when they determined it was plausible Atwater was actually unaware of the explosives, which were lodged inside the lumbar padding of his backpack.

Atwater had returned from a third tour in Afghanistan eight months previously, where it was routine for soldiers to carry large quantities of C-4. Because Atwater reportedly was an excellent soldier, the FBI supported his claim that he had not realized C-4 was in the backpack and didn't knowingly bring it with him. Incidentally, the explosives were *not* discovered when Atwater departed from North Carolina.

"There's a lot of people who are very nervous to fly. If you have more than two of these [suspicious] behaviors together, they're going to pull you aside and go through your things and talk to you and give you an extra screening," Carrie continued, talking about the SPOT checklist.

"My brother's friend, it happened to him," Carrie clucked, referring to behavioral profiling. "He asked me why. 'Well,' I said, 'you have very short hair. You have two tattoos of, like, barbed wire around your arm. You wear a cut off . . . I don't know what you would call that—a muscle shirt? And you have a big earring in your ear like Mister Clean.'"

Carrie and I both sniggered.

"And then I said, 'They're looking at you. They're profiling you as being a white supremacist.' Truly, that's what I believe," Carrie claimed. "Even though they can't profile."

But that's probably exactly what they were doing.

Since its inception, the behavior detection program has drawn fierce criticism for suspected racial/ethnic profiling. In fact, thirty-two TSOs at Boston Logan reported complaints to the Department of Homeland Security about coworkers singling out people of color for additional screening. They claimed that upward of 80 percent of those detained for extra screening were people of color. Since then, the TSA has retrained all BDOs at that facility, but complaints about behavior detection persist.[11]

"When I interview passengers, they often talk about being anxious in the security area, afraid to talk to TSOs," I explained to Carrie. "They talk about never wanting to bring attention to themselves. Even if they notice that something is a little off, they're afraid to say something. I'm wondering what you think about that."

"I think it has a lot to do with the BDO program," Carrie conjectured, "because the flying public knows that they're being scrutinized."

And so are the officers, in some cases.

"[My manager] stands there and watches me. You know when someone's looking at you, you can feel it? I can feel her eyes on me almost all the time that I'm at work. I know how that makes me feel," Carrie huffed, explaining how she fumbles and is terrified of making mistakes when she's being watched by management. "I know how the flying public must feel having behavior detection officers standing around looking at [them] and watching everything [they] do. That's where I come in. I try to make them feel a little bit easier," she said, citing examples of how she has given advice about how to arrange a bag, and has helped carry strollers for parents.

"Given everything we've talked about," I said, "what advice would you have for new travelers or for people who don't travel very often?"

"Just to not worry about it," she said, "just to be themselves and they'll be fine."

That's the hope, anyway.

Pro Travel Tip #10:

Use Risk-Based Security to Make Your Travel Life Easier

Since embracing risk-based security techniques, the TSA now assumes that most travelers, especially frequent fliers, are low-risk passengers. It introduced its own "trusted traveler" program, TSA PreCheck, in 2011. Essentially a "fast pass" for security, PreCheck requires that passengers apply, pay a fee, submit to a background check, get fingerprinted, and show numerous forms of identification.

In return for being deemed low-risk, PreCheck passengers enjoy a designated line where they do not have to remove shoes, belts, and jackets before screening or take laptops or liquids and gels from their carry-ons. Passengers still must comply with the 3-1-1 rule and with advanced imaging and pat-down procedures where appropriate.

So far, the program is only available on certain airlines and at some airports.

A frequent business traveler, Alice said she was in favor of PreCheck because she likes "the idea that you can just go through. They have all your information down, they know you're a passenger already. You could just walk through, shoes on, stuff in your bag, throw it in, and walk through the metal detector."

For those of us who have survived the sky warrior life, the thought of reducing hassle by any means is novel. I finally enrolled in PreCheck after my time flying weekly was over (only because it wasn't invented back then) and can report that it's worth it.

Although there are some limitations to PreCheck—it's not available everywhere, and occasionally you might be diverted to the regular line as part of spot checking—it's a lovely experience to keep your shoes on in the airport. And significant peer-reviewed research about TSA PreCheck says it is actually effective in mitigating risk.

10

Even Pilots Have Pat-Downs, Sometimes

Flight Crew Tales

Fall 2010.

"Can you tell me what going through security is like for you?" I ask. I'm sitting down with "Flyboy," a flight attendant with a major air carrier.

"Just another day at the office. No big deal," he says, acknowledging that being in uniform generally helps the security process.

"I've noticed that flight attendants don't take their shoes off," I mention, recalling flight crew skipping to the front of the security line, shoes still on.

"Right," he confirms. "It's something that was implemented [to help] crew members [get] through security after 9/11. But prior to that, we just went underground and got to the airplane that way. A large majority of airport employees don't go through security," at least not through TSA checkpoints, Flyboy explains. "They show Port Authority or airport ID. And they just go underground without ever being searched, which is something of concern to the aviation security industry."

And indeed, ten years later, it is still a concern.

"So when you go through as a normal passenger?" I probe.

"We can use our credentials to get through, but unless we're in uniform, we have to follow the same procedures that other passengers have to follow. But we can go first," Flyboy shares. "I pull out my bag of liquids and my shoes and my computer, which doesn't bother me at all. But I think if I had to wait in line all the time, it would be frustrating. But I haven't ever had to wait in line."

"Why would you find the line frustrating?" I query.

"Because it is something that takes a considerable amount of time out of one's day and if I had to do that consistently day after day after day, as part of my job, it would not be productive. It would be quite wasteful," Flyboy notes.

And in fact, within a year of our conversation, airline organizations recognized that the amount of time their employees were spending in airport security was causing flights delays and frustration. So they aimed to remedy the problem, at least for pilots.

In 2011 the TSA announced the creation and testing of the Known Crew Member (KCM) program, which streamlined security processes for airline pilots in uniform. Developed in collaboration with the Air Line Pilots Association (ALPA) and the Air Transport Association, KCM gives the TSA access to employment and identity verification.[1] In exchange, pilots can enter the "sterile area" of the airport, also known as the post-checkpoint terminal, without the typical security screening.

"KCM is a life changer for any commuting crew," said "Wild Bill," a pilot with twenty-six years of experience in the airlines. "Being able to move from terminal to terminal when required to chase a flight . . . has been streamlined, and minutes often make the difference."

Based in part on the Crew Personnel Advanced Screening System (Crew-PASS) deployed at three East Coast airports in 2007, KCM is an example of the TSA's implementation of risk-based security, the idea being that pilots are not likely to be safety threats.

Indeed, "Weeble," a captain for a major airline with twenty-five years of commercial experience, described her general feelings about the TSA. "Mostly, I feel like it's a placebo. As for flight crew, we have the keys to the jet, so why screen me and take away my butter knife?"

Other pilots agreed with her sentiment, including Jim, a thirty-six-year airline veteran, who complained, "Searching me for a pen knife when there is a crash ax in the cockpit, instead of verifying that I am who I say I am, is the worst part [of security]. Fortunately, that doesn't happen very often."

However, while the TSA relaxed security requirements for pilots from certain airlines at certain airports, it initially did nothing for flight attendants, even though they were undergoing the same fingerprinting and ten-year FBI background checks as pilots. Instead, flight attendants continued the practice of jumping the line in security, something that regularly caused uncomfortable interactions with passengers.

Eighteen months later, in late 2012, thanks to complaints from the Association of Flight Attendants, the Association of Professional Flight Attendants, the Transport Workers Union, and Airlines for America, KCM benefits were extended to flight attendants.[2]

Similarly, when advanced imaging scanners were deployed across the country in 2010, airline pilot unions encouraged pilots to boycott the scanners, citing increased radiation exposure to pilots who already experience large amounts of radiation as part of flying. During every flight, crew and passengers are exposed to "cosmic ionizing radiation," which is naturally occurring radiation that comes from outer space and is more pronounced at high altitudes than on the ground. The National Institute for Occupational Safety and Health notes that by virtue of their time spent flying, aircrew receive larger doses of radiation every year than all other workers in the United States who are exposed to radiation.[3] The organized call for AIT resistance prompted the TSA to exempt pilots from advanced imaging in late November 2010.

But again the courtesy was not extended to flight attendants. In order for flight attendants to avoid AIT, they would have to opt out like passengers and receive an enhanced pat-down. Critics complained, accusing the TSA of sexism because pilots (95 percent of whom are men) could avoid invasive security but flight attendants (almost 75 percent of whom are women) could not.

Investigative journalist Lindsay Beyerstein pointed out the discrepancy in calling flight attendants "the last line of defense against terrorist attack" but subjecting them to "degrading and demoralizing" pat-downs while in uniform.[4] She argued, "Our society takes it for granted that men have absolute bodily autonomy; whereas women are often expected to subordinate their bodily autonomy for someone else's idea of the greater good."

Despite these challenges, Flyboy said, "I'm always respectful [in security]. I recognize that [TSOs] have a job to do. And you know, I see it as we're working as a team to secure the airport and secure the aircraft, which I have to fly on regularly. And so I'm always respectful. I smile, say hello, please, thank you. And I know their job must be quite difficult because they deal with individuals all day, every day who aren't happy to see them."

To be sure, many crew members take this same attitude.

"I have seen far more passengers be unruly dicks than I have seen bad TSA agents," said "Nasty," a captain with twenty-two years of airline experience. "The public can be a bitch to work with, and [TSOs] get it all day long. Just like customer service agents and flight attendants, TSA is on the customer front lines, and some people are just plain assholes. Most TSOs are observant, friendly, and honestly try to do a good job. A few appear lazy or incompetent, and a few are on power trips, but they are the small minority."

Likewise, pilot Jim said he gets along fine with TSOs. "I try to treat them as professionals and with respect."

However, some crew members also maintained skepticism, tinged with memories of past challenges.

"Useless. They have gotten worse," said "David," an airline pilot of thirty years, reflecting on the TSA. "Think teenagers with power, looking for a place to flex said power. Most likely the TSA agents were bullied in school."

Wild Bill chimed in, "They are doing their job, although some may 'do their job' too much. Much has changed over the years since 9/11, and we went through some adversarial times. For the most part, the system has settled down. And as KCM and other programs have been instituted, the mutual respect between crew and TSA has improved. Once you realize that the 'system' is operating, good or bad, and that the TSA guy/gal in front of you is only carrying out their directions, it all gets easier to tolerate."

Bill, who served in the U.S. Navy, acknowledged, "I just chalk it up to the government/military mentality. They do what they're told. The biggest issues were likely based around a sense of 'power trip,' possibly on both sides of the conflict, that elevated everyone's blood pressure. That has calmed down a lot over the years, though."

Part of the tension seems to be a matter of perspective, like the conflict between infrequent passengers and TSOs who are steeped in TSA rules.

Thanks to KCM, pilot "Tac" said, "I generally don't get searched or have to go through the passenger lines. However, when I do, it seems the protocol is always different."

Despite eighteen years of airline experience, pilot Tac mentioned that he gets confused about laptop and shoe rules in various airports.

"The agents generally seem irritated that I don't know the protocol, and act as if it is common knowledge," Tac explained. "It always seems to be a little different, station to station, and is definitely different among different countries. While the TSA agents generally work the same location every day, it seems they don't understand that pilots travel and go to many different locations."

Of course, it doesn't help when flight crew get an attitude. When asked about experiences with passengers who were rude, TSO Alexa explained, "It's not even just passengers! There's been pilots and flight crew who have started getting funny [having attitude]."

TSO Elizabeth admitted, "I hate Known Crew Member. They're so entitled."

"Talk to me about that," I prompted.

Elizabeth launched into a story about a time when she was working the KCM station and had to wait for her computer to reboot before she could scan crew badges. "It was taking forever . . . so I left my window closed while I was doing that. . . . It's like a drive-through window," Elizabeth said, explaining that she knew the crew would complain because it was taking a while. "As soon I opened it, [a crew member] gave me attitude. 'Oh my god, why did this take so long? You're awful! This is horrible! I can't believe we have to do this.'" Elizabeth mimicked the woman's whininess. "I'm like,

'You gotta be screened. Sorry.' She didn't get the random [screening], so it's not like [it was] the end of the world." Because the crew member wasn't selected for random screening, she wouldn't have to have a bag search or pat-down, or even go through the PreCheck lane.

"You just get to walk right through," Elizabeth explained, not understanding why the crew member had such a disdainful attitude, slamming doors as she left. She also divulged that one time an airline employee got so frustrated with the TSA that she threw her radio. "It smacked the wall and a whole battery popped out. And now she's under investigation."

The TSA takes aggression against TSOs very seriously, especially from flight crew. Flyboy said, "The company mandates that we follow and obey all security measures and TSA directives. And if we do not, and we're reported by the TSA, that puts your job in jeopardy. And there are people who get terminated for doing so. Most recently I can recall a flight attendant who was at home and commuting in on a flight. She got loud and nasty with the TSA and made comments about, 'Oh well if I wanted to, I could take down the aircraft, I have access to the flight deck. This is ridiculous, why are you making me take out my stuff' and blah, blah, blah. They arrested her, and as far as I know they are now prosecuting her. And the airline terminated her shortly thereafter. She had over twenty years of tenure with the company. I actually was sitting in on her termination hearing.... All because she got frustrated and had an outburst."

Consequently, some airlines give crews explicit instructions about inter-acting with the TSA. Nasty warned, "In the event of a conflict, keep your mouth shut, comply, and take the complaint to the chief pilot. Don't get thrown in jail!"

David emphasized his airline's directives. "Do what they ask/demand [or] you will lose," he said.

Bill added, "Our company and the union [ALPA] work tirelessly with the TSA to make our lives easier. When you are in an airport, you are subject to their [TSA] rules." Thankfully though, he said, "My company at least will not enforce any action against a crew who is late because of TSA issues."

In general, Bill gets along with the TSA officers, he said. "[It's] fine, as long as you don't say anything and comply with all their demands. . . . I have had issues [with the TSA] but have learned to go along and get along."

TSOs don't always agree philosophically with crew, though, especially lax attitudes about contraband.

"I have found so many things in their bags that they know they're not supposed to carry," Elizabeth said. "Somebody had a huge ceramic knife, like butcher-level knife. They said it was just for vegetables. I'm like, 'You still can't have it!' We've had a pilot who had a gun in his bag. Only reason we found it was because he wound up having to go through screening for a random check. They're like, 'Well I'm the pilot. I should walk right onto the plane.' We had a pilot actually tell us, 'Oh, I can bring the plane down if I wanted to.' I was like, 'Is that a threat?'" Elizabeth exclaimed, incredulously. "'Are you threatening the three hundred passengers on your plane right now?'"

"Yeah. That's not the argument to make and he knows better," I chimed in.

"That was his excuse for not having to be screened," Elizabeth recalled, shaking her head and explaining how she is obligated to report any type of threatening comment to her superiors. "That's nice if you want to lose your license."

In contrast, though, TSO Carrie said, "I believe that if you work for the airlines, you shouldn't have to go through security. There has to be some line . . . you have to start trying to trust people. We, as TSOs, are trusted. We can use side doors. We don't have to go through security. We can use the door. We put our badge up. We go through the door and we go to work."

Citing that airline personnel all have good background checks, Carrie implored, "There has to be some level of trust between the workers and the airlines and the police department."

Pilot David agreed. "Forget the random selection. Does it really matter what we carry? We fly the airplane."

Greg, an aviation security specialist, also emphasized a trust-oriented, system-level view of security. "It's like an onion the way the thing is set up now. . . . The government works well with the airlines. At the airport, you can see that the law enforcement agencies, the TSA screeners, the ground security coordinators for all the airlines—they're all working together first to identify any potential things that happen, like people leaving bags on the curb," Greg explained. "All the skycaps, everybody that has a security badge, or anybody that's an airline employee or contract employee, they're required to go through a certain amount of security training."

Greg emphasized the importance of a coordinated system with well-trained and trustworthy employees. However, there have been instances where that trust has broken down.

In March 2016, Marsha Gay Reynolds, a flight attendant for JetBlue airlines, was arrested for working in a multimillion-dollar drug-smuggling operation. After she fled a security checkpoint at LAX, authorities found her carry-on bags contained almost seventy pounds of cocaine, worth around $3 million.[5] Similarly, in December 2017, American Airlines flight attendant Scott McKinney was arrested for running an unlicensed money-transmitting business and smuggling packages containing $50,000 or more.[6]

Consequently, and without warning, the TSA changed its KCM procedures. In late summer of 2019, the TSA decreed that flight crew could only use KCM benefits when traveling in uniform, significantly curbing their freedom.[7] After considerable backlash, the TSA rolled back the changes, saying that crew out of uniform could use KCM, but they would have to show extra identification. In addition, the TSA added more random screening measures.

None of these changes have been popular with crew.

Pilot Tac complained, "[They should] make random checks targeted . . . for those who might commit infractions of KCM policy. When you do catch someone, take their KCM privileges away, knowing you solved part of the problem, rather than punish everyone else who obeys the rules."

Tac's comments illustrate much of the TSA's typical way of responding to threats—abrupt and blanket policy changes seemingly aimed at singular or high-profile incidents.

"If terrorism continues with a 9/11 scenario, they will gain access through catering, cleaners, vendors, flight crews, etcetera," Weeble commented.

"They won't necessarily try to sneak their weapons through a security checkpoint."

Indeed, security experts have long argued that future terrorist attacks will not likely be by the same means as those used on 9/11.

Pro Travel Tip #11:
Don't Begrudge Your Crew a Line Cut

As the KCM program is not available in all airports, you might notice flight crew in the security line. Consider letting them go ahead, and if they cut the line, keep any sass to yourself.

Pilot Bill expressed consternation at passengers who give crew a hard time. "Most of the TSA are understanding when we need to cut" in order to make a flight, he said. "Passengers, not always so much. [It's] hard to imagine holding up your crew so you as a passenger can be at the gate early."

So do them a favor. Forget the "racing" mentality and let the crew through.

Addressing Insider Threat

So if the TSA is watching the flight crew and passengers, who is inspecting the TSA?

As high-profile cases of TSA gun smuggling and drug running have hit the news, some might wonder who's keeping an eye on America's fifty thousand TSOs. It turns out, TSOs are watching each other.

"Insider threat" is the possibility that current or former employees, contractors, or others with access to sensitive areas or information might use their status to facilitate crime or other illicit actions. And it's been a major concern for the TSA.

Discussing advanced imaging, TSO Elizabeth shared how even officers are limited in their knowledge about how the machines work and what precisely they scan for. "They say it's a security thing. You're not allowed to know how it works for certain things. Because the biggest threat is an insider threat," she explained. "The biggest threat is my people doing something versus the public doing something."

Elizabeth described how she is part of the ATLAS—Advanced Threat Local Allocation Strategy—program, which screens and observes employees as well as passengers. ATLAS is meant to reduce the possibility of harm from the 1.8 million aviation workers throughout the United States.[8]

And it seems necessary. According to the Government Accountability Office, from June 2017 through June 2019 an average of 138 insider threat referrals were made per month, including attempted maintenance sabotage, jet theft, drug trading, and weapons smuggling.[9]

11

On the Front Lines with "Screener Joe"

On Ideal Transportation Security Officers

"I've been peed on twice and hit three times," says Elizabeth.

"Who peed on you?!" I exclaim. "Please say they were children!"

"Nope."

Elizabeth, the TSO I'm interviewing, explains that one peeing passenger was in her thirties and the other was an elderly woman. I realize I had first expected children because, who hasn't been peed on by a small fry at some point in their lives? Then I assumed that the urine-spraying assailants must've been men. Who else can pee standing up with reasonable aim?

Realizing I've made a lot of assumptions, I perch at the edge of my chair and wait for Elizabeth to continue. She clarifies that the older female passenger was in a wheelchair and struggled with bladder control. Her story tugs at my heart.

"I'm like, 'Oh, she's wet . . . why?'" Elizabeth recalls. "And then I noticed the smell."

Because the woman had peed in her wheelchair and then again during the pat-down, Elizabeth explains, a whole section of the security checkpoint had to be shut down for biohazard cleanup. Apparently the woman didn't have a change of clothes and probably had to fly in her pee-soaked duds.

"I felt bad for this lady," Elizabeth recounts. "It really wasn't her fault."

But the other urinator? "She came in with the intention of peeing on an officer," Elizabeth says. *Say what now?*

"So I was patting her down. She got a groin anomaly," Elizabeth says, explaining that the body scanner alarmed and indicated something strange in the belt-line area. After giving the passenger instructions, Elizabeth started to do the pat-down. "Totally fine. But as soon as I went under her inner thighs, she peed all over me."

At this point I am in full shock and stare in rapt attention.

"I'm like, 'Are you serious? Are you kidding me right now?'" Elizabeth sputters. "Because I'd been on the job two years. I thought it was a lie. I thought people really didn't do that 'cause it never happened to me."

Apparently peeing passengers are a feature in TSO lore? I chime in, "I've been studying the TSA for a decade and this is the first pee story I've ever heard."

Elizabeth says she called her manager and seethed, "'Hey, she just peed on me. She openly admitted she did it on purpose.'"

The woman had decided before she got to the airport that if she got selected for a pat-down, she was going to pee on the officer. "She just didn't want to be touched," Elizabeth says, explaining that the woman was protesting the "meeting resistance" aspect of the pat-down policy.

"Was she intending to fly in her pee clothes? Did she bring a change of clothes?" I ask.

"I have no idea," Elizabeth laughs. "She had a purse with her and that was about it."

My mind spins off into so many directions. She better have had a ziplock bag in her purse. And if she didn't have a change of clothes, did she know what, if any, clothing retailers were in the airport? Most big airports sell logoed clothing, so now I'm picturing someone in head-to-toe "I Heart Sacramento" gear having to explain her strange outfit to others on the plane.

While struggling to figure out the logistical implications of Elizabeth's story, I also can't stop thinking, *Who would do such a thing?!* Purposefully urinate on someone else? To *plan* to purposefully urinate as an act of resistance against a TSA policy? But more than that . . . who, other than maybe medical or childcare professionals, would still cheerfully work for an organization where getting peed on was a legit possibility?!

Elizabeth's willingness to continue as a TSO and aspiration to climb the TSA career ladder surprised me. In addition to her anecdotes about urinating passengers, she described being assaulted—physically and sexually—by passengers (mostly women, by the way), sexually harassed by coworkers, stressed out by management, and overwhelmed by the ongoing pressures of work. But she also mentioned how she prioritized work over her personal comfort and safety, appreciated the pay and opportunities, and was even encouraging her sibling to join the organization.

In fact, Elizabeth exemplified one of the types of TSOs who most surprised me during my research. Virtually unrepresented in popular culture and passenger interviews, some agents like Elizabeth embody idealized TSO identities that directly reflect their organizational training and inculcation. In other words, some officers drink the TSA Kool-Aid and embrace their roles as TSOs.

Officers demonstrating what I call the Ideal TSO identity showed a significant and clear connection with their organization, what scholars call *organizational identification*.[1] They integrated their roles as TSOs and their status as members of the TSA into their self-concepts.[2]

This identification process isn't unique to the TSA. Many organizations—the ones we belong to and the ones we buy from—invite us to identify with them all the time. Think about your brand loyalties. Perhaps you think of yourself as a Mac person or a PC person. Although you're probably referencing your preference for a type of computer, you've linked that choice with your description of *yourself*.

When organizations can get us to identify with them—to believe in them, to like them, to feel connected—they are better able to persuade us. This is how Apple gets people to shell out so much for their new iPhones, and it's how the TSA encourages its officers to overlook the difficult aspects of their jobs and focus on the bigger organizational mission.

Ideal TSA officers sometimes connected their work in airport security to patriotism and a higher calling. In fact, TSO Carrie shocked me when she described her job as "how I serve my country." In the middle of discussing significant challenges at work, including abuse by supervisors, she said, "I really feel very proud that I do this. And maybe not for the people, but for my country that I care about."

It never occurred to me that TSOs would frame their jobs as a duty and public good, yet several specifically highlighted the civil service aspect of their work. For instance, TSO Jonathan remarked, "Being a TSO is a test of strength and perseverance—being able to take abuse from all directions, from within and without. It means flexibility and endurance, to be able to perform a variety of functions at the same time while [being short-staffed]. And, in the middle of all that, being a TSO means being a protector."

Despite being peed on and screamed at, some TSOs stressed that their job is an important public service with a tremendous amount of responsibility. For instance, in my interview with Skeet, I asked, "[What happens] when you make a mistake at work?"

"There's this little thing called, people die," he said, straight-faced. As I worked to bring my eyebrows down to their normal height, he chuckled at my startled expression. "If I miss something at work, and let the terrorists go through one time, people die. That's the extreme, okay. It can be as little as, 'Oops, I missed that water bottle.' Okay. Nothing happened. Nobody knew about it. I'm the only one that knows. [Then there's] the breach that we had, where it gets on the national news," Skeet fretted, describing an incident where TSOs had left a security lane unattended and four passengers walked into the airport terminal without being properly screened. The TSA shut down the entire terminal for more than an hour, delaying twelve flights, while they reviewed security footage to find the unchecked passengers.

Skeet discussed how much national news attention the breach caused, and how mistakes like missing a water bottle or not screening passengers can have serious consequences: "Like I said, people die."

But in reality, no people died. Not from any missed water bottles or from the unattended security lane.

Later in our conversation, Skeet asked if I remembered "the Christmas Day bombing attempt"—the "shoe bomber" story. He cited the incident as a reason for TSO officers to be constantly vigilant, and described the story as if it had happened the day before, not more than a decade ago.

It was during that very first TSO interview with Skeet that I realized how dramatically different TSO and passenger perspectives are, not to mention the discourse that shapes their work and worldview. In fact, that conversation and my subsequent interviews revealed that terrorism events are *constantly* on officers' minds. Every day, TSOs start their shifts with team meetings that routinely mention the larger purpose of the TSA. TSA leaders emphasize that another 9/11-style terrorist attack is not going to happen on their watch, and how it is the TSO's responsibility to prevent one. While all TSOs get regular messaging about duty and patriotism, some embrace and embody these ideals, which shapes how they work and interact with passengers.

During my early years of observing TSOs without actually talking to them, beyond casual conversations, I assumed that officers were as they appeared: bored, apathetic, just collecting a paycheck, or power-hungry jerks who got their kicks controlling others. It wasn't until I sat down with Skeet that I realized that some TSOs view their jobs as an important mission or even a calling.

So what do these Ideal TSOs look like? Broadly speaking, TSOs who embrace TSA ideals demonstrate precision and expertise in their work. They maintain strict vigilance and situational awareness, project an authoritative presence as per TSA training, and stay "calm, cool, and collected" under pressure. They are serious about their work and they talk about it as a career, not just a job, even if they envision TSO work as a stepping stone to other roles within the federal service system. Within the Ideal category, I noted officers who perform their duties with serious enthusiasm (Zealots) and others who bring a punitive edge (Disciplinarians).

Zealots

Ideal-Zealot TSOs embody TSA ideals to the extreme, a quality that emerges from TSA training rhetoric. Identifying as "patriots" on a "mission," the Zealot TSO draws on discourses of nationalism, "serving one's country," and the TSA's early but still often used catch phrase "Not on My Watch!"[3]

Zealot characteristics include personalizing job duties and clearly demonstrating organizational identification. "Carol," a TSO I encountered on a number of occasions, tailored her approach to work, taking time to tell passengers their gate locations while checking their tickets, and describing parts of a pat-down as a game of hokeypokey. Carol, who reminded me of a dialed-down version of Carol Burnett, enacted policies with precision and ownership.

During one of my trips, Carol bounded up in response to the call for a "female assist on B!" She wears her coarse red hair in a short crop and sports blue eye shadow harkening back to the seventies. I have been patted down by her before and I know it's probably going to take a while.

At the screening area, I face my belongings without being asked. I want Carol to know that I know the drill. She speaks with an affected tone, similar to Jane Lynch's deadpan delivery as Sue Sylvester in the television show *Glee* but without the menace. She performs her role as if she is talking to children or acting on stage—somewhat exaggerated and just this side of obnoxious.

Explaining procedures slowly and loudly, Carol acknowledges that I may know them already, but she has to review them with me. When I verify that I have no sore or sensitive areas, she leans in to whisper reassuringly, "Well, I don't want to hurt anyone."

After confirming that I do not need a private room or have any medical devices, I stand in the proper position—feet spread, arms like airplanes—before she can ask. She begins her work methodically, slowly brushing hair from my collar (turning my tag under as several TSOs have been wont to do) and dragging her blue-gloved hands down my back.

"I'm going to need to see that waistband," Carol says when she gets to my lower half. Automatically, I lift the edge of my shirt to make the hem of my pants visible. Carol continues, brushing down my legs, coming to rest her gloves on my ankles. Given her measured tempo, I am far too aware of how long it is taking today.

Intriguingly, as she finishes her work, she compliments my outfit—black slacks and a close fitting shirt—saying it's "easy" and that I wore "the right thing." She doesn't explain, but I infer that she means easy and right for her to search without trouble.

In this scenario, I played an Ideal passenger—someone prepared, organized, compliant, and unquestioning. Carol caused me great frustration with her dramatized performance of the pat-down. It took longer than normal because of her exceedingly thorough, plodding pace. I found myself struggling to contain my irritation, wanting her to move faster, but my attempts to speed the encounter along by anticipating her moves were to no avail.

Furthermore, Carol linked the pat-down process simultaneously to care and authority. She said, "I'm going to need to see that waistband," calling to mind a police officer during a traffic stop. ("I'm going to need to see some ID.") Yet she also demonstrated a caring attitude—she didn't want to hurt anyone; she turned down my collar tag.

Although these gestures may come across as helpful or nurturing, they also take time, which is at a premium for passengers trying to make flights. Officers exhibiting Ideal-Zealot behavior often prioritize security above all else—clinging to and enacting ideals, regardless of the time required.

"It's important to get people through quickly, but ultimately it's about security," admonished a young TSO I spoke with during his lunch break at a large Los Angeles airport. He said he tries to screen people as fast as he can, "but if it takes ten minutes to check a bag, it takes ten minutes to check a bag." The officer emphasized that it's critical to be thorough when searching baggage, and not unlike Skeet, he implied that there are significant consequences of shoddy work, both moral and material.

Although many are fastidious, some Zealot-type TSOs use discretion when enacting the rules—helping passengers deposit belongings into bins for scanning, *not* rescreening bags containing innocuous identifiable liquids/gels like the lotion I refuse to remove from my purse. However, this type of discretion typically is exercised to achieve *organizational* goals such as making the lines go faster, rather than to be helpful to passengers.

As a rule, Ideal-Zealot TSOs display clear organizational identification, using "we" frequently and prioritizing organizational goals. You might notice divestiture officers proclaiming, "*We* need you to remove all liquids and gels from your bags" or, "*We're* here to protect you." Such language puts a clear demarcation between "we" TSOs and "you" passengers, which reinforces the us/them dichotomy for both groups. As a case in point, consider the disparate perspectives of passengers and TSOs regarding TSA work as a mission, patriotic duty, or service.

TSO Carrie described her work in the following terms: "I come home every night with the feeling that I know I did my job, that I am not just doing it for a paycheck. That I'm there because I truly want to do something to help my country and this is a way I feel I can help my country—by being a transportation security officer and doing the best job that I can."

Carrie spoke passionately about her former caregiving roles and how she brings that nurturing orientation, along with a fastidious approach to the rules, to work at the airport.

TSO Jonathan said, "First and foremost, I needed a job." But he also became a TSO to give back. "I also looked to it as a way to serve. I am excluded from military service because of a medical condition, so this is really the best way for me to do so."

Passengers, however, did not seem appreciative of a rules-forward perspective, and they never discussed TSOs work as related to mission or patriotism. World traveler Kristine described TSOs as less friendly and more robotic, although she emphasized routinized professionalism and did not frame TSOs themselves as robots. "They take what they're doing very seriously," she observed.

Similarly, Alice, a business traveler, said, "They seem like no-nonsense and they just follow the rules. They kind of throw the rules at you. Not all the time, but they definitely are very strict. Some of them are nice when they want to be, but they don't have to be," she added, underscoring the discretion TSOs can use when showing emotion.

Reacting to my question about the TSA's larger mission of protecting freedom of movement for people and commerce, Sue reflected, "I would say [TSOs] exemplify that mission very well and I think it probably explains why they don't seem very humane in their treatment. They're not there for us, they're there for transportation. They're there to keep the system running smoothly. They're there to make sure no terrible things happen at the airport. I realize that, but I think when it comes to how they interact with people, they should try to treat people as people."

Others were a little more pointed.

Passenger Mac gibed, "They're taking their jobs too seriously. That's a good description. They take their job way too seriously. I know it's a serious matter if there's a terrorist in the airport, but how often does that happen? Come on."

Indeed, as of the writing of this book, the TSA has yet to catch a terrorist in the airport. The threat persists and organizational rhetoric has TSOs constantly on high alert, yet neither passengers nor my observations framed TSOs in terms of patriotic service or personal mission. These specific organizational constructs (patriotic service and personal mission) seem to go unrecognized, and are even challenged by passengers who question why officers act so seriously.

Maintaining a sustained level of seriousness also takes concerted energy. Consider the following excerpt from my airport travels:

> The twenty-something TSO working the walk-through X-ray machine reminds me of a dark-haired Ken doll—six feet tall, short dark hair, glowing skin, warm eyes.
>
> He smiles vaguely as I approach the AIT line. When I ask to opt out, "Ken" startles me by belting into his walkie-talkie, "Female opt-out on Baker! Female opt-out on Baker!" He overenunciates the words in a way that reminds me of an overhead page in a grocery store, à la "Clean up on Aisle 3!"

Within moments a young female TSO appears and taps him on the shoulder from behind. Tapping must be protocol as I see it frequently and hear references to people being "tapped in" and "tapped out" of position. Ken does not turn or take his eyes off the crowd in front of him. He maintains constant vigilance.

In this scenario, Ken demonstrated an exacting, if not embellished, performance of professionalism, which mirrored his organizational training in continuous situational awareness and precision. However, by sustaining strict focus on the scene—indeed refusing to look back at his coworker or even make eye contact with me—he misses opportunities to connect with passengers and coworkers. Such missed connections can make work less enjoyable for him and also reinforce the "us versus them" perspectives among passengers and TSOs, as well as among TSOs themselves.

When emotionally contained TSOs like Ken meet hostile passengers, the potential for conflict intensifies. For instance, during fieldwork I met a TSO at a large Southern California airport who had recently learned that he was going to be promoted to lead TSO. During our conversation, he admitted frustration when passengers acted "noncompliant," "irate," or "demeaning" toward TSOs.

He shared a story about a passenger who was randomly chosen for an enhanced pat-down. The passenger ranted that the TSA was a waste of tax dollars. The TSO retorted, "I'm sorry you feel that way, sir," and indicated that the passenger's feelings were not going to change the fact that the screening must take place.

The TSO admitted that dealing with passengers can be difficult, but he still insisted that the TSA was a good organization to work for. "They take care of you," he said. "There are lots of opportunities."

When faced with a passenger who questioned his professional identity, invoking broad social conversations about waste and TSA spending, the TSO bottled his anger and responded in a manner appropriate to his training. When describing the confrontation, he clearly identified with the TSA, contextualizing interpersonal conflicts with passengers as part of his service and highlighting his pride in his workplace. In fact, he talked at length about how the organization rewards and promotes good work from employees.

During interviews and in the interactions I observed between Ideal TSOs and Ideal and Hostile passengers, the passengers propagated mainstream stereotypes of the TSA as government waste and of TSOs as robotic dolts. Having bought into these stereotypes to make sense of security, passengers then find that their views are reinforced when they encounter TSOs who act according to their training. Although TSOs may initially try to school travelers about security procedures when engaging with passengers like Carol, above, they are trained not to let emotional situations escalate.[4] Yet when TSOs do not show emotions, passengers may be more likely to treat them not as human beings who can be hurt by rude words and actions, but as extensions of the TSA, presumably without feelings.

TSO Jonathan, for instance, described being "physically assaulted and verbally threatened" by passengers. He learned to activate what he calls his "Screener Joe" persona so that he could be "all business" and deal with problems efficiently.

While TSOs see themselves as being trained to work with an emotional public, their use of Screener Joe–type façades reinforces the TSO view that passengers are stupid and that TSOs must be tough and emotionless in dealing with them. This type of emotional labor is constructed as a patriotic duty and a badge of honor, although Jonathan confessed that his Screener Joe persona helps keep him from "questioning my faith in humanity" when dealing with passengers every day.

For TSOs, organizational ideals can generate much personal conflict as well. Take, for instance, the tension between the ideal of efficiency and the ideal of thoroughness. Although both are important to the TSA, TSOs must decide which one takes priority—thoroughness, which equates with better safety, or efficiency, which equates with greater customer/managerial satisfaction (or at least fewer complaints).

When efficiency and thoroughness conflict, TSOs can face a paradox. There's no way to reasonably choose both, so they must weigh the consequences of picking one over the over, which can lead to cognitive dissonance, stress, and eventually burnout. Consequences for prioritizing the wrong one also loom large for TSOs, especially because the prevailing organizational discourses such as "security," "safety," and "not on my watch" emphasize moral failing for not being thorough enough.

Some research suggests that hanging on to the broad ideal of work as mission or service can help people manage this type of cognitive dissonance.[5] On the other hand, stressing mission can mask important underlying tensions for agents who identify strongly with their workplace. Dr. Sarah Tracy, a qualitative methods expert and organizational communication professor at Arizona State University, examined burnout among correctional officers to understand why correctional officers have a drastically lower life expectancy than the general population.[6] She found that correctional officers who strongly identified with their work environment and who viewed it as central to their identity experienced more confusion and frustration with the job than did officers who did not link work and their identity.

Most of the TSOs I interviewed—regardless of their TSO identity—seemed irritated by bureaucracy that they felt interfered with their work. However, some officers who enacted Ideal-Zealot behaviors, including Carrie and Rick, managed this frustration by continually referring back to the broader goals and mission of the TSA and its discourse on safety and security.

Officers' ability to manage the efficiency-versus-thoroughness paradox may depend in part on whether they hold a career orientation or a calling orientation to their work. Dr. Amy Wrzesniewski, a professor at the Yale School of Management, worked with colleagues to understand how people identify with their work.[7] If you have a "job" orientation to work, for instance, you might talk about "working to live" instead of "living to work." In this view, work is a means of providing for family and pursuing meaningful hobbies. In contrast, a "career" orientation is associated with ladder climbing, advancement, and promotion, as well as material benefits. The third orientation is a "calling," which emphasizes emotional connection to one's work, with work providing a means of personal fulfillment and self-expression.

TSOs who conceptualize their work in terms of mission and service may view their employment as a calling. Unlike the correctional officer "lifers" in Dr. Tracy's research, some of whom managed frustration with workplace bureaucracy by breaking with institutional policy, some TSOs are able to transcend the paradoxes in their work by emphasizing overarching institutional goals, such as keeping the public safe and preventing another 9/11. Those who get mired in the conflict between efficiency and security, however, can choose to enact a different type of identity, such as that of a Stereotypical TSO who does not see their job as intricately connected with personal identity.

In my research, some TSOs with Zealot characteristics, who otherwise suggested that their work was about "giving back" and "serving their country," also discussed—in markedly jaded tones—their frustrations with work politics. For instance, BDO Steve ruminated about being passed over for several promotions and advancement opportunities. "Am I going to do my job? Absolutely. I signed and I'm under oath of protecting and defending the elements of the constitution. So I am not going to back down as a government employee. I'm not going to be a shitbird employee. . . . The shitbird person is the person that doesn't give a rat's rear end but isn't going to do their job."

A ten-year veteran of the TSA, Steve began our conversation espousing organizational ideals. But as he spoke about paradoxes in his work, he seemed more apathetic and not in tune with the TSA. In fact, Steve insinuated that he might even need to "get out of government work" to clear the "sour taste" in his mouth. Over time, employees may shift from identifying positively with their organization to greater ambivalence or even disidentification and distancing.[8] The second Ideal TSO character type I found, the Disciplinarian, has sometimes taken a step along this path.

The Disciplinarians

Similar to the Ideal-Zealot in terms of organizational identification, the Ideal-Disciplinarian TSO acts with a more punitive edge. These TSOs take vigilance to the point of paranoia, exacting the letter of the law instead of the spirit. They demonstrate an extreme acceptance of organizational policies, seemingly without question.

When discussing security procedures, Neecie, a TSO at a large international airport, framed TSA rules as superseding the tenets of constitutional freedom. "I feel like civil liberty goes out the door when it comes to security," she stated. "If [people] want to go the route of the airlines, they're going to comply with what's explained or they need to get a train, a bus, drive, or stay home."⁹

In our conversation, Neecie said she couldn't see anything troubling about her statement or empathize with other viewpoints. Such a black-and-white approach to TSA practices definitely contributes to friction with passengers.

TSOs who enacted Disciplinarian characteristics did so primarily as a result of organizational-level policy and training. In our interviews, TSOs regularly referenced organizational training, saying they prioritized internal standard operating procedures and published policies in their interactions with coworkers and passengers.

At the same time, they emphasized some societal-level discourses, presumably at the risk of alienating others. Neecie placed "security" above the ideals of "freedom" and "liberty" in her depictions of security procedures.

Likewise, TSO Carrie, who confessed that she did not agree with the age-related shoe policy, because "over-seventy-fives have nothing to live for," argued that parents can take advantage of children by using them to smuggle contraband. Carrie extended her thoughts about safety to the extreme, exhibiting paranoia as she argued on behalf of some TSA policies.

Despite feeling some of the Stereotypical TSO's malaise, especially when passengers make mistakes or act rudely, the Ideal-Disciplinarian TSO upholds the rules fastidiously. For example, instead of punishing a rude passenger by slowing down or unnecessarily repeating a screening, as Skeet described, Disciplinarian officers act above reproach in their adherence to the rules.

That said, the Ideal-Disciplinarian officer often *avoids* making discretionary decisions to help individual passengers, sometimes at the expense of organizational goals. Recall TSO Alexa, who described her conflict with an older man who refused to take his shoes off because he thought the new policy for over-seventy-fives applied to him, although he was younger than seventy-five. When Alexa enforced the rules, the man "started getting really mean," calling her "Missy" and throwing major attitude. Although the passenger actually had a medical condition and would likely have been granted an exemption had he explained it early on, Alexa insisted that she *has* to be "a little tough sometimes with the passengers."

She said, "This is partly my home. This is where I'm at—my rule, my regulation." Then she corrected herself. "It's not *my* rules, but I'm here to implement them."

Alexa enforced and took ownership of the rules and her work environment. As the passenger acted more and more erratic, she enforced the rules with even more sternness, even though letting it go would have been faster and less stressful for all involved.

Unlike Carol and others who personalized and customized the enactment of rules as Ideal TSOs with Zealot inclinations, Alexa's Disciplinarian mindset involved internalizing the rules even while suggesting they were not hers per se. One result of enforcing the letter of the law and deferring to the rules is that it puts distance between TSOs and their actions—that is, "It's not *me* doing this, it's *the rules*." While this explanation may help TSOs deal with aspects of the work they find displeasing, it also releases them from personal accountability for the way they treat passengers.[10]

Investigating idealized TSO identities shows how employees use discourse as a resource, a screen, and—in the case of Screener Joe and "the rules"—a shield against uncomfortable emotions. And what's interesting is that passengers do something similar.

Pro Travel Tip #12:

Don't Take Offense at Screener Joe

Some passengers feel disgruntled at TSOs who seem emotionless and robotic. Remember that they might be enacting their Screener Joe persona for reasons that have nothing to do with you. Consider giving these officers a pass and recognize that they are likely trying to accomplish their work mission or survive the rude passengers who came before you.

12

Lemmings and Sheeple

On Ideal Passengers

November 6, 2012.

Between the creeping checkpoint lines, the petite divestiture officer paces around, practically whispering instructions. If I concentrate, I can hear her plaintive pleas about taking liquids, gels, and aerosols out of carry-on luggage.

Meanwhile, the metal detector officer stares as I wait to guide my last bags into the X-ray tunnel. With an acerbic air, he snaps, "Hold on!" as if I'm trying to force my luggage through, which I'm clearly not. I resist the urge to roll my eyes.

Luggage through, I walk over and he points me to the advanced imaging machine.

"I'd like to opt out," I state, firmly.

Instead of telling me to wait alongside the AIT as usual, he curls an index finger toward me, beckoning me closer. Now two feet apart, I feel his eyes boring into mine.

"I have to tell you, if you opt out—you know what we're going to do to you?" he asks, in a near-menacing tone.

"Yes," I counter, returning his steady gaze.

"We're going to pat you down, head, chest, waist, legs, breast, buttocks, groin, sensitive areas," he continues, leaning even closer.

"Yes," I reply, not shrinking back. *Who does this guy think he is?!*

"You know this is a millimeter wave scanner and doesn't have the radiation?"

"Yes," I say, while thinking, *Well no, dumbass, it absolutely uses radiation.*

Exasperated, he directs me to wait. I'm surprised and annoyed by the coercion. But then it occurs to me that I don't look like a business traveler today. I'm wearing jeans and sandals instead of slacks and heels. Inwardly, I laugh at myself for feeling a momentary blip of indignation: *Don't you know who I am?!* Did he read me as a Stereotypical Inexperienced traveler, someone likely to freak out over a pat-down? He clearly didn't recognize me as a frequent flier.

My mental dialogue becomes all the more amusing moments later when TSO Roger walks behind the conveyor belt, apparently recognizing my baggage. He looks at me, holding up four fingers to ask if all the items were mine. I nod, mouthing "thank you" since he's too far away to hear.

A moment later a TSO comes to collect me with a "sweetie" on her lips and a smile across her face. She asks me to point out my things, and I motion to Roger, who walks the baggage over to the pat-down area. As she changes her gloves, she advises me to keep an eye on my things but not touch them. Smiling amiably, the TSO talks through her instructions carefully. Even though she knows I know what they are, she repeats them without rushing. When I stand in the proper position without being asked, she praises me. She pats my hair, exclaiming how much she likes the color. I share that my mom is a stylist, and she lavishes more compliments.

The pat-down feels thorough but not invasive. Blue hands sweep my bare arms and palms. When she comes around front, I automatically point my toe and lift my heel off the floor. She again commends me, saying I'm making the process easier for her. I repeat on the right side, aware that I am enacting the role of the Ideal passenger.

She tells me to wait while she tests her gloves. I look over to where she's standing, at a computer behind a partition. "Ten more seconds," she calls, and I smile. When the beep sounds, she wishes me a nice day. Although I didn't write it down in my field notes, I'm positive I wished her the same right back. It's what an Ideal passenger would do.

My passenger and TSO interviewees constructed the same picture of the "ideal" or "perfect" traveler. Ideal travelers were described as those who fly most often and who arrive at the airport prepared, organized, and familiar with rules. When going through screenings, Ideal passengers listen, comply with directions, do not question TSOs, and complete tasks largely without expressed emotion. In short, Ideal travelers enact docility and do not trouble TSOs or fellow passengers.[1] They recognize the roles they must play in order to make security successful.

From a TSO perspective, compliant passengers come across as unremarkable. As Rick, a TSO manager, described, these passengers are easily forgotten because they do not stand out, cause a scene, or do anything to be remembered. Many business travelers fit into the Ideal category because the process of travel is routine to them.

Casual traveler Rachel described the Ideal traveler like this: "A perfect traveler, I suppose, would just have everything in line, ready, organized to go. Whether that's checking your bag, being ready to go, and hav[ing] everything in order. Your ID, your luggage ready to put up on the cart."

Rachel trailed off for a second, before admitting, "It's sad to say this, but like doing what you're supposed to do in line. Being ready to go at your gate, knowing where you're going, getting in your seat right away at the airplane without holding people up. Someone who does what they're supposed to do . . . who does what they're told. It sounds like the person would not have any sort of personality or assertiveness. They do not have any sort of human interaction . . . just sitting there like a plain robot-travel kind of person."

When asked whether she considered herself a perfect traveler, Rachel initially said yes, noting that she was familiar enough with travel and thought of herself a "rule follower." However, after giving it some thought, Rachel seemed upset by the realization that she conformed to the rules unquestioningly and would not, for example, display negative emotions for fear of getting in trouble or stand up for another traveler who was being hassled.

Poignantly, Rachel mused, "That's not the person that I strive to be." She indicated she would be giving the matter more thought after our interview.

Days later Rachel contacted me and described how upsetting she found the idea that she acted as an Ideal passenger. She said she viewed herself as someone who stands up for herself and others, and was dismayed that she so easily fell into unquestioning compliance. But it's perhaps not surprising, given her life-long rule-following training in school and church.

"It's interesting because I have that stress of coming through security. But I am a Catholic. I generally don't do anything 'bad.' I don't break laws. I don't try to cause mischief," Rachel explained, describing how her faith shapes her actions.

"You're in the line so long, though. It's generally a longer line. It goes pretty fast but you have time to look at everyone else. You have time to see the security officers looking through people's bags, if needed. There are pat-downs, checking IDs. You see what's coming—that they're going to do a whole check of you and what you have on your person."

Rachel discussed how passengers have extended time to think and worry about the type of screening that's coming—metal detector, imaging, or pat-down. "In general, you don't have much time to think about something like that. The only thing I can compare it to is when you're driving your car and there's a police officer behind you. I'm not doing anything wrong. My tags are all in order. They're not expired. I'm not driving crazy. I haven't been drinking or anything like that. I know I'm doing everything right," Rachel explained. "But you get those nerves of . . . I guess, maybe, there's an authority figure looking for something wrong. In general there isn't really too much in my day-to-day life where I see someone looking at me to see what's wrong."

Rachel continued, reflecting on following rules in security and feeling conflicted about her willingness to comply. "Like I said, that's not the type of person that I want to be. I want to be interactive and have my own thoughts and feelings, and not necessarily do everything that I'm told."

During our conversation, Rachel wrestled with wanting to be the type of traveler who shows personality and acted happy but also the type to stand her ground and refuse to comply with uncomfortable requests—like the time a TSA officer made her take off her outer sweater and left her feeling extremely exposed in a skimpy camisole. But she also described being acutely aware of the airport environment and the very long lines that she and hundreds of others were trying to traverse. In that context, defiance means "not getting on your plane, or everyone else in line's going to be really frustrated with you," she said.

"It's kind of contradictory," Rachel said, referencing her desire to be unique while also doing what you're *supposed* to do—"like standing around like cattle," she noted. "Maybe it's that in the airport it's a whole different world. Out of that world, I wouldn't necessarily act like that. Unless it's like a police officer and they're telling me to pull over. I wouldn't necessary be like that, compliant I mean."

Like Rachel, other passengers who demonstrated Ideal characteristics seemed to draw on societal discourses related to authority and compliance, enacting social norms from a lifetime of rule following and deferring to figures of authority.

As Ideal passengers interact with TSOs, they may feel emotionally at odds, even though they do not readily demonstrate emotion. In fact, most of my interviewees described feeling uncomfortable expressing emotions, especially negative feelings, in security settings. As a result, Ideal passengers likely engage in emotional suppression, which can have significant consequences for their interactions.[2] When you try to suppress negative emotions, you end up feeling them even more acutely, which makes managing emotions during interactions even more difficult.

I asked frequent traveler Kristine, who has flown to many of the major airports in the world, if she feels comfortable expressing emotion in airport security.

"Why would a person do that?" Kristine asked. "Keep your feelings to yourself in security. They don't care. It's just going to cause problems. Move through. I am not expressing anything in security."

"Why?" I probed, knowing that Kristine is a larger-than-life character whose emotional expressions are a prominent feature of her personality.

"Because there is no reason to draw attention to myself. That's the deal," she said. "I don't want to draw any more attention to myself than is already there. You get it, right? If there's nothing out of the norm, less attention is paid to you."

Referring to the security process, Kristine said, "There's an antagonism, of the TSA wanting to protect that bigger picture so that the whole nation can move around . . . [but they see] individuals being [threats] to the whole big system. As you're going through the TSA checkpoint, each individual has the potential for breaking down the whole system with their actions. What the TSA is trying to do is to find that really small percentage of individuals that have that in mind. I think that goes back to not wanting to bring attention to myself. I want to make sure they put me into that much bigger category of people just trying to get on their flight. Just a normal traveler."

"You said the normal traveler. What is a perfect traveler like?"

"That's me, of course," Kristine quipped. "I think a perfect traveler is just . . . well, yeah, I'm going to describe myself. [It's] somebody that knows that they have to go through TSA, wants to be respectful of the process as much as they can and make it as painless on them and the TSA as possible, and the rest of the passengers around them. That would be the perfect passenger to me."

I asked Mac, a regular traveler, how comfortable he was expressing emotion in security. Laid-back but confident, Mac spoke freely with me. Bantering and joking, he had no trouble critiquing the TSA. So his answer to the question surprised me.

"Not very comfortable at all, actually. I would do my best to avoid all problems," Mac explained. "I feel like my vision of the TSA and airport security is very . . . I feel like they're all machines and robots. If I do something wrong, I'm going to be yanked aside and interrogated. I am not comfortable with them as an agency, I suppose."

Mac struggled to put his feelings into words. "I just feel strange. I'm just trying to figure out how to describe it. As an individual, I feel like they don't have your best interests in mind. If you do something wrong, you're going to pay for it. I have a friend who is from Saudi Arabia, and he really gets questioned every time he flies. I don't know why. This guy is loaded. He is absolutely loaded."

I know exactly why a young man from the same country that supplied most of the 9/11 terrorists would get hassled, regardless of his finances, but I didn't interrupt.

"He is a twenty-two-year-old college student," Mac said. "He gets drunk every time he flies now, just because he hates dealing with it. He's always pulled aside every single time he flies."

"My goodness," I replied.

"Yeah, it's probably the fact that I have that vision in my head: If I express my emotions, I will be pulled aside," Mac said.

While Mac admitted that it's different for people like his friend from Saudi Arabia, he was adamant about how the airport environment shapes his emotions. "In society we feel like there's a lot more risk inside an airport than there is at a department store. Whether that's true or not, I don't know. We feel like there's a lot more at risk because, I feel like we're trained to believe there's terrorists running through our airports at all times in our life." As a result, Mac indicated, he feels less free to express himself emotionally.

While casual travelers like Rachel, Mac, and Kristine emphasized rule following as deference to authority, frequent-flier business travelers underscored compliance primarily for efficiency purposes.

Portlander, a business traveler from Portland, Oregon, who flies an average of 120 times per year, described the airport as "kind of like another home. I know the people in the lines. I know the people at the bar. I know the people at some of the restaurants."

He laughed while admitting that flying out of different airports can cause anxiety and sometimes distress if the food isn't good. "I usually feel moody, fat, and bloated when I fly from Sacramento," he said. As a Sacramentan, I pretended not to take offense.

"It's just different at each airport. It's kind of like going to your grandma's house versus going to [the home of] some crazy lunatic friend that you once knew back in college, and you never know what's going to happen when you go to his house."

Portlander explained that when he travels to a new place, which is often, he learns ways to limit his exposure to the craziness and minimize negative emotions.

"How do you manage that?" I asked.

"I usually have very tight control of what's immediately around me. My bags are very specifically packed. I usually will pack them the night before. I have specific places where I put my sunglasses, my car keys, my wallet."

"Mm-hmm," I said.

"When you're traveling, you're always worried about losing something. So I have copies of my driver's license and passport in different bags," Portlander continued. "And if someone's right around me . . . I just kind of watch the lines. If you watched *Up in the Air*, you know that's what we do, we profile, right? I know which line to get into."

Portlander was referring to the ultra-frequent-flier's ability to assess inexperienced passengers and their line-slowing tendencies, as showcased in the George Clooney movie about a corporate hatchet man on his way to earning ten million frequent-flier miles.

"What do you make of the people who just can't figure it out?" I asked. "I mean I've observed a lot of people seeming really stressed out about flying."

In a knowing tone of voice, Portlander said, "Yessssss. People who are genuinely stressed out—that's where I'm kind of just a helpful person. So I'll come over and go, you know, 'Here is the container you put your stuff in.' You know? Unless I'm feeling a real rush, I don't exude impatience. It just scares people and makes them move slower," Portlander laughed. "I usually just genuinely try to help."

In talking about his extraordinary flying experience, Portlander described his empathy for TSOs and acknowledged how, just as passengers are governed by lots of rules, so are the TSOs who have to enforce them. "Nine times out of ten, they're just trying to get the three hundred people through the line and just trying to follow the rules."

But empathy doesn't equate to approval. Recalling a time when a TSO confiscated his asthma inhaler because it didn't have its original prescription on it, Portlander admitted, "They're definitely not customer service [oriented]. Most of the people are . . . I don't want to say low class, I'm not saying that at all, they're just . . ."

Struggling for polite wording, he continued. "Their job detail should have more of a customer service component and then more of a way to move people through faster. You know what I mean? The ability of a well-trained person in having [passengers] go through [security without] . . . feeling rushed or threatened, who will work *with* you and move through the line faster," Portlander said, describing the ideal. "And the people being hired for this job, 95 . . . 98 percent of them are not in that vein. I have very, very little poor interaction with them, but I'm also not the kind of person that picks fights. I just try to get through and realize they're just trying to do a job."

In so many words, Portlander highlighted how non-service-oriented TSOs act, and he speculated that better service would mean better security, or at least more palatable experiences. And probably less monetary waste.

"The rules about all these different types of fluids . . . it would be amazing, absolutely stunning, to figure out the hours of time in lost productivity due to these types of rules. It would be truly astounding, like billions of dollars, you know, a week, probably," he marveled, and we both laughed.

"Maybe getting people who are more customer service [oriented], that are more educated?" Portlander imagined, when asked to describe what he might change about security. "That [lack of service is] why you see all of these people harping on [the] TSA. When you travel like me, you see that you hardly have any rights anyway and you just want to get through and get it done. So you can call me a 'sheeple' because I'm just trying to get through and get to the other side. And my experiences are pretty short. I mean, I can count on one hand how many times . . . I've been in a TSA line that's been over fifteen minutes. So I've been pretty blessed."

In reflecting on his travel experiences, Portlander emphasized efficiency and understanding, recognizing how his personal feelings take a back seat to the bigger picture of airport security.

TSO Lucky described appreciating passengers like Portlander. "Business-type passengers, they do this every week and they understand how it works and how the process is, so they're very compliant. If we ask them to do something, they'll do it right away, no questions asked. They know. It's a routine to them."

But of course, not all frequent business travelers act as kindly or have the same perspective as Portlander.

TSOs described their frustrations with business travelers who think they "know it all." For instance, with an authoritative tone that bordered on snide, TSO Peter stated, "Just because you've been through it at one airport doesn't mean it's the same here."

TSO Skeet concurred. "You can tell by people's attitudes that they have a dislike for us. Especially a lot of business travelers who do it every week. [They're like,] 'I know what to do. Don't talk to me,' and I'm like, 'Okay, sorry, I didn't know that.'"

Peter's and Skeet's comments, which were echoed throughout my research, suggest that passenger behaviors can also influence TSO reactions. When passengers act like know-it-alls, threatening TSOs' presumed authority, TSOs may in turn amp up expressions of control. In fact, some of the more outrageous news stories about airport security revolve around passengers or aircrew who frequent the airport regularly. For instance, John Brennan, a Portland business traveler, was detained when a TSO's gloves tested positive for explosives after a pat-down in 2012. When the TSO wanted to perform additional security measures per protocol, Brennan started removing his clothes, piece by piece, to prove he did not have explosives on his person. Eventually peeling off *every* article of his clothing,

Brennan was arrested for disrupting security. Courts later upheld his nudity as an act of free speech and protest.[3]

Having been accused of smuggling something in my bra, I understand the exasperation of getting hassled during what should be an extremely routine interaction. Of course, some people who *look* like Ideal business travelers are really just Stereotypical jerks in Ideal clothing. It can be a challenge for TSOs to predict when they are going to meet a helpful Portlander- or Alice-type traveler and when they are going to encounter an entitled ass.

Like most people, TSOs use heuristics to "interpret" the identities of people in their environment.[4] They often assess attire as a signal for expected behavior. When people arrive in security wearing business suits and carrying briefcases, TSOs probably presume the travelers are experienced Ideal passengers who need little help through security. Likewise, they may assume that passengers who arrive in casual or complicated (i.e., difficult to quickly remove) clothes are Inexperienced passengers and treat them accordingly.

Passengers who fly frequently use similar rules of thumb to judge TSOs and other passengers they encounter, as Portlander described with his reference to the movie *Up in the Air*. When quick categorizations are violated and then challenged, there is an opportunity for surprise and sensemaking. For instance, this extended field note excerpt depicts what happens when a TSO encounters a Hostile passenger who only *looks* like an Ideal business traveler:

Inside the security checkpoint, I wait for a female TSO to perform my pat-down. The X-ray TSO scrutinizes items intently, the line of waiting passengers backing up.

I notice a bag getting rescanned belongs to an A-lister who cut me off in line earlier. We'd both approached the deserted security checkpoint at the same time, him rushing past me to the priority screening lane and me entering the general boarding line because it was completely empty. Clad in a smart suit, dragging a premium carbon fiber carry-on,

"A-Lister" avoided eye contact and hustled to get to the TSO checking IDs first. To save himself approximately five seconds.

A TSO with a sweet demeanor and lilting voice finally arrives for my pat-down. She directs me to the screening area next door to the A-lister, who watches his suitcase being searched by a male TSO. The officer is in his late forties and wears a red braided cord over his left shoulder that I will later learn signifies an honor guard. As the woman rubs her gloved hands over me, I watch A-Lister get snooty with the TSO.

As blue fingers comb through A-Lister's suitcase, the TSO tells him that liquids and gels need to be removed from the suitcase and scanned separately. The A-lister spits out a haughty "I know" as he fiddles with his phone. At least when I get caught knowingly flouting the rules, I act somewhat abashed. Instead, A-Lister stands, pin-striped legs akimbo, brown leather valise resting at black tasseled feet, intentionally ignoring the proceedings.

I ask my TSO how her day is going and she replies, "Good, it's my Friday!" to which I respond, "Hooray!" with enthusiasm. It's mine too.

As her pastel blue hands arch around the curves of my breasts, she glances toward her colleague and confides, "I can't wait to get out of this place." *No kidding.*

While she scans her gloves, I watch A-Lister plunge in earbuds and tap furiously on his iPhone, although the TSO is still checking his bags and talking to him. A-Lister stands erect and I can sense his utter disdain for the process, if not the man, who is holding him up.

The TSO, however, remains pleasant—seemingly oblivious to A-Lister's scorn. I am disgusted by this passenger's nonverbal behavior—the dismissive tone, use of technology for distancing, and disregard for the person just trying to do his job. And I can't hide my smirk as I see the TSO take the bag back to the scanner, having found the errant liquid or gel, furthering detaining the condescending passenger.

In this example, A-lister—who was likely used to being treated as an Ideal passenger—was challenged by the TSO, who did not acknowledge his status. Like the many passengers who describe not feeling like customers in airport security, A-Lister seemed to believe that "the customer is always right," taking a position of privilege. He exuded irritation and disgust, while the TSO completed his work impassively, not reacting to the degrading behavior. The TSO kept his emotions buried, despite the A-lister's apparent loathing. With his behavior strictly professional, the TSO attempted to explain how to avoid a bag check in the future. This further infuriated the A-lister, who took the lesson as another affront to his Ideal presentation.

Although TSOs described seeing all sorts of rude passengers—TSO manager Rick reminded me that "you can't classify stupid"—the officer in this interaction might initially have been surprised by the passenger's behavior. Wearing the trappings of a business person, the passenger first appeared to fall into an Ideal, low-effort category. But his Hostile behavior contradicted his business suit wrapper.

The TSO also acted Ideal and indeed wore accoutrements such as a red-braided cord to suggest his elite status. He almost certainly had extra training that equipped him to deal with the passengers without conflict. However, a newer or more Stereotypical TSO in the same situation might have approached it with less sensitivity and greater susceptibility to conflict.

The vignette from my field notes emphasizes how emotions influence people in dynamic organizational settings as well as people not even directly involved in an interaction. For employees, emotional residue from passengers can accumulate over time, especially in airports that see thousands of customers every day. It's not hard to imagine a TSO tolerating demeaning behavior from passengers at the beginning of a shift, but acting less patient as the day wears on.

But thankfully, most Ideal passengers are not like the A-lister, instead causing minimal consternation for TSOs.

Pro Travel Tip #13:

Nobody Likes a Know-It-All

Leave your A-lister attitude at home. Channel your inner Portlander, think about the good of the group, and recognize that no one has clout in the security checkpoint, no matter how many frequent-flier miles you have.

13

Nice TSOs Finish Last

On Mindful Transportation Security Officers

April 25, 2012.

It's 5:25 a.m. I'm at the airport having barely slept the night before—a theme for my years of early morning commuting despite over-the-counter sleep aids and bedtime relaxation exercises. You'd think I'd be better at this by now.

I pass through document screening without issue. Ahead I see a young TSO, "Maria," working the X-ray screener and Roger, a friendly TSO I've come to know through my travels, working behind the scenes, ostensibly collecting bins. He's someone I've been hoping to interview, and we've corresponded over email. I don't catch his eye, though, and instead turn to request my usual opt-out pat-down.

Maria directs me to wait. Standing next to the millimeter wave scanner, I crane to keep an eye on my laptop bag. Almost immediately, though, TSO "Becky" comes to claim me. Literally, the words "female assist" have barely left Maria's mouth when Becky materializes. I hear her tell Maria that Roger summoned her because I always opt out.

Does it weird me out a bit that a TSO knows my pat-down preferences without me having to ask? Uh-huh. But I try to think about it like being a regular at Starbucks. Maybe it's like a barista remembering I prefer a grande latte with one raw sugar? I keep telling myself that.

Drowning me in "sweeties" and "dears," Becky guides me to the screening area. She asks if I've had a pat-down before, apparently not recognizing me from our pat-down interaction last week. So much for feeling like a regular.

Roger sweeps in to help her move my bags from the conveyor belt to the extra screening area and says "I got your message." I'd emailed about setting up an interview. He looks uncomfortable and I'm afraid he's going to back out.

When he says, "I can't do it at work, in uniform," I reply, "Of course not."

Before I can say, "I'll email you with more information," he asks, "Do you like sweets?"

Quizzically, I reply, "Yes."

"I have something for you," he says and runs off. *Okaaaaay.*

I turn back to Becky. After giving me the usual instructions, Becky says that because I'm wearing a short dress, she is only going to pat-down my legs and not go up my skirt. I'm bemused because when I wore a similar outfit last week, she said she would skip patting down my legs because they were obviously bare. Are TSOs not always allowed to trust their eyes?

Starting with my collar, Becky moves my hair aside and slides her gloved hands down my back. I remark that the checkpoint seems busier than normal, and I ask why the center line is closed. She ignores the question and says, "It's always busy this time of the morning," as if on autopilot.

"Yeah, I fly every Wednesday morning," I remark.

She's not picking up on my "I'm clearly a regular and we have done this exact same interaction before" signals. I keep trying though—I'm always on the hunt for interviewees—and we get to talking about busy times at the airport. I wonder aloud why the airlines stack their flights so early and at the same times. We chat about her job, and she says that she doesn't work the evenings. I explain how busy the airports are on Thursdays and Fridays, at least in Phoenix. I'm regularly surrounded by sales and business people going home from visiting their territories.

Becky says she's heard it's busy in Sacramento, too, at least for the Las Vegas flight. She sniggers as she makes fun of the "Las Vegas crowd" and how you can tell where they're heading by how they dress and how they act. "I've never seen it, but I've heard," she admits.

Waking every day at 3:30 or 4:00 a.m., Becky is off by noon, so she never sees the apparently scantily clad women. That Becky seems to know what it means to be a "Las Vegas passenger" without ever working the evening shift intrigues me and leads me to believe that TSOs do share knowledge about passengers frequently. If someone appears to be a Las Vegas passenger, do they get treated differently? How is that different from a sleep-deprived parent passenger or a business executive passenger? I muse.

After her gloves test negative for explosives, Becky comes over and chats with me more about the Vegas crowd while I reshoe myself. We both smile and laugh. When we're talking here (as opposed to during screening), she stops calling me "sweetie" and "dear." It feels like I'm meeting a more genuine Becky—Becky the person, not Becky the TSO. And she seems to recognize me as a person rather than just a passenger too.

Of course, I notice other passengers and TSOs watching us, and Becky clearly has to get back to work after a couple minutes. I collect my belongings and walk out, smiling at the TSO manager behind the counter. I leave security and walk to Starbucks, following three sheriff's deputies who saunter slowly together, blocking my path. The men take up space, with holsters and belts making them appear wider than they really are. Their ambling reminds me of Wild West movies. We all join the line for coffee.

Just then, TSO Roger materializes behind me with a large brown paper bag, the edges rolled under to keep it loosely closed. I jump, startled.

Holding the sack out to me, he says, "I made this last night."

"Thank you," I reply, tentatively. I reach out to take the bag; it's heavier than I expected.

Wanting to end the interaction immediately, I'm grateful when the Starbucks line moves forward and I need to continue inside. I offer more thanks and tell Roger to have a good day. He walks off, leaving me holding the sack. The three deputies eye me curiously but say nothing.

What am I supposed to do now? I want to interview Roger and that means not offending him, but I'm also not really wanting to eat homemade goods from a virtual stranger. What the hell am I supposed to do with this bag?! As I ponder my state of affairs, three flight attendants join the line behind me and I hear them wondering aloud if they will "make it." I let them go ahead of me, and they ask, "Are you going with us to Phoenix?"

"Yes," I say. "And I want my flight crew well caffeinated."

They laugh and promise to "take care of me" on the flight—meaning they will give me a drink. I laugh, saying it's a little too early in the day for liquor. It's really fun to have them be so friendly, though. (Later, when I get on the flight, they say, "That's our girl!" and people crane to see what makes me so special.)

After securing my second coffee of the day, I visit the ladies' room—the only place I can think to get any privacy. Setting the bag on the counter near the sink, I unroll the edges and peer inside. I have to at least peek at the contents, in case Roger asks me about it later.

Inside the bag sits a foil container that looks like restaurant takeout. I lift it out and pry open the silver lid to discover a giant flan. Yes, flan, the Spanish caramel custard dessert. It's by far the strangest gift I've ever received ever, from anyone, let alone from a mere acquaintance. (And it's super funny because I'm obnoxiously vocal in my personal life about how much I *hate* flan.)

So now I'm standing in an airport bathroom at 6:00 a.m. with a cup of coffee and a flan large enough to feed a small family, unsure of what to do. I'm truly troubled by this turn of events, feeling tension between my desire/need to collect TSO interviews and my anxiety/fear about a stranger in a position of authority giving me gifts. Did he make the flan just for me, knowing that I fly every Wednesday? Or was it a flan he just happened to have in a takeaway container? Who just happens to have a flan with them? Are there rules about TSOs giving passengers gifts? Was he assigned dessert for the weekly TSO potluck, and has he just ruined everyone's day by giving it away? What if he put something untoward in it? Later, when I tell my friends, they joke that Roger must get excited for Wednesdays, and that he might be crafting a Shawna shrine somewhere. I watch far too much serial killer TV programming for this type of talk.

My impulse is to ditch the flan immediately. But I worry that Roger might've doubled back and will be standing outside the bathroom waiting to ask me about it, which feels eerie but possible. Instead, I replace the flan's lid, return it to the bag, and carry the sack out of the bathroom. I hear boarding calls for my flight and drag my flan with me to line up, seeing no sign of Roger. As soon as I get down the gangway, I toss the flan, rationalizing that it won't be good by the time I get to Phoenix anyway. (Sorry, Roger!)

Months later, when Roger and I finally sit down for an interview—at an ice cream parlor of all places—I realize that Roger is a sweets fiend like me and definitely not the creepy shrine-making type. I am not brave enough to ask him about the flan, nor does it come up in conversation.

As we speak, Roger describes how much he cares for his job, the people he works with, and the passengers they serve. In fact, TSO Roger explains that by being friendly to passengers, he lets them "know that we care about [them]."

When asked to explain the "we" in that statement, he says, "Us, the company, the TSA."

(At this point, gentle reader, I must tell you that I half-hid behind my Leatherby's Black & Tan sundae to mask the "say what now?" expression on my face.)

"We're all people. We're not robots that just do our jobs and don't care about the passengers," Roger emphasized, digging into his caramel and marshmallow confection. "We do care. We care so much. That is why we are there for them, to make sure that they are safe when going through the checkpoint and traveling in the air."

Whereas from some people this might feel like lip service, Roger's words aligned with his actions. Roger made a point to go out of his way to help passengers—joking with them, helping heft their luggage, trying to get them to smile during screening. Roger described these actions as demonstrating the care that he and his organization feel. While not all TSOs would describe their work as caregiving per se, one type of TSO identity allows them to express care about passengers and coworkers as fellow human beings worthy of respect and kindness: the Mindful TSO.

This TSO identity surfaced rarely in my interviews with passengers but more frequently in my interactions and interviews with TSOs themselves. I call these officers Mindful TSOs because they are aware of yet able to resist the dominant discourses of the security context—namely, the pressure to exert authority and to practice strict emotional containment. Instead, Mindful TSOs transgressed norms of the security context, most often emotionally, in order to make travel easier for passengers and work better for their fellow employees.

TSOs appeared Mindful when they described their work as helpful and service-oriented, and maintained friendly, engaging, and supportive relations with passengers. For instance, one TSO greeted me prior to a pat-down by saying, "Hi love, what's your name? I'm Andrea, I'm going to be taking care of you tonight." Few TSOs ever introduce themselves and definitely do not frame pat-downs as caretaking.

Importantly, as Mindful TSOs expressed affirmative emotions and practiced excellent customer service, they also appeared well trained and professional. Often they used their discretion to help passengers—perhaps allowing Grandma's homemade jelly to be carried on or enabling someone younger than seventy-five to keep their shoes on—but made sure not to compromise security. Unlike other TSOs, who might use discretion to speed up lines or to skimp on steps, a Mindful TSO helps because "it's the right thing to do." Mindful TSOs infuse work with humor and humility, while still doing the job well. Mindful TSOs might also draw on the TSA service and mission discourses, but they do so in less militaristic/patriotic ways than their Ideal-Zealot counterparts.

Mindful TSOs recognize negative views of the TSA and, in many ways, work to counteract them. For instance, TSO Carrie acknowledged attitudes toward TSOs. "There's a lot of negativity out there about being a TSO, but if you came to my airport and you met me, and you didn't know me, you would be so surprised at how great of a person a TSO can be. We don't have to be nasty or rude to be professional. You can be professional and still do your job and be nice."

In fact, TSO Roger lamented training that requires TSOs to reflect a "commanding presence" and how the emotional rule affects both him and passengers. "When [passengers] get stressed out, they make mistakes. Not through their own fault, it's because the way they see things. . . . Eventually they do something wrong because of fear."

The fear and mistakes "can be avoided if you have more friendlier [TSOs] . . . [with a more] approachable presence than a commanding presence," Roger said. "I know they [the TSA] try to implement a commanding presence in everybody because we are in charge of security. But, like I said, we are also people. Being commanding sucks."

As one of the few officers I had the opportunity to both interview and observe, Roger consistently resisted pressure to be intimidating. Instead, with a soft-spoken and helpful demeanor, he employed humor and kindness in his work. Importantly, it seems that empathy, kindness, and humor are not mutually exclusive of security goals, but instead reinforce the value of communicating *with* passengers instead of *at* them.

Underscoring positive communication, Ty, a TSO at a small airport in the Southwest, described how he interacts with passengers. Ty said, "I'm a people person. I'm friendly to people. I can get them to lighten up. Every day I hear at least one to ten people say, 'We wish we could have it like this everywhere.'" Admitting that it is often easier to be friendly and engaged with passengers in a small setting—his rural airport serves less than fifty people per day—Ty said he responds to passengers who compliment his service by saying, "'Well, I'm glad that we were able to make you feel better.'"[1] He added, "At least they know that there are places where they don't have to feel like a cow," explaining that some passengers describe feeling like cattle getting herded through security. He offers them more personalized and courteous interactions.

Likewise, TSO Neecie said, "I go over and beyond. I talk with the passengers. If I have to pat a passenger down or do bag checks, I tease them. I have a conversation with those that are willing to have a conversation. I get to hear life stories in a ten-minute time frame. I laugh, talk, cry, whatever it is the passenger wants to do. I listen. I assist passengers that need help information-wise, getting from terminal to terminal and whatnot. That sort of stuff."

She sounded more like a counselor than a security officer.

I thought about Neecie's comment regarding life stories in a ten-minute time frame—how amazing that part of the job must be. To hear about people's lives in snapshots. While some research describes the phenomenon of "reluctant confidants"—people like bartenders and hairdressers who hear all of our secrets and are privy to "too much information"—Neecie's perspective seemed more hopeful.

"Can you recall a favorite passenger moment?" I probed.

"I have a few favorite passenger moments," Neecie replied. "I had a passenger come up to me needing help. She was convinced someone was out to kill her."

"Oh my goodness," I sputtered.

"I got the law enforcement involved, [got] our behavior detection officers involved, and made sure that someone stayed with her at all times," Neecie explained. "Even after my shift was over . . . I stayed with her four hours after my shift, on my own time, making sure that she boarded the plane and that no one was actually following her. I made sure the plane took off before I left."

Neecie's comments made me think about the training flight attendants receive to identify and help stop human trafficking, and I wondered if TSOs get the same type of education. I was impressed that she would stay on her own time to help a stranger, especially because many TSO shifts are long and some start in the middle of the night.

"Then I had another passenger who was a diabetic and I had to screen her," Neecie recalled. "She was looking for her luggage. I assisted her with trying to find her luggage, which took like two hours." Apparently the woman's carry-ons contained her insulin, and she had misplaced one of the bags.

"She didn't have any money and I gave her money to get something to eat on her flight. I made sure we found her bags and retrieved her diabetic medication that she had gone without. Those are two of my favorite passenger moments."

"What makes them your favorite?" I asked, marveling that in all of my years studying the TSA, I had never heard stories like this. Concern for *individual* passenger safety and protection had not been a common theme in my conversations with TSOs.

"I was actually helping someone, physically helping someone," Neecie replied. And this I understood. A lot of TSOs talked about job satisfaction at a meta level, like the abstract satisfaction of helping society or helping "the public" travel safely. But being able to help specific individuals, especially in extreme cases like someone feeling unsafe and escaping an abuser or an elderly woman needing medication, must make the job so much more meaningful.

"How often would you say that you get to have that type of satisfaction in your job?" I asked, thinking about other TSOs who talked about the thousands and thousands of people they see every day.

"Not often. Not often," Neecie repeated. "It's a rare moment situation, for sure. Other than that, it's business as usual every day." And by business as usual, Neecie meant managing the usually negative interactions with passengers.

TSOs who act friendly and empathetic can challenge passengers' negative impressions, particularly Inexperienced passengers who might be nervous about interacting with TSOs whom they envision as scary and aggressive. TSO Peter described acting friendly and engaged with passengers: "We're taught over and over and over, body language speaks volumes. If you've got a smile on your face . . . versus arms crossed with a look on your face that says, 'You're an idiot.' [If you were a passenger,] how would you respond?"

When TSOs go out of their way to be helpful and friendly, inexperienced passengers may feel less stress in security and potentially change the way they think about TSOs. Affirmative interactions can produce more satisfied customers. That said, when Mindful TSOs interact with hostile passengers, conflict can result. Recall that TSO Roger described a scenario in which he had to perform additional screening on containers of breast milk. The passenger grew irate, accusing Roger of trying to put something in the milk and ranting about her civil rights being violated. Finally, the passenger became aggressive.

Still visibly angry, Roger recalled the incident. "She said, 'Did they teach you how to be rude?' I was so, I was so shocked I couldn't say anything. I was so mad because I'm being blamed for [being] something I'm not, and I don't like that. I try my best to be a very good person, a courteous person. But to tell me I've done something that I haven't done is unforgivable. I don't like people judging me. They don't even know me. What did I do, though? I just walked away."

Roger reacted to this hostile passenger by controlling his anger and surprise in the moment and by asking a supervisor to help him. As a TSO who prides himself on being kind and helpful, Roger's identity was challenged by accusations that he was acting in a rude Stereotypical TSO manner.

But Roger described with satisfaction that this type of heated exchange is rare for him. In fact, a number of TSOs bragged that they use their helpful demeanors and excellent communication skills to diffuse hostility, and that they experience far less antagonism from passengers than their less-friendly colleagues.

Interactions between Mindful TSOs and Stereotypical-Hostile passengers can change Hostile passengers' perspectives too. For instance, TSO Peter recalled a situation where he had to perform a pat-down on an elderly man, and the man's son grew upset.

"I was working with one of the original members of Easy Company, the Band of Brothers, the real deal," Peter recalled, explaining that the elderly traveler was a World War II veteran and a member of the E Company, 2nd Battalion, 506th Parachute Infantry Regiment, 101st Airborne Division—the subject of the HBO miniseries *Band of Brothers*.

"I had to do a pat-down, and his son was just livid—a war hero getting a pat-down? He [the father] couldn't put his hands in the proper position because he was ninety years old and he had more metal in him than he had bones. If he walked through the metal detector he'd light up like a

Christmas tree. We know he's not dangerous, of course we do," Peter admitted. "But the guy's son, he's really upset about it. . . . So I spent the next twenty minutes bringing him [the son] back down to earth. If my father was a World War II vet, a hero, I'd be pissed, too. But I just treated him with empathy."

Peter took care not only to perform a gentle and compassionate search of the elderly man but also to calm down the son. He counted this interaction as successful because his communication skills and empathy helped the passengers walk away feeling good, or at least better, about the experience.

While good for passenger morale, however, Peter's Mindful approach took much longer than a typical screening, keeping him away from other duties at the checkpoint. While paying such close attention to this pair of passengers, Peter could not be vigilant and aware of others around him, as the TSA requires.

Many TSOs described the hyper-awareness of managers who prioritize efficiency, and in fact, being an especially helpful TSO may lead to trouble with management. This conundrum is typical in high-stress service environments where employees must decide whether to appease a customer or attend to and prioritize higher-level organizational goals.[2]

Indeed, communicating with a particular passenger, whether engaging in small talk or addressing questions/concerns, can result in slower security screenings and delays in lines, which irritates other passengers who are concerned about getting through security quickly. Mindful TSOs who take time away from the screening process, even for helpful purposes, can face consequences from their coworkers and managers.

TSO Carrie described how her supervisors did not appreciate the extra time she took to help passengers. "[They] don't like people who are nice . . . who go out of their way to help people. I've been told I am unprofessional, unprofessional, unprofessional, unprofessional. That's all they keep telling me because I help old ladies with their carts. I tie people's shoes for them. I help people with their coats when they need it, and that's being 'unprofessional.'"

Carrie emphasized her approach to taking care of and respecting passengers as well as protecting them: "I go home at night . . . knowing I did the best job I could to make sure that everybody who went through that checkpoint when I was on the X-ray, or if I was at tickets or if I gave a pat-down, wasn't getting anything through that they shouldn't have. I go home and I sleep well at night knowing I did the best job I can."

Carrie spoke emphatically about her job, with a sense of duty. "I don't do it for the money. I do it because I care about my country. And they get mad at me."

"Mad?" I asked.

Carrie described a passenger who approached the walkthrough metal detector in tears. "I said, 'Ma'am, what's the matter?' She said, 'My fifteen-year-old daughter just died, and I'm going to where she is,' and she grabbed a hold of me and put her head on my shoulder and started weeping. I held her in my arms, and I said, 'I'll say a prayer for you,' and I comforted her. And they said I was unprofessional."

Explaining that "they" meant her TSA supervisors, Carrie complained that her training conflicts with her inclination to offer care. "I can't hug anybody anymore. I used to hug soldiers all the time. There were a few times these young kids were going to Iraq or Afghanistan, and I would always stand up. I would shake their hand and tell them they're my hero—because they are—and how I am proud to shake their hand, because they deserve it.

"Sometimes their moms are behind them, and their moms come and hug me. . . . They're crying because they're so surprised that somebody would care," Carrie gushed. "Well, I come from a military family. I know what it's like. My father served in World War II, Korea, and Vietnam. My brother served in the air force, and my other brother served in the army, and I served in the army."

Carrie reiterated that she does her job every day to serve her country, and that it's service and family that "really" matter in life.

Her supervisors?

"They don't matter to me. I respect them because they're my bosses, and I have to do what they say, but that doesn't mean that I agree with it,"

Carrie said, citing their mandate that she stop her familiar behavior with passengers.

Depending on which station a Mindful TSO has in the security line "chain" (e.g., from ID checker to divestiture officer to walk-through metal detector officer), conversations and helping can cause passenger bottlenecks that back up lines and breed resentment in coworkers who must then deal with cranky fliers.

It is interesting that Carrie's perception of what management defines as "unprofessional" differs so starkly from the way a passenger might define it. Likewise, our understanding of "professionalism" depends on the context and our perspective and past experience. During traditional customer service encounters, professionalism often means doing the job right, as in the way the customer wants it. In security, professionalism as management defines it may mean stoicism and strict adherence to protocols, but those behaviors might not satisfy passengers who need extra help and care.

I know that despite the no-hug rule, Carrie will still be determined to show care to passengers, no matter what her managers might think. Her perspective reminded me of an analysis of "workplace selves" by Dr. David Collinson, a critical management scholar, who compared the types of identities that people demonstrate at work. He described "resistant selves" as people who use satire, irony, and whistleblowing to express dissatisfaction with workplace policies.[3] His concept of resistance is entirely pessimistic, though (at least in terms of employees' feelings toward their organization). Carrie and the other Mindful TSOs—Ty, Roger, Peter, and Neecie—each displayed positive emotions in ways that transgressed and resisted organizational norms. And this cheerful resistance still allowed them to identify with their workplace.

When TSOs resist dominant organizational and societal discourses about what it means to be a professional TSO, interactions with passengers can be positive, surprising, and even transformative, as passengers' preconceived notions about TSOs are challenged. Mindful TSOs often infuse their work with kindness and humor, relying heavily on interpersonal communication skills. TSO Peter boasted, "I can communicate pretty well with passengers because I can empathize. . . . I treat them as humans. With humor, empathy."

In my observations, helpfulness and humor seemed to make the security process less onerous. For example, when TSO Roger was aiding a group of elderly travelers, a wheelchair-using member of the group stood up next to her chair, and Roger murmured to her companions, "She got free. I don't think she plans to go back." The group and surrounding passengers chuckled. TSOs describe these instances of connection as what make their jobs satisfying and fun.

Pro Travel Tip #14:

Cycle Up Gratitude and Courtesy

In the research about emotions, there's a concept called "emotion cycles." Based on emotional contagion theory, which suggests that we can "catch" emotions from other people, emotion cycles emphasize the sharing and perpetuating of emotion in social situations.[4] Think about when your significant other is in a bad mood and you soon find yourself in a bad mood too. The literature on emotion cycles examines how these shared emotions can spiral and influence organizational settings, but it focuses almost exclusively on negative emotions like anger.

The good news? We can "cycle up" gratitude and courtesy as well. Friendliness and empathy are not antithetical to security procedures, but they are not "normal" in airport security, nor are they often rewarded by TSA management. However, friendly and empathetic behavior not only helps passengers, it also helps TSOs have better work experiences, even preventing burnout and anxiety.

So if you meet a Mindful TSO, consider amplifying your positive emotions in return. You might even create a cycle of gratitude, courtesy, and happiness that can improve the moods of other officers and travelers—and, of course, yourself.

14

The Traveling Unicorn

On Mindful Passengers

April 6, 2012.

It's evening in Albuquerque. At the checkpoint, TSOs outnumber passengers, and for once I'm annoyed that I arrived at the airport so damn early. The TSO working the documents station does not look at me, just reaches out for my ID and boarding pass. Without a word, he scans them, then abruptly looks up, smiles, and wishes me a nice Easter. The interaction feels strangely robotic, but I return the greeting and walk on to baggage screening.

After loading my baggage for the X-ray scanner, I approach the young male TSO who is working the millimeter wave scanner. Confidently, I say, "I'd like to opt out, please."

He looks at me with something like concern and warns, "Okay. You'll have to get a full-body pat-down, you know."

"I know," I say, smiling. A moment passes and the woman behind me declares she wants to opt out as well.

A second TSO insists, "There's no radiation here. It's radio waves."

"I know," I assert, not wanting to argue the finer points of the technology. "I'd still like to opt out."

"It's nice to have some support here," the woman behind me blurts, gruffly. She's maybe five feet two and swims in faded, baggy jeans. I mentally nickname her "Alex" because she reminds me of actress Alex Borstein, the star of the TV show *The Marvelous Mrs. Maisel*. I nod. She's not wrong. I haven't had very much experience opting out with someone else and the solidarity is pleasant.

While we wait, the first TSO tells Alex, "We need your shoes."

"Sure you do," she spits. "Sure you do." She rips off her white sneakers and slams them on top of her suitcase, which is awaiting a trip through the X-ray machine.

The second TSO silently hands Alex a gray bin for the shoes while making eye contact with me. The first TSO, speaking calmly into his microphone as if not wanting to startle a wild animal, says, "Female assist times two."

I offer a half-smile and continue to wait. Sizing up Alex as a potential interviewee, I comment, "I fly every week, so I always opt out."

Before she can reply, though, an unsmiling, stern TSO—"Nancy"—opens the gate for me. She snaps at a coworker, "Gerald, you're in the way!"

Gerald moves aside with an upward flick of his eyes. I walk around the metal detector and point to my belongings. Nancy glares as I gesture to my suitcase, laptop bag, and two gray bins. She calls for a lanky redheaded TSO to help carry the luggage and snipes at him for taking too long.

Nancy talks through the screening protocol in precise detail, without ever looking at me. I clear her by at least six inches and watch the top of her messy brown hair flop around as she talks. She scowls as she opens the drawer holding a supply of latex gloves, and I wonder how invasive this pat-down will be.

As I stand spread-eagle, facing my belongings, I see the male TSOs from earlier staring at me from across the checkpoint. Nancy roughly rubs me, getting uncomfortably close to my lady parts. My skin tingles as she touches me, and I almost flinch. She completes her work quickly, though, tests her gloves, and walks off.

"Have a nice weekend," I say to the back of her head, and then chastise myself. Why am I trying to be nice to her after *that* interlude?

Meanwhile, I notice that sneaker-slamming Alex's screening is taking twice as long as mine. A second TSO stands nearby, asking questions about her trip—where's she headed, how long she's been in town—standard questions for a behavior detection officer. Alex is assertive and just this side of rude as a saccharine-sweet TSO checks the turned-down waistband of her jeans. I lollygag while putting on my shoes and repacking my luggage, but she is still getting her pat-down when I walk into the terminal.

I wonder if Alex received extra scrutiny simply because of her attitude. Was her wee bit of interpersonal resistance punished with an excessively long pat-down and interrogation? Perhaps.

Most of the passengers I've observed over the last ten years fall into either the Ideal or Stereotypical-Inexperienced passenger identity buckets. Even if they are disruptive like Suzanne or Ronny, they ultimately comply and avoid asking critical questions or expressing displeasure. Many *feel* upset but don't express negativity out of either fear for repercussions or pragmatism—not wanting their emotional displays to disrupt security, especially when they realize their feelings won't matter in the grand scheme of things. Even a pee protest doesn't shut down security for long.

However, I did find a small segment of passengers who resisted regularly. They pushed back against norms in the security context and against views of passengers as Stereotypical (unprepared, emotional) wrecks or Ideal (unthinking) automatons. As with TSOs, I describe these passengers as Mindful to reflect their awareness of the airport's context and their willingness nevertheless to reject its social norms.

Prepared and familiar with organizational rules, Mindful passengers demonstrate resistance in two primary ways—by being militant about civil rights and openly critical of the TSA and also, perhaps counterintuitively, by demonstrating empathy.

The Militant

Mindful-Militant passengers frequently demonstrated a deep concern for civil rights and protest that more closely aligned with employee resistance in organizational settings. They knew policy and security procedures, showed up prepared, and were not afraid to stand up for their beliefs. More likely than other passengers to opt out of advanced imaging and receive pat-downs, they often described opting out as a political stance and, like Alex, made efforts to develop solidarity with other opt-outers.

In the extreme, some Mindful-Militant passengers set up TSOs to make them look bad and record supposedly improper actions in an attempt at civil disobedience. For instance, in 2011, a woman receiving a pat-down screamed at the top of her lungs, "For [god's] sakes, somebody help me!"[1] As she carried on a ten-minute tirade, her son Ryan recorded the incident. When asked by airline and TSA personnel, he declined to stop recording because they could not cite a law requiring him to stop. As it happened, Ryan and his family were regulars in the TSA protest genre; several YouTube videos show Ryan and his parents in confrontations with the TSA. In one, Ryan compares the TSA to the secret police of Nazi Germany, indicates he prepared all day for his protest, and declares that fliers must choose between being "molested" or being "microwaved like a TV dinner."

Occasionally, some Ideal passengers are pushed to the brink and veer into protest. Recall John Brennan, the Portland business traveler who stripped in protest. In practice, of course, Mindful-Militant passengers usually stick to describing their feelings rather than acting them out. During my interviews with them, many discussed feeling highly critical of the TSA as well as the organizational and societal discourses that promote security and compliance. Mindful-Militant passengers analyzed TSA policies and used terms like "security theater" to insinuate that TSA protocols are largely farcical performances designed to make passengers *feel* safe without actually increasing safety.

For instance, Leroy ridiculed the TSA, saying, "Ideally, a country that cares about security as much as ours supposedly does would back that commitment with security policies and staffing decisions that value actual assessment of threats rather than inane policies about liquids and shoes. I'd like to see more people who study psychology and fewer metal detectors. I'd like uniform searches rather than racial profiling or silly no-fly lists. If we really care about security, maybe we should quit hiring the dregs of society.

"My general attitude toward air travel is that it is a series of inconveniences and lunacy run by toothless government agencies, profit-hungry companies, and an army of undereducated, overempowered dolts. My job when traveling is to limit their ability to ruin my trip, and thus happy air travel entails lots of preparation and an abundance of margin for their inevitable errors. I generally try to be friendly and approachable [to TSOs]. Their responses are generally nondescript. Despite being employed to be on the watch for potentially dangerous people, they seem to pay my actual personality zero attention. Their concern is that the name on my license matches the name on my boarding pass. Then again, I also suspect that their lack of concern about me has to do with the fact that I'm unremarkable to them as a white male. I'm not the person they're looking for."

Although he generally acts like an Ideal passenger, Leroy described a razor-sharp awareness of the discursive context surrounding airport security protocols and a willingness to fight back against perceived TSO misbehavior—politely, if necessary.

Dirk, a frequent flier who exhibited extreme skepticism toward the TSA, echoed Leroy's thoughts. He described how he interacts with TSOs by being prepared, direct, and calm. "I'm ready for them," Dirk remarked. "I try not to offend them or humiliate them. . . . Usually, I very clearly and very plainly [say], 'Scanner, no thank you. I don't think so.' I'm not aggressive, but I don't act wishy-washy. They have a job to do, whether or not they like me. I try not to take it as a personal affront to the people that are there. . . . I try to jump through the hoops as much as I can to make life easy. Really, I try not to make the situation more aggressive or uncomfortable than it needs to be."

With more forethought than many of the passenger participants I spoke with, Dirk described his discomfort with the mission and goals of the TSA, and the tension he felt between his goals of travel and his desire to "take a stand" for his rights. Despite deep convictions about what he described as the irrationality of TSA policies, Dirk also recognized that frontline TSOs were not to blame for the creation of those policies. He resisted the view of TSOs as inhuman and instead treated them civilly, albeit firmly, when it came to asking for alternative screening.

One thing that sets Mindful-Militant passengers apart is their willingness to communicate discontent and actively showcase their resistance, although they do so in ways that do not generally disrupt security. As with Alex's shoe slamming, these passengers ignore organizational norms that teach passengers to bottle emotions, and instead take latitude to *express* rather than suppress their annoyance.

Passenger Sue described how she disagrees with TSA policies and always has "run-ins" with TSOs. "Each time I have been fairly accommodating, but I really felt when they implemented the scanners—the full-body image scanners—I thought they just crossed a line."

Sue described her experiences as a frequent flier for her PR job, saying she watched "irrational" policies like the liquids and gels rule without much comment, but advanced imaging had pushed her over the edge. As an example, Sue shared that the last time she had gone through the backscatter scanner, she held her hands over her head and flipped off the camera.

"I decided it would be comical to flip off the cameras, and they did not find that comical," Sue admitted. "When I got out of the scanner, they pulled me aside and patted me down. They tried to say it was the little metal details on my jeans that had set off the imaging thing. But . . . I always wear the same jeans in the airport and that was the only time I had ever had a problem. So I'm under the assumption it's because I was being a terrible person in the scanner."

To Sue, being punished for her resistance was comparable to when passengers who "mouth off" have their screenings repeated or last longer than normal. Although the connection between flipping the bird and receiving an enhanced pat-down might have been coincidental, Sue believed they were connected and said she complained vigorously via social media to anyone who would listen. However, despite being a self-described advocate for social justice, Sue did not think to formally complain on her own behalf.

Militant behavior—beyond negative nonverbal communication and opting out of screening—was rare in my observations. Much more frequent were passengers who described *feeling* like Mindful-Militants but *acting* like Ideal passengers.

For instance, "Bob" eloquently described how he disagreed with TSA policies and their impact on individual civil liberties. "I feel like my only choice is to basically not get treated like a citizen anymore, or [not] fly," he said. Nevertheless, he did not opt out of screenings, express emotion, or question protocol for fear of being singled out and punished. Like Mindful TSOs, Mindful-Militant passengers did not emerge frequently in my research and do not surface often in popular portrayals of airport security.

Furthermore, during my interviews and social media discussions, TSOs seemed likely to deride passengers who "take a stand" by opting out or complaining. For instance, in a LinkedIn discussion, TSOs debated whether passenger behavior had improved since the removal of backscatter scanners in January 2013. When some TSOs complained that passengers were still opting out, others made fun of passengers for their obvious lack of understanding of security protocols and technologies. Moreover, TSOs seemed to view Mindful-Militant behavior as just a "hassle" to deal with and control.

And sometimes TSOs choose to control the Mindful-Militant "hassles" by creating obstacles during screenings. For example, passenger Sue discussed how TSOs made her request to opt out of advanced imaging difficult. "I'd already unpacked all of my stuff and I was waiting to go up to the agent because I didn't want to distract him from the other people," Sue said, showing that she wanted to assert her rights but was also mindful of not interrupting the security process. "I said I wanted to opt out. Then he questioned me for about three or four minutes, and he's like, 'This is completely safe. I don't see why you wouldn't want to use this.' I said, 'Well, I just don't. I don't think that this measure is necessary. It's a little bit of an invasion of personal privacy. I don't like having an individual image of me floating around. I would just prefer a pat-down.'"

When the officer asked Sue if she knew what a pat-down consisted of, she said, "Yes, I've been patted down before. It's fine." She waited a couple more minutes for a TSO. And then kept on waiting.

"The first time was probably my worst experience because that was the time it took twenty minutes for them to get an agent over. . . . When she finally came over, she had a bad attitude. My husband had been trying to help so that my personal items weren't getting stolen by people on the other side of security. She was yelling at him not to touch anything and so she got gruff with him," Sue continued.

"I was trying to be patient because I realize you don't need to yell at TSA people because they can kick you out [of] the airport or whatever," she said, showing a clear knowledge of societal discourses related to the TSA's power. "I was already in a bad mood because I had to wait so long. Even the general banter you have with TSA people had an edge to it from both her and I, which I'm sure didn't help the situation. Once the pat-down happened, I just complied with everything she asked me to do."

When I asked Sue how she generally interacted with TSOs, she said, "I realize they're just trying to do their job, but I feel put out or annoyed by the extra security measures they've installed. I try and just be neutral," Sue said. "I realize I have a tendency of going into it with a bad attitude, but I try and not let that show because I realize if I reflect that, then they'll obviously reflect that back onto me."

Sue said she would regularly read the TSA policy brochures at airports, and despite being a frequent flier, she still visits the TSA's website. Most recently, she wanted to learn more about opting out.

"I read over their policies because I wanted to know exactly what my rights were," Sue said. "Is this opt-out thing still valid? Because I've been told by TSA people that it's not. That worries me. If I'm getting misinformed by them or lied to by [officers], that concerns me."

But Sue also mentioned that despite being someone who regularly emails the TSA to complain, she keeps her interactions with TSOs in context. "I try to keep it in perspective that they are just trying to do their job. They're earning a paycheck. They're trying to support their family. It's their job. They're probably not as emotionally invested in this as I am."

Intriguingly, Sue draws on societal pragmatism—the view that officers are just doing what they have to do to feed their families—humanizing them despite her personal discomfort with how they accomplish their jobs. And given her awareness of the larger context of their work, Sue makes a point to stay apprised of TSA policy and procedures. "I try and be an informed consumer of their services," she said, "and not get so jaded by other people's experiences."

Sue explained that she does not allow her interactions with TSOs to be influenced by hearsay or gossip from other passengers. Rather, she collects information for herself. "What is their policy? If I get in trouble, what are my rights? That sorta thing. I would say I have only just recently started looking into that because of the problems I've been having [with officers]," she said. "Because I am concerned that one of these days they're just going to pull me into an office and put me on a list and say I can't fly."

While I wish that Sue was a Mindful-Militant passenger who just sounded paranoid, my TSO sources indicated that continued passenger "misbehavior" is sometimes flagged.[2] (However, my sources assure me that the flagging is usually related to verbal and physical abuse, not standing up for one's rights.)

Sue mentioned her awareness of public discourses about the TSA, admitting she'd recently become more "susceptible to media portrayals of [the] TSA just because they're funny." (As a fan of *South Park* and *Saturday Night Live*—two shows that routinely lampoon the TSA—I would agree.) "Also, because I think they are accurate to my experiences," she said. "I realized my experiences [must] be completely abnormal [compared] to the rest of the world. I would hope that not everybody [gets] treated this way or else nobody would fly."

Sue said she feels that typical passengers don't encounter the same type of harassment that she's endured. "[Although] the media portray TSA, I think, in such a negative light . . . I feel like that reflects my experiences."

Even with her negative experiences, Sue was aware of how Stereotypical passengers view the TSA and how officers are treated. "I don't see [officers] mistreated, but I'm sure they are." Likewise, she admits the media probably prioritize sensational passenger stories, "not the average individual's experiences, which . . . are normal and not negative encounters with TSA."

Sue's ability to view the TSA and its officers within the prevailing personal, organizational, and societal discourses is remarkable, considering how much pressure passengers feel from their exposure to negative accounts in media and organizational pressure to conform.

"I mean, they just seemed like average people. Which is why I try to keep it in my head that they're just trying to earn a paycheck," Sue said, reflecting a working-class discourse of pragmatism. "I think if I put it in that perspective I can at least deal with them a little bit better than if I put it in my head, 'They're doing this for their country and they see me as a potential threat.' That would annoy me."

I make a mental note not to describe the Ideal TSO to Sue. Her orientation to the TSA also points to the second category of Mindful passenger behavior—Mindful Empathy.

The Empathetic

Even more exceptional than Mindful-Militant passengers were those who demonstrated positive emotions toward airport security—specifically, empathy for TSOs. Prepared and informed, Mindful-Empathetic passengers resisted the emotional norms of airport security, but in largely affirmative ways. For instance, they shunned the pressure to tightly control their emotions in order to "get through" security, and unlike the majority of passengers I spoke with, they did not describe feeling anxious about TSOs.

More to the point, Mindful-Empathetic passengers recognized the humanity of TSOs. They offered friendly smiles and jokes, making connections with officers and other passengers as they traveled. Unlike their Stereotypical and Ideal counterparts, some Mindful-Empathetic travelers seemed to relax in security, have brief conversations, and not rush through line.

Mindful-Empathetic passengers explained feeling compassion for TSOs and the stressful job they have to do. "Tigger," an infrequent flier, said she wished people would not give the TSOs "such a hard time." As a retired firefighter, she described identifying with the task of needing to get large groups of people to comply with orders. Depicting her interactions with TSOs, she said, "I'm usually pretty friendly, because there's really no point in not being friendly, because they have to do what they have to do."

"What do you mean by that, 'They have to do what they have to do?'" I asked.

"Well, they have to check for dangers. I know I'm not one of them, so I don't expect to have a problem, but I want them to check everybody because somebody there might be a problem," Tigger said.

When I asked how officers interact with her, she repeated, "I'm usually pretty friendly, and they usually respond in the same way. Some of them are, [it's] not like they're unfriendly, but they're a little quieter. Going through security, I don't think of myself as a customer," Tigger explained. "It's like dealing with the police. I don't consider myself a customer. I consider having the service provided, not just for me, but for everybody."

Here Tigger linked to a view of public safety that helps to explain the less-friendly treatment she experiences sometimes, and also how her personal friendliness usually results in a positive interaction. And I have found other examples of noticeably friendly people, usually business or frequent travelers. Portlander, a more-than-weekly frequent flier, described his often-friendly demeanor in the context of security and empathy. "The point for security is to be safe overall. . . . They're not there to block your time, they're not there to invade your privacy. . . . They're just human beings, too, just doing their job, right?" More than any other type of passenger, Mindful-Empathetic passengers are able to see TSOs as individuals rather than as a construct of "The TSA."

Although many passengers evoked this argument—TSOs are just doing their job and the whole point is to be safe—the majority of passengers do *not* act friendly toward TSOs. Lucky, a TSO at one of the busiest airports in the country, described meeting only a handful of exceptionally nice and gracious passengers in his two years of work as a TSO. However, friendly faces are welcomed by TSOs—at least by Jonathan, who described his favorite types of passengers as those who "respond to my greeting and allow us to interact as people."

Intriguingly, though, those who do respond cheerfully may be "marked" by other officers. I often portray an empathetic persona when I travel. Yet I learned from several TSO interviewees that as a result of my joking, well wishing, and small talk, I likely stand out in security compared to passengers who act reserved or demonstrate negative feelings. In fact, TSO Steve, a behavior detection officer, said that his entire job revolves around spotting "difference" in line and assessing those passengers who stand out from the rest.

Passengers deemed different enough can be detained or flagged for further screening. Even though Steve said he most often tries to assess people who might "snap," he emphasized that *any* deviation from the emotional norm in the line at any given time could be cause for further investigation. Given that security lines are typically not places brimming with positive emotions, the few passengers who do demonstrate empathy, kindness, and humor may draw extra suspicion.

But they can also have a lot more fun at the airport.

May 31, 2012.

"I'd like to opt out."

The twenty-something TSO shrugs, poking his bottom lip out in an exaggerated pout. "Was it something I said?" he asks, working his face into an admirable puppy dog expression as he leans through the metal detector rails.

I laugh. "Sorry," I reply, moving to the side without being asked.

The person behind me gets waved through the AIT machine. A woman nearby asks to go through the metal detector and the now not-pouting TSO says he needs everyone to go through the millimeter wave scanner. The metal detector is reserved for "overflow, employees, and kids."

Swiftly, he pivots back to me. "Do I smell?" he inquires.

"I'm sorry," I say, opting in to the joke. "I really wasn't going to say anything."

We're both laughing as he shouts, "Female assist, opt out! Female assist, opt out!"

Ahead, I notice TSO Roger. While I wait for my pat-down, he mouths to me and points down the conveyor belt, "Is this yours?" I nod yes, grateful that, as always, he is keeping an eye on my luggage while I wait for the advanced screening.

Soon a female TSO with dark hair and wide eyes appears. The now-pouting-again TSO complains to her, while nodding at me, "She doesn't want to be my friend anymore."

"It was never meant to last," I sigh.

Feigning despair, he clutches his hand to his chest, declaring, "I'm hurt!" before turning back to the stream of passengers behind me.

I walk away, chuckling.

Pro Travel Tip #15:

Yes, You Can Take Snaps in Security

TSOs might not like it and might even tell you no, but according to the TSA, photography and video recording are not prohibited in security checkpoints. As long as you don't interfere with security processes or reveal sensitive information—such as images from equipment monitors that are shielded from view—you're welcome to record your experiences.

15

Traveling with Identity Baggage

How Security Challenges Intersecting Identities

In early November 2010, Thomas Sawyer was traveling from Detroit to a wedding in Orlando.[1] A bladder cancer survivor, Sawyer wore extra-large clothes to accommodate his urostomy bag, which collects urine from an opening in his abdomen. The combination of the bag and baggy clothes triggered the security body scanner and necessitated a pat-down. The TSOs refused to acknowledge Sawyer's attempts to explain his medical condition. Despite his pleas for them to be careful, the TSOs broke the urostomy bag during screening, soaking Sawyer's clothes with urine. It wasn't until Sawyer had boarded his plane that he was able to get cleaned up. The TSOs involved never apologized. That same month, TSOs forced a flight attendant and breast cancer survivor in Charlotte, North Carolina, to remove her prosthetic breast and show it to officers during a pat-down.[2]

Five years later, Shadi Petosky, a transgender woman, missed her flight from Orlando to Minneapolis when TSOs detained her for forty minutes, apparently unsure of how to screen her.[3] After the body scanner showed an anomaly in the groin area, Petosky explained that she was trans and, per TSA rules, was traveling under the name and gender on her license.[4] However, TSOs argued about whether she could be rescanned or if she would need to be patted down. They ended up detaining her in a private space, patting her down twice, and searching her luggage. Despite being told not to use her phone, Petosky live-tweeted the ordeal using the hashtag #travelingwhiletrans, bringing to light a troubling issue that in subsequent years would spawn a record number of complaints and, ultimately, lawsuits from other trans people.[5]

Five years after Petosky's experience, in January 2020, a TSO in Minneapolis–St. Paul grabbed an indigenous woman's braids behind her shoulders during a pat-down. Laughing, the TSO said, "Giddyup!" and snapped the braids like reins on a horse. That passenger was lawyer and indigenous rights activist Tara Houska. When Houska confronted the TSO about her racist behavior, the white officer apparently claimed it was "just in fun" and complimented Houska's hair. In her Twitter account of the incident, Houska said, "My hair is part of my spirit. I am a Native woman. I am angry, humiliated. Your 'fun' hurt."[6]

A month later, TSOs at JFK International Airport in New York disassembled and destroyed the instrument of world-renowned Malian kora player Ballaké Sissoko. The kora is a twenty-one-stringed instrument, and its string, bridge, and entire sound system were torn apart in a security search. The TSA left Sissoko a note in Spanish, saying that his case "may have been searched for prohibited items." On Facebook, Sissoko lamented, "Would they have dared do such a thing to a white musician playing a classical instrument? What does this tell us about the attitude of the administration towards African musicians? This is an unprovoked and sad act of aggression, a reflection of the kind of cultural ignorance and racism that is tak[ing] over in so many parts of the world."[7]

What these news stories have in common, aside from people feeling humiliated and dehumanized, is identity. In early chapters, I described how passenger and TSO stereotypes and identities are constructed through discourses at the personal, organizational, and societal levels—for example, how TSA rules and societal requirements to comply with authority produce Stereotypical passengers like the unforgettable Ronny and Suzanne. And how discourses regarding duty, safety, and "not on my watch" combine with organizational-level rules to produce Ideal TSOs who prioritize policies over people's dignity.

But it's also important to understand how personal identities are woven into the discourses about airport security, making security experiences even more challenging for certain people. At the beginning of this book, I mentioned the concept of emotional taxes, the idea that all of the emotion management required of passengers in airport security can be likened to taxes or tolls. For instance, we pay the emotional toll of keeping our mouths shut when a TSO confiscates our property, or we dampen our nerves to seem "normal" in checkpoints, even if we're anxious.

For me, a now-middle-class white lady with tons of airport experience, that emotional tax is usually small. The tax might be linked to my gender, if you recall my terrible pat-down story, but it's not normally tied to other aspects of who I am such as my ethnicity, culture, country of origin, sexuality, health status, or abilities. And that's because those aspects of my identity—being white, a U.S. citizen, cisgender, feminine-presenting, heterosexual, healthy, and able—are deemed "normal" and even "ideal" in this context. Those accident-of-birth identity markers are easy for the TSA because they are among the least threatening, according to TSA organizational discourses. But for other travelers, personal identity can make security more difficult and the emotional tax much larger, because of the ways that they are discursively constructed, marked, and marginalized.

Consider passenger Nate, a lawyer, father, and community advocate. In our interview, Nate discussed the emotional tensions that emerge in security regarding his racial identity and appearance.

"The security line has always been a little bit stressful," Nate said. "I'm half-Mexican. I don't know if that means that I would be singled out, but it has felt that way. Since September 11th, I've gotten singled out for special, not excessive, screenings. They watch you through the metal detectors. They pull random—supposedly random—people out and pat [them] down. I've gotten patted down many, many times."

Nate suggested that the reason for his additional screening is his appearance—dark skin and beard. As a brown man, Nate is also extra-suspect, because media portrayals and stereotypes perpetuate the image of terrorists as almost exclusively brown and male.[8] While we could say Nate, as a male professional, has masculine privilege in this context, his ethnicity, skin color, and appearance are framed negatively, rendering him a possible suspect far more often than if he were Caucasian or even brown skinned and clean shaven.

Considering multiple, overlapping aspects of identity and how they are subjected to discrimination is a hallmark of intersectionality. Coined by Black feminist scholar Dr. Kimberlé Crenshaw in 1989, the term *intersectionality* explains how "interlocking systems of power affect those who are most marginalized in society."[9] In an interview for Columbia Law School celebrating the twentieth anniversary of Crenshaw's groundbreaking article, she describes intersectionality as "a lens through which you can see where power comes and collides, where it interlocks and intersects."[10] Intersectionality often considers how aspects of identity like gender, race, and class operate to produce privilege or discrimination.

Intersectional theorizing helps explain why security experiences, which are already difficult, can become excruciating for some people. Passengers whose interconnected identities shape their lived experiences of discrimination, stigma, and violence in the United States are more likely to endure compounding challenges during travel and security.

At their core, security procedures can be onerous for passengers because they are compulsory interactions where passengers have no authority and little power. Passengers maintain a keen awareness that TSOs hold all the cards and can wreak havoc on passenger travel plans whenever they feel like it. Very often, TSOs' displays of authority relate to their perceptions of passenger identities, perceptions that might derive from their personal biases or from structures outside of their control, such as TSA rules, technologies, and social discourses. In taking an intersectional approach, we can consider how these structures contribute to systematic oppression and discrimination against certain identities and lived experiences.

Consider appearance. TSOs frequently single people out based upon their looks—be it skin color, religious head coverings, medical equipment, clothing, or hair style. If you have big hair, for instance, it's going to get patted down. But how that pat-down affects you will depend on your intersecting identities. Hair pat-downs stem in part from policy. TSOs are directed to search anyone's hair if it "looks like it could contain a prohibited item or is styled in a way [that] an officer cannot visually clear it." And that goes for anyone blessed with bountiful hair.

Rachel, a white woman with exuberant red curls, emphasized that TSA hair checks feel "violating." Describing an instance where she wore a big bun through security, she said, "I fe[lt] someone come up behind me [after she went through the scanner], and the TSA agent had touched my bun a couple seconds before they actually said, 'Oh, I need to check your hair.' Instead of saying, 'Ma'am, I need to check your hair,' and then asking to touch your hair, they can just grab it. It wasn't as invasive as 'I need to check your breasts' or something like that. It wasn't that part of my body, but it still felt very intimate because someone had just come up and touched a part of my body. I did feel a little violated."

Now imagine if that bodily violation happened *every* time you flew *and* reinforced racist stereotypes.

Black women report being regularly singled out for hair searches. One cause might be that AIT itself is discriminatory. Government and advocacy reports show that machines are frequently triggered by certain hairstyles (i.e., thick hair, braids, dreadlocks) and have higher false alarm rates for turbans, wigs, and religious headwear like a hijab. In case it isn't obvious here, these false alarms disproportionately affect Black and brown people, especially women. The rate of passenger complaints about hair and headwear searches was significant enough that the TSA reached out to vendors in 2018 for ideas "to improve screening of headwear and hair in compliance with Title VI of the Civil Rights Act."[11]

During my interview with TSO Elizabeth, I asked her about race and ethnicity issues, citing the news story about Tara Houska, the indigenous woman whose braids were snapped.

"So, honestly, Black women can be pretty bad about us having to touch their hair," Elizabeth said. "I have had multiple [people] stop screening[s] because they didn't want me to touch their dreadlocks."

Elizabeth sounded very frustrated by this, viewing the situation as if it were about the hair itself.

"If I have braids in my hair, they're going to alarm," she said, pointedly. "I've tested that one before because at times we do have to go through the scanners. . . . I know if my hair is braided, which I typically braid it for work and then pull it up in a bun, it's alarming 100 percent. 'Cause it's dense. Dreadlocks are very, very dense. Very, very dense hairstyle. You can hide something in there, especially with how thick that hairstyle tends to be. I know that that was a big thing in LAX recently. They were getting called out as racist—TSA as a whole—because they were screening Black women's hair when in reality it's, 'I'm just trying to do my job.'"

And yet, doing the job clearly perpetuates stereotypes and suspicion about Black people in a country where wearing Black hair naturally or in culturally relevant styles is still regularly deemed "unprofessional." In fact, in 2019 California passed a law banning employers and schools from discriminating against natural hair. The CROWN (Create a Respectful and Open World for Natural Hair) Act has since been implemented in several other states, and Senators Cory Booker and Cedric Richmond introduced the act in Congress to pave way for federal-level protections.[12] Without federal protections, and despite promising to stop singling out Black women, the TSA continues to operate as if hair checks are simple security protocols and not symbolic and emotion-laden acts.

"Braids of all kinds are gonna alarm," Elizabeth emphasized, pivoting away from race and toward assessing risk. "I've seen them alarm on a thirteen-year-old girl. . . . I felt bad [but] it was just pat, pat, pat. 'Okay, go on your way.' That one's hard to work."

Elizabeth recalled a time when a passenger had to be escorted out of security three times before she agreed to having her hair screened. "She changed her hairstyle on each one. So that should have been enough for my supervisors to go, 'something's not right with you.' You're obviously hiding something at this point."

I didn't say it, but I speculated that the passenger rearranged her hair not to conceal anything, but merely to avoid the pat-down.

"There's always a level of suspicion on these people," Elizabeth warned.

I held my breath when she uttered "these people," worrying our interview was going to take a more decidedly racist turn. But, as ever, Elizabeth emphasized protocol.

"There's always a level of paranoia where you're like, 'As soon as you [passengers] start acting weird, as soon as you're lying to me, you are hiding something.' And it can be a gun. It could be a knife or it could be a bomb. How am I supposed to know which one it is?" Elizabeth asked. "Most of the times it's drugs."

Chuckling, Elizabeth continued, "Weaves are a big thing or extensions. I've had so many white women get mad at me 'cause I've patted them down and you can feel the clips and all the little pieces on the back of their skull."

Elizabeth described how she inquires, "Are you wearing hair extensions?" and the women reply, affronted, "Why would you ask me something like that?"

"Either this is hair extensions or an explosive. So which one is it?" she asks.

"It's just hair extensions."

"*Thank you*," Elizabeth said, with a hint of exasperation as she recounted the scenario.

While I appreciated Elizabeth's frankness, I also knew that her discursive context was telling her hair is just another place to hide contraband. But as the daughter of a hairdresser, I understand that hair is so much more. It's personal. It's intimate. It's political. In some religions, it's even sacred.

Taking an intersectional approach means looking at how the components of identity are inextricably linked and how they work together to inform peoples' experiences in the world. Rachel, a white woman with bountiful hair, mentioned the discomfort of having her hair touched against her will. For her, this invasion was uncomfortable, but ultimately based on one physical aspect of her identity. For women of color, hair searching touches on not only physical appearance, but also race and gender, *together*. The intersections of these identities heighten the complexity of the situation and the severity of the emotional consequences. For women of color, hair searching reflects upon deeply embedded historical systems of racism and sexism *as well as* the discourses of security, safety, and surveillance.

For other people, the intersections of identity include observable aspects like physical appearance, but also invisible components like sexuality or health status. Passenger Sammy, who discussed her challenges related to gender identity and advanced imaging, related how they intersect with her health status, making her experiences in security more difficult and unpredictable.

"Actually, one of the funniest experiences with that is I was flying back from Salt Lake City . . . and I had this heart monitor. There was so many wires cause it was like a really big one. And it was awful," Sammy remembered.

"And when I told them [the TSA officers], I was like, 'You know, I can't go through the machine.' They were like, 'Oh hey, no problem. Come around,'" she said, explaining how the TSO led her away for a pat-down. "And then I didn't even think about it because, to me, the gender of the person who's frisking me really doesn't matter. I don't see that as an issue for me. And this guy started frisking me . . . they start at the back, patting down."

Sammy explained how the officer then came to her front side. "And he places both of his hands on my chest and immediately went, 'Whoaaaaaa!' His arms went out to the side in a crucifix position," she said, describing how the officer jumped back to get away from her.

"And then he was like, 'Oh my god, I'm sawwwrrry!' and yelled, 'We need someone else!'" Sammy imitated the voices to get me into the scene as we both cackled. "He made this big scene," she said, laughter in her voice. "And I was laughing and he was like, 'Why didn't you say something?' And I was like, 'I didn't even think about it!'"

Sammy related how she had just cut her hair short, and with her androgynous style the TSO mistook her for a young man. I chuckled, imagining the scene—the TSO completely freaked out, Sammy amused.

"It doesn't matter, just finish it, you've already done it," Sammy recounted. "Whoever does it, it's a stranger feeling me up. So I just don't care who's doing it. There's probably no one who works there that has the same gender expression as me, which is fine. So just pick someone,"

Sammy continued, referencing the TSA policy that passengers can choose someone who matches their gender expression to pat them down.[13]

"So did he finish the pat-down or did he get someone else?" I asked, knowing that if they'd gotten to the front side, her pat-down was almost complete anyway.

"No, he was like, 'I can't! I can't! I'm not allowed to!'" Sammy said, conveying the man's obvious sense of panic. "So then I had to wait for a woman to come over who was busy doing something else."

During our conversation, Sammy repeatedly emphasized using humor to cope with the absurdity of her experiences, especially as they related to gender. For others, though, the confluence of security and sexuality generates unsettling emotions.

Passenger Ramona, a white woman in her late twenties, told me about a trip from Houston to Denver when she was stopped by a TSO working the X-ray scanner.

"The TSA officer said 'Is this your bag?'" Ramona recalled. "He said that he needed to look at it. And so I said sure."

Ramona explained how her backpack alarmed and she was left awkwardly holding her laptop, trying to figure out how to manage the rest of her belongings. As she struggled, the TSO said, "I'll wait for you. I don't mind waiting. Take as long as you want, because I like looking at you."

"*What?*" I shouted.

"Yeah. It gets worse," Ramona said. "So this guy's probably, like . . . midthirties, could be forty. African American . . . taller, pretty good-looking guy. And he said that, and I said, 'Umm, okay.' One of the things, I guess, to note about this is, I notice now that I live in Colorado, when I go back to the South where I am from, how forward men are in terms of their commentary about your body or how you look. And that that is much more socially accepted there."

Ramona added that many Southern people are socialized to view open, sexualizing commentary on women's bodies as a "normal compliment."

Mm-hmm, I thought, my California brain very skeptical.

"So, in this case, it's particularly uncomfortable because the TSA officer is in a position of authority . . . so I go with him. I get my stuff and then I'm holding my computer, and we go over to [the] stations where they check [for] chemicals or they look at stuff. I had gone to this church bazaar with my grandfather," Ramona said, explaining how she bought a Christmas candle with a decorative mirror. "The mirror must've looked strange on the [TSO's] screen. When he was actually looking at it and investigating it, I was just kind of standing there. And he was like, 'You know, you should keep smiling. You have got such a pretty smile,' and, 'I guess I'm going have to go and run this now and leave you by yourself.'"

"Wow," I commented.

"He goes to run it and comes back, and then I said, 'Okay, am I good to go?' And he said, 'Yeah, you can go, if you want.' And I said, 'Okay.' And he's like, 'Take me with you. I want to go with you.'"

"Wow," I repeated, at a loss for any other cogent comments.

"It was blatant sexual harassment that, in his mind, I'm sure was not at all problematic," Ramona said, acknowledging how culture, context, and gender influence interpretations of harassment, and how if confronted, the officer might have said he was simply being complimentary. "And as I'm packing up, he was just [staring] at me, and I was just like, 'Get me out of here!' basically."

"That is such an abuse of power," I remarked.

"And my flight was about to start boarding, because the security line was so long," Ramona continued, explaining how she didn't report it or complain. "The fact that I was flying really early in the morning . . . If it weren't so early and I hadn't left my grandfather's house at like 3:45 a.m., I probably would have said something to him. I'm generally pretty comfortable saying, 'That's really not appropriate.' And to me, that probably would have been the best way to handle it, but at that point, I was just like, 'I need to get to my gate.'"

I understand this pressure. I suspect that many conflicts are not reported to TSA management because of the time pressure of flying.

"It felt especially uncomfortable because of his position of power, and I have to follow him and go with him?" Ramona balked. "The other thing that I think made this TSA encounter really creepy was he had my boarding pass, and he kept saying my name. And just being like, 'Hey, Ramona, blah blah blah.' It was creepy the way he was saying my name over and over. And like, 'It's okay, take your time, Ramona, I like looking at you.'"

"Oh no, no, no!" I exclaimed.

"It gives me chills when I think about it now. It was just very creepy," Ramona admitted.

Like other people represented in this book who have compared and contrasted the security scene with other contexts of life, Ramona keyed in on a critical difference. In contexts where power is more equal, like at a bar or in the grocery store, Ramona could have walked away from the uncomfortable interaction or felt empowered to tell the guy to knock it off. Instead, she recognized the officer's positional authority as well as his ability to punish her by detaining her if she rejected him. Rather than reacting negatively, Ramona concealed her discomfort and complied with his orders. What sets this example apart from many other compliance-oriented stories in this book is the connection to sexuality and gender as well as power and culture.

Unfortunately, as with allegations of racism, the TSA is routinely accused of gender and sexual discrimination. In fact, as of the writing of this book, the TSA is fielding numerous lawsuits about profiling and discrimination, including one from a woman in North Carolina, alleging civil battery by the United States via an unreasonable search. The lawsuit alleges that a TSO groped the passenger's vulva *underneath* her clothes for self-gratification and to "humiliate, dominate, and control" her. It charges that when the officer's hands went inside the passenger's shorts and contacted the woman's genitals, she flinched and complained. Purportedly, the officer said, "If you resist, I will do this again."[14]

While examples this grievous do not seem common, the everyday discrimination described by Sammy and Ramona, as well as the numerous other examples in the news such as Shadi Petosky and Tara Houskas, illustrates why advocacy groups have launched lawsuits and petitions aimed to reform TSA screening policies.

Likewise, as a result of the TSA's frequent discrimination against and excessive screening of trans people, Representative Kathleen Rice introduced HR 6659, the Screening with Dignity Act of 2018, which promised to "appropriately and respectfully screen self-identified transgender passengers."[15] The bill included a provision for TSO training, as well as the right of passengers to request same-gender pat-downs, have private screenings with a chosen witness, and "only be required to lift or remove clothing exposing sensitive areas of the body or to remove prostheses when no less intrusive screening method is available and the passenger is provided with visual privacy via a drape or other means in a private screening area." Importantly, the bill also prohibits "profiling or other discrimination on the basis of race, color, national origin, sex, religion, age, disability, genetic information, sexual orientation, parental status, or gender identity." Unfortunately, the bill was not enacted, and until reform happens, passengers must continue to navigate complex and uncomfortable screenings.

Security is also often difficult for those who manage health conditions and/or disabilities, especially the many that are invisible to TSOs. Sammy shared how in addition to difficulties related to her gender presentation, she also deals with challenges related to her autoimmune disorder, dysautonomia.

"My body doesn't regulate temperature, so if I don't want to pass out and then throw up on the airplane, I have to be able to cool myself down quickly," she said. She travels with a collection of health aids—instant cold packs that can be activated when needed, juice, supplements, walking sticks.

"A lot of this stuff is equipment that isn't even wildly medical looking, which I think is what sometimes throws them off," Sammy added, saying she regularly has to negotiate with TSOs who don't always understand that she's traveling with these items for her health and not as a convenience. "Then just other things, like they want your pills to be in their original containers, and like, I don't do that. I put them in a pill sorter because if I were to bring all of the original containers, I'd need another bag," she quipped.

Although she mentioned that "[most] every rule at TSA becomes void if it's medical equipment," she said that the interpersonal interactions with TSOs make traveling with medical conditions difficult. When she advocates for herself, "TSA makes it clear that I'm being irritating."

She said, "Almost every time, I have to tell people about the rules. Like, 'You work here, yes, but no, you can't take that [medication or device] away.' And they argue with me, and I'm like, 'Okay, well, bring your manager over.' And I hate to be, you know, that 'Let me talk to your manager' person," she said, mimicking an entitled whine, "But at the end of the day, I just have to, which sucks."

Sammy revealed how she's argued about all of her medical equipment, including the adjustable hiking stick she uses for mobility when she's feeling dizzy coming out of the airplane. "They're like, 'If you have a mobility [issue], you have to use it all the time. Otherwise you don't need it.' And I'm like, 'Well, that's not true, although that's something a lot of people believe,'" she said, explaining how TSA officers tell her the walking stick might be a weapon, not a mobility aid. But it would be a mobility aid and not a weapon if she had to use it full-time? It's no wonder people find the TSA confusing.

"So there's a lot of arguing, which makes me feel uncomfortable because these people are just trying to do their jobs," Sammy remarked. "They probably hate this as much as I do, but I have to kind of be a bit of an asshole so I can get through." And by asshole, Sammy means standing up for her rights as a person with legitimate medical conditions.

"Then there was one who just told me that I flat out couldn't have my medical equipment, which included the ice packs. [And] this device that I had to measure heart conduction," she recalled. "It was more intense than a heart rate monitor. But because it wasn't attached to my body, they were like, 'That's ridiculous. That's not what it is.'"

Apparently the TSOs wanted to confiscate the monitor. "It was really expensive and I was pretty pissed. So that was definitely a conflict just in terms of . . ." Sammy paused briefly. "You know, my life already sucks enough with all of this stuff, so make it worse? Also, what could I possibly do with this device that would become a security challenge? I guess I could throw it at someone. I could do that with a laptop, too."

We laughed.

"And so I was getting very testy at that point," Sammy recalled. "I was also very tired. When I travel, I usually feel really sick because all of my symptoms get worse. So I did definitely . . . like I was a little bit more . . ." Sammy trailed off, searching for the words.

"Well, I guess I was *less kind* than I could have been at that point. [They] also tend to get really frustrated when I ask for someone else. Like, 'Can I talk to another agent or can I talk to your manager?' And then they're like, '*Oh my gawd!*' And they make it a thing. So that is always irritating because then I feel like that meme of, like, the mom with the haircut."

"Karen," I chimed in, both of us referencing a meme stereotyping middle-aged white women who complain to management and/or call the authorities on people of color doing normal things in public.[16]

"Conflict-wise, that has happened more than once. But now I just have this, like, conviction that I'm right every time, because legally, I know that I am. So I just am, like, 'I will argue with you until you get sick of me and then you will let me go.' And a lot of that, I mean, comes with my other identities. I'm a nonthreatening person in the eyes of TSA. I'm a small person. I am female. I'm, you know, white as hell. Generally speaking, if I get testy with TSA, they're not gonna freak out."

"Right," I chimed in. "So how do you think it would be different if you were larger and male and a person of color?"

"In general, because most perpetrators of violence, especially in the U.S., are men, there would be a lot more fear surrounding that for sure. But also I think there's probably more respect."

"Interesting," I replied, prompting her to say more.

"Like, they might not argue as much with someone who's male because I think there's this idea that if you are female . . . your body . . . you're already irrational and your experience of your body isn't as true."

She continued, describing the prevailing attitude. "'You're overreacting. You don't need all this equipment,'" she said, suggesting TSOs buy-in to stereotypes of women as hysterical, unstable, and dramatic. "But in terms of being a person of color, like to be honest, I don't know what I would do because I'd probably be screwed," Sammy admitted.

"If you are already framed as a threat and then you have all of this extra stuff, you know, I could see me having to leave way more extra time to go through security and having to have, like, documentation of citizenship or things like that."

"Yeah," I remarked.

"I often travel with my classmates and a ton of them are from the Middle East. They're all women and they're all traditionally feminine presenting women," Sammy explained. "And they get a ton of shit in TSA and they *don't* have any of this weird stuff in their bags."

"Right."

"Every time we go through TSA, they're like, 'Who's going to take longer? The brown ones or the cripple?' And I'm like, 'Oh my god! Jesus. Don't say that out loud!'"

We both laughed for a minute. The candor was strangely refreshing but also heavy. We abruptly paused as I sighed, not knowing how to transition.

"'At least I'm white' is what is literally in my head half the time I'm in TSA," Sammy admitted, filling in the silence.

"Yeah," I commented, and I took a breath, understanding her sentiment but also hating it.

Sammy reflected on her whiteness as one piece of privilege that supports her medical and safety needs, something she understood would be further compromised if she was a woman of color.

"Have you thought of getting a letter from your doctor?" I asked.

"So, I have, um, a medical ID on my wrist," she said.

"Oh, and they still don't believe you?" I suppose anyone can buy one on the internet, but still. Does everything have to be so hard?

"So it has helped, but then because they don't know what it [her medical condition] is . . ." Sammy said, trailing off. I'd never heard of it either, not even with my Google MD.

"Maybe I need to lie and just pick a different medical condition," she joked. "Just because they don't know what it is, they don't seem to care. Whereas I think when someone goes 'I'm diabetic,' everyone is like, 'Oh, I guess you probably need these needles.' Whereas when I'm like, 'I have dysautonomia or POTS or like such-and-such an autoimmune thing, they look at me and they're like, 'Yeah, right.' The other thing is having letters from your doctor often doesn't . . . I mean, they might believe you and not take away your stuff, but you're still getting frisked for sure," Sammy added. "Even if they say, 'Okay, this is real,' because so much of my medical equipment is not medication or something that is clearly a medical device . . . it's just harder."

"God, that is so frustrating," I commented, recognizing how often I, as an able-bodied person who routinely bitches about security, takes so much for granted. And from what other passengers have told me, it's frustrating even with equipment that is clearly medical. Passenger Tigger described flying with a TENS unit, an electrical nerve stimulator used to treat pain.

"It was the first time I traveled since 9/11. I was trying to tell the security lady about my device," she explained. "She starts getting pissed at me because she had to do something. She had to go get the wand instead of having me walk through the gate. So, that was not pleasant."

"How did it make you feel?" I asked.

"Well, it didn't make me feel too secure, because she didn't want to do her job."

"She didn't want to scan you?" I asked.

"She was bothered that she actually had to do something rather than just have me walk through the metal detector," Tigger said, disgusted.

Echoing Sammy's comments, Tigger described how frustrating it was to travel with her necessary medical equipment. Equipment requiring extra attention moves passengers from "easy and nonthreatening" into another category of scrutiny, which spells more emotional work for passengers.

And a lot of it seems to involve uncertainty, according to passengers with medical conditions and disabilities. In some airports, security might be no big deal. In others, it might be a long, drawn-out process of having to reveal intimate personal details. And all of that is on top of managing the sometimes exhausting difficulties of long lines and treks to far-off gates.

It can be especially hard when the person with the medical issues can't readily communicate and the caregiver has to negotiate security on their behalf. Passenger Kristine discussed such a travel experience with her mom.

"She has Alzheimer's and doesn't always get cues. So I told TSA [about the Alzheimer's]," Kristine stressed. "Because if she gets pulled to the side and they start asking her questions, their training's going to see something's really wrong. She can't answer coherently."

"What did they say?" I asked.

"We were at the regional airport in Nashville. It's a smaller airport. It tends to be more friendly there, the TSA," Kristine explained. "This is exactly what I said: 'She has Alzheimer's, so if you need to ask her questions, I need to stay close to her.'"

"They called her through [the advanced imaging] and then they wanted me to wait a long time [to go through]," Kristine said. "I said to the guy, 'You know what? She has Alzheimer's, so I need to stay close to her.' He goes, 'Oh, okay.' And I said, 'Mom, just wait right there.' Normally, they don't want you talking to people on the other side of security. They were okay with it this time," Kristine explained, sounding relieved. "I've just sort of made it known now that she has Alzheimer's."

Unfortunately, for travelers like Kristine and her mom, as well as Tigger and Sammy, navigating security with medical conditions requires disclosing private health information to absolute strangers. In a public place that's under heavy surveillance. In ways that can be difficult or demeaning. With little control over the outcome without intense persistence.

Reading these accounts might feel discouraging, but the good news is that the TSA has a history of *eventually* responding to passenger concerns. The problem is, most people don't complain or share their stories, or make recommendations to the TSA about how to improve. But my interviewees, as you may have noted throughout this book, were not short on suggestions. When I asked Ramona what she would change about security, she didn't hesitate.

"For sure, diversity training," she said. "I think that one way that it can impress me, with the amount of work that officers must do, is to be more progressive as an organization. [To] think about difference differently and not just be a product of the same system."

By "difference," Ramona means the identity categories discussed in this chapter, especially the ones that are regularly discriminated against.

"What would it be like to have folks in there thinking a little bit differently about issues like gender—but also age and disability, and all these different identities that people have—and being receptive to [them]?" Ramona asked, citing examples such as race, sexuality, and nationality. "[The TSA] could be more informed to avoid stereotypes or perpetuating these systems of inequality that are already an issue in the U.S. It would be really cool if the TSA was progressive, and moved to be like, 'Yeah, we're this governmental agency. Yeah, we have this mission.' What did you say? It was like the freedom to . . . ?" Ramona asked.

"Freedom of movement," I replied.

"Yeah! What if they re-scripted what this freedom of movement meant? If their idea of being progressive was that 'you can travel no matter who you are, and we support who you are as an individual' or something like that. I know it's hard in such a big system to do that, but there are little micro-moves that they can do to make inclusivity happen," Ramona said, citing examples of accommodations for children and seniors. "I think they're receptive to the fact that once this rule has been created for a security measure, it doesn't mean it's stuck [forever]. So, continuing to be reflexive about how to make travel more comfortable and safe for all people is something I'd like to see them continue to push themselves on."

And this writer completely agrees.

Pro Travel Tip #16:

Avoid Co-creating Hidden Taint

As you read this chapter, you might have wondered, "But what about intersectionality and TSO identities?" Indeed, identity challenges apply to employees as well. Facets of identity can sometimes contribute to passengers paying high emotional taxes in security. It works the same way for TSOs. Their emotional labor is made more challenging when parts of their identity are implicated in their interactions.

For instance, consider Sammy's story of accidentally getting a pat-down from a male TSO and his extreme reaction. We could read that as the TSO being generally embarrassed for accidentally touching a woman's breasts. But in the context of pat-downs, as other TSOs have said, eventually TSOs become unfazed by bodies. Like Alexa said, "We've all got boobs and butts and whatever."

But consider the conservative context of Salt Lake City, where fully half of the residents are affiliated with the Church of Jesus Christ of Latter-day Saints. It could be that the officer's gender and religion—potentially significant aspects of his personal identity—were challenged in the interaction. His strong reaction and mortification seem to suggest that there was more at play than simply making an embarrassing work mistake.

However, Sammy reacted graciously amused. She could have flipped out and yelled at the officer, calling him names and insinuating that he was a sexual predator, as TSOs have all described experiencing throughout their careers. Had she done so, Sammy would have helped create what organizational communication research calls "hidden taint."[17]

Remember the discussion of dirty work in chapter 2? The TSO's job—having to touch strangers' bodies in this context—is already physically and perhaps morally tainted. Mix in a negative reaction from Sammy and the stigma would be compounded, adding unexpected layers of emotional taint too. The interaction would become even more difficult because Sammy would now have more power to punish the officer emotionally.

When passengers co-create hidden taint—for instance, by sexualizing pat-downs or stigmatizing aspects of officers' identities in complaints—they reclaim some power in the interaction. But they also make work extremely challenging for officers and travel more emotionally taxing for themselves.

Conclusion

What an Undercover Look at Airport Security Reveals about Communication, Emotion, and Identity

February 1, 2013: The last pat-down.

"Oh, she always opts out," a TSO with short spiky highlights says to a white-shirted officer working the walk-through metal detector. "Kate" is a manager and she smiles at me with recognition when I ask to opt out.

I quickly realize that the TSO's white shirt indicates trainee status. The newbie, "Nellie," looks confused as she directs me to stand aside and wait. Behind me the divestiture officer stops his instructions to passengers and asks Nellie, "Was she given her options?"

I guess this is a team effort?

Laughing, Kate answers for her. Nodding toward me, she says, "She always gets a pat-down."

A few seconds pass. Kate opens the gate to allow me through, bringing Nellie with her. Nellie asks which side my belongings are on and I gesture to the right. She points to a place at the end of the conveyor belt, commanding me to "stand right there." She reinforces her message for me to stay by extending a flat palm, putting distance between us, as if I am a dog.

Kate comes over and tells me that Nellie is in training—as if to explain the gestures—and that I am a "perfect person to learn from." I laugh, assuming she means because I am a nice passenger with no history of troublesome emotional outbursts.

"In that case, should I give her a hard time?" I joke.

Kate chuckles and confesses, "She'll get that soon enough."

"You do this more than we do," she adds, suggesting I could probably train new people myself. She's not wrong.

The three of us meander to a set of chairs and mats just past the X-ray lines. Kate stands nearby as Nellie starts the process. She stands close, and even barefoot, I must gaze down to meet her eyes. Her speech comes in short gasps—she's so nervous, she can't quite catch her breath. The litany of advisements seems longer than usual, and she explains the motions she is going to use in full detail. There is apparently way more to this spiel than I've ever heard before.

The pat-down begins as if in slow motion. I stand in the proper position—feet wide, arms outstretched—trying to move things along, but to no avail. She carefully inspects both of my empty, upward-turned palms before starting the pat-down proceedings.

Gloved hands pause on my skull, palming my hair but halting at the collar. Nellie's hands freeze and her head snaps toward Kate, who reminds her that she can ask me to move my hair aside. As I lift my long brown locks, she methodically sweeps my collar and then begins the tedious process of scraping her fingers down my back, inch by careful inch until she gets to my waist.

Nellie asks me to lift up my shirt. "But only enough so that I can see the top of the waistband," she says. She's the only TSO to ever say this to me.

She pauses again and then Kate jumps in to indicate that when she encounters pants like mine, without belt loops, she should pinch together the fabric in the back so it bunches away from the body. That way, she can clear the waistband without touching the skin. Apparently that is a rule! How, after more than a hundred pat-downs and lots of swipes of my bare skin, am I just learning this?

Kate says "seam to seam," and I guess that's a mantra from training. After completing the waistband work, Nellie bends to "clear" my lower half. With the same measured, firm pressure, she sweeps down my hamstrings, squeezing calves and ankles before tracing up fleshy inner thighs until her gloved fingers brush my groin. The contact feels like a zap to the system. Being touched on the arms, back, and head seems more clinical, ordinary, but contact to the inner thighs and groin always feels reprehensible.

When Nellie transitions to face me, she stutters, stops, and then stumbles as she tries to explain the breast check. I somehow refrain from finishing her sentences and stifle a smile, realizing that I really *could* give the advisements if I wanted to.

Eventually, clumsy fingertips press down on the top of my breasts and around my collar bone. She swipes through cleavage, squashing the underwire into my ribcage. She repeats on the other side and I feel fabric biting my skin. I recall Carrie mentioning that TSOs can get in trouble if they don't press down firmly enough during "secret shopper" tests, where unfamiliar TSA trainers come through checkpoints to test security procedures. This newbie will never be in trouble on that score.

Nellie performs "seam to seam" work on my front side before sweeping down to clear my legs, again gripping my ankles. As she stands, her radio goes flying. Immediately, she lunges to retrieve it, but Kate orders her to leave it until she finishes up.

When Nellie goes to test her gloves, she again gestures for me to wait. After a moment, she says, "You're free to go and have a nice day," but Kate scolds her—she can't say that until the buzzer goes off.

When the signal finally sounds, indicating that I have not touched any explosives, Nellie repeats herself, with the exact same phrasing and intonation. I look at the clock and realize this pat-down took more than twelve excruciating minutes. Her very first pat-down and, coincidentally, my last. For the purposes of data gathering, anyway.

I met Nellie during the last research flight of my dissertation project, after three and a half long years of flying regularly and well over 101 pat-downs. (That's when I stopped counting.) Since then, I've spent seven more years analyzing and writing about the TSA, especially how we express emotion and identity in a heavy discursive context.

My goal in this chapter is to bring all of the stories and ideas full circle and to address what an undercover exploration of the TSA reveals, broadly speaking, about communication, identity, and emotion. As I promised in the introduction, this exploration requires us to think about the discourses of history, power, and politics, as well as identity and emotion.

Although airport security has been in existence since the early 1970s, it wasn't until the aftermath of the September 11, 2001, terrorist attacks that "airport security" became a dirty phrase in the popular imagination. In my scholarly work, I suggest that the events of 9/11 and the resulting creation of the TSA are examples of cultural-level meaning making.[1] Put simply, the United States made sense of a major terror tragedy, in part, by creating the TSA.

By design, the events of 9/11 shook our collective sense of self for a time, shattering what it meant to be a citizen in "the land of the free and the home of the brave." I invoke this patriotic phrase as a cliché purposefully, because the events that killed thousands of people and decimated an entire branch of the travel industry also prompted us to prioritize social discourses regarding safety and security over discourses about freedom and courage.

At the time of the TSA's creation, the visceral impacts of terrorism were fresh for everyone. When President George W. Bush launched the war on terror, his rhetorical move introduced the country to terror as a discourse and as a problem to be solved. U.S. citizens were asked to do their patriotic duty to prevent another attack, and that included supporting a contested war, accepting freedom-eroding laws like the Patriot Act, and tolerating a dramatic increase in airport security measures. It also positioned airport security work as emblematic of patriotism and the enactment of duty and honor.

However, the memory of 9/11 has faded for passengers who have not remained steeped in the discourses of terrorism and patriotism. Although the charge of terror prevention still reinforces the mission of the TSA, for the last twenty years it hasn't provided the fearful motivations for most passengers that it once did. Airport security is now taken for granted as a part of travel. In fact, many millennials probably don't even remember the time before the TSA, when we could fly without removing our shoes or submitting to a full body search. Gen Z definitely doesn't.

What once was achieved by stoking passengers' fear of terrorist attacks is now accomplished through conditioning and apathy (e.g., "I can't change it, so why bother?"). Fear appeals initially resulted in eager compliance, but over time compliance without meaningful complaint turned some people into sheeple—unthinking, docile, go-with-the-herd rule followers. Or at least that's one theory. Even freedom lovers who once protested that screenings undermine constitutional rights to privacy and lawful searching have largely let their struggles go in order to travel.[2]

Of course, it may also be that the worry has shifted—from fear of terrorists to fear of the officers supposedly responsible for protecting passengers from terrorists. Many of the passengers I interviewed described being afraid to talk to TSOs, hesitant to question procedures that induce discomfort, and conflicted about certain aspects of airport security protocol.

Passengers primarily focus on themselves and their individual travel experiences. In contrast, most TSOs keep a broader perspective, thinking of the flying public as a whole. This is not terribly surprising given that TSOs and passengers have different roles. However, the *framing* of roles can affect how we express emotion and identity.

TSOs receive messaging from their initial training, monthly education, daily briefings, annual evaluations, and frequent surprise inspections. A constant refrain is that the TSA is responsible for "taking care of the flying public"—an abstract ideal that connects the mission of TSOs to lofty and noble goals that extend beyond the material realities of the job itself. At the same time, TSOs are trained to see individual fliers as potential threats and to gaze on them with suspicion until they are proven innocent through screenings.

Organizational policies actively constrain the ways that passengers and TSOs relate. Security lines physically orient passengers. Scripts and strict protocols structure communication. Blue gloves, stanchions, partitions, pseudo–law enforcement uniforms, and a commanding emotional presence create barriers between TSOs and passengers.

With a few exceptions, passengers react to these cues by acting compliant and ceding to TSO authority in the security checkpoint. Compliance and anxiety are not necessarily surprising, considering that passengers know they are being viewed with organizationally mandated suspicion. In fact, passengers are cast in a dubious role in the security process: They are relied on to make the process function smoothly by complying, yet they are fundamentally not trusted until they have cleared multiple layers of security. (And even then, TSOs still cast aspersions on passengers by performing random security screenings outside of the checkpoint.)

Passenger roles are further complicated by the expectation that they participate in ensuring airport security. While they are treated as untrustworthy, passengers are also asked to facilitate security by viewing *others* with suspicion and reporting suspicious activity through the Department of Homeland Security's "If You See Something, Say Something" campaign. The expectation extends to onboard flight safety as well. Even as early as Flight 93, the third hijacked airplane in the 9/11 attacks, passengers succeeded in subduing would-be bombers.[3] Since then, passengers have subdued would-be attackers, including erratic passengers, flight attendants, and even a pilot.[4] These actions helped to set the assumption that passengers will actively participate in ensuring flight safety and security.

Thus, passengers must make sense of contradictory pressures—submission as the target of suspicion, on one hand, and participation in active scrutiny of peers, on the other—from officers who engender more fear than cooperation. However, the discursive, relational, and physical environment of the checkpoint makes it easy to comply. And conformity keeps passengers focused on their individual role in security rather than on the big picture.

This structure positions passengers as "conformist selves," which people like critical management scholar Professor David Collinson suggest can have detrimental consequences because it encourages people to unwittingly obey authority.[5] Whereas extreme examples of such consequences include the Holocaust and the Milgram experiments, in airport security we see the implications in passengers' acceptance of increasingly invasive protocols and the erosion of civil liberties.

It may seem easy to dismiss—as some passengers and TSOs do—current protocols as simply an outcome of and response to terrorism. But the consequences can extend beyond the airport. If passengers are willing to put up with indignity and, some would argue, lawful-only-by-a-technicality search and seizure in the airport, why not in other areas of transportation and interactions with actual law enforcement as well?

In airport security, compliance means not only opening bags and proceeding through scanners but also managing emotions and identity in particular ways. This book shows how identities are constructed, enacted, and occasionally contested by passengers and TSOs. Likewise, it emphasizes how personal, organizational, and societal discourses normalize and emphasize some identities (the Stereotypical and the Ideal) while obscuring others (the Mindful).

Many interviewees described mostly subtle but occasionally overt conflicts between who they felt like (what type of passenger or TSO) and who others *thought* they were or treated them like. This tension was most apparent for TSOs, who consistently reflected on the differences between their identities as individuals and their identities in their roles as TSOs and members of the TSA. They also compared how their self-concepts conflicted with media portrayals and public opinion. Security professional Greg lamented, "The media is not very kind. . . . There's been a lot of negative press about the Transportation Security Administration. There's even a nickname. I think *USA Today* [said,] 'TSA stands for Thousands Standing Around.'" Not exactly an identity that matches how any of the TSOs I met described their work.

In framing roles, whether as traveler, customer, hassle, herded cow, or suspect, passengers also compared how they appear and are treated in security with how they feel and act outside of the airport. Recall how Rachel was upset at the thought that she had conformed to TSA norms. These identity conflicts, however ephemeral for passengers or embedded for officers, can spur painful cognitive dissonance, which can influence interactions at the checkpoint. I suggest taking inspiration from communication scholars Professor Sarah Tracy and Professor Angela Trethewey, who use the metaphor of a crystal when they write about identity. A "crystallized self" is multifaceted and changeable. Thinking in a crystallized fashion considers not whether certain identities, like how we act in security, are "fake" and others, like how we are at home, are more "real," but whether our identities might be multifaceted, performative, and preferential.

For instance, I consider myself a Mindful traveler of the Empathetic variety, but I am also someone who remains skeptical about authority and critical of infringements on civil liberties. I also think empathy and compassion are important, especially for bureaucratic workers who are steeped in tedious and emotionally arduous work environments. My preferred way of being in the world is to act friendly and helpful, but also to stand up for myself when needed. Of course, I also lean toward the pragmatic, so in more challenging circumstances like airport security, I will regularly default to the easy, neutral, and unemotional Ideal passenger version of myself, if it means getting through a difficult interaction faster. It's not my preference, but it's a type of identity I can embody for a time. It's not more or less "real" than any other version of me.

Cultivating a preferred self, even in scenarios like security where emotions run high, experiences are unpleasant, and discourses impinge on available meanings for identity construction, can help us navigate identity conflicts. Identity performances are flexible. Airport structures and some discourses tell us to quietly conform and submit, but we have other options. Like the TSOs and passengers who appeared as several types of characters in this book (myself included), we aren't just one type of person.

To evoke the spirit of the great philosopher Aristotle, "We are what we repeatedly do."[6] If we want to be mindful and empathetic in security, we can practice that. Identity performances don't have to be essentialized or dichotomous—"real" or "fake"—because they are malleable and driven by context. We can *play* certain characters without having to *be* certain characters.

I suggest that, whatever type of identity we try to embody, we infuse the security process with more humanity and compassion.

The enterprise of airport security—its rigid protocol, expensive technology, and regimented practices—makes it easy to forget that beneath the uniforms and behind the boarding passes are human beings. TSOs complain about feeling like "just a number" to their management and as "robots" to passengers, whereas passengers decry feeling like "cattle" or "widgets" being "processed." Discourses that constrain the demonstration of emotion also objectify passengers and TSOs, and make it easier for people to treat others with disdain and incivility.

Airport security is an emotional context to work in and travel through. The TSA clearly trains its employees to perform emotional labor in specific ways—by staying "calm, cool, and collected" while also using a "commanding" presence to control passenger behavior. Passengers also perform emotional management, controlling how they express their feelings and keep them in line with presumed emotional norms for the context. Although helpful for efficiency in security lines, these emotional management processes may have unintended consequences for personal well-being and TSO-passenger relations.

TSOs and passengers perform emotion work differently, depending on the identity they are portraying (Stereotypical, Ideal, or Mindful). For TSOs who have worked in security for long periods of time, emotional suppression or masking—displaying one emotion while feeling another—can generate stress and promote tension, emotional exhaustion, and burnout.[7] Even though passengers in airport security only have to actively manage their emotions for a short time, this emotion work is critical too. The way passengers manage their feelings—swallowing them or spewing them— can directly affect the TSOs they interact with as well as the people around them. Interactions that are negative can trigger negative emotion cycles that follow them out of security and onto their planes.[8]

As illustrated, passengers have much more license to express emotions in security than they might realize. But passengers of all experience levels described feeling hesitant and uncomfortable about expressing emotions, especially negative feelings, because they wanted to avoid conflict with and potential consequences from TSOs. Given that unusual emotional displays are grounds for extra screening from behavior detection officers and are often featured in stories about security in the popular press, passengers' fears are not unfounded.

Nevertheless, a number of TSO interviewees discussed wishing passengers would relax and recognize that they will not "get in trouble" for communicating their feelings. In particular, TSOs Jeff, Ty, Rick, Roger, and Carrie encouraged passengers to feel comfortable and ask questions. According to these TSOs, passenger stress could be alleviated if they asked questions, admitted being nervous, and did not trying to overmanage their feelings by "acting right" (like our dear friends Ronny and Suzanne). In fact, TSOs *expect* passengers to be worked up simply by virtue of the stress that travel brings in terms of time constraints, fear of flying, and so on.

Of course, travel stress doesn't give anyone license to be a jerk. And in fact, being kind can bring significant *positive* consequences to organizational settings. Cultivating positive emotions such as empathy, compassion, humor, and warmth can help alleviate the consequences of emotional management for passengers and TSOs alike. Affirmative emotions are associated with creativity, openness, flexibility, increased trust, and strengthened interpersonal relationships, as well as positive physical and mental health outcomes.[9]

And what's more, positive emotions help people build other resources such as mindfulness, intellectual depth and complexity, resilience, and optimism. Positive emotion cycles "broaden and build," which translates to important outcomes in organizational environments such as good relationships, enhanced productivity, and increased pro-social actions like being helpful and supportive.[10]

Now, it might be radical to promote fostering positive emotions in airport security, a context built upon fear, authority, and intimidation. However, security interactions that included friendliness, humor, and helpfulness resulted in less need for emotional management and less conflict for both the officers and the passengers I interviewed, *without* compromising security procedures. The TSA needs passengers to comply with security in order to keep the system functioning well, and an open, more affirmative environment can help passengers move from unthinking compliance to cooperation. Moreover, engaging passengers may be easier when security interactions feel safe and secure instead of irritating and threatening. And TSOs would experience less abuse, stress, and burnout if passengers felt more comfortable.

By juxtaposing the experiences of passengers and TSOs, this exploration of airport security also sheds light on contradictions in the ways that TSO and passenger roles are enacted. TSOs are often cast as interminably powerful by passengers who act with deference and comply with "the rules." But TSOs who appear to wield authority actually possess very limited discretion.

Whereas TSOs enforce policies while wearing uniforms similar to police officers, their actual influence is limited to detaining passengers and calling upon law enforcement. The fact that TSOs maintain a façade of authority that engenders deference sparked the ire of many people I interviewed. In fact, Nasty, a U.S. Navy veteran and airline pilot, said he wished TSOs would "stay in their lane" and leave managing illegal activity to law enforcement. Intriguingly, many TSOs I met spoke candidly about their limited authority, seeming surprised that passengers blame them for the rules they have to enforce.

From an organizational perspective, "the rules" and "need to know" policies set passengers and TSOs up for conflicts. Passengers described tensions about rules that seemed illogical and are arbitrarily enforced by TSOs who couldn't or wouldn't explain. Meanwhile, TSOs insisted that rules are "there for a reason," but they are not at liberty to discuss rules with passengers due to security protocol. In many cases, detailed rationale for security is hidden even from TSOs.

In theory, a "need to know" attitude toward TSA policies is meant to deter potential terrorists with "constantly changing" security procedures. In fact, past TSA administrator John Pistole responded to criticisms about TSA policies by invoking obscurity as a deliberate strategy to remain secure.[11] However, in practice, unsubstantiated policies provoke confusion and consternation for passengers. Without a compelling rationale besides "it's for your safety," rules appear to be enforced solely on the basis of authority and compliance.

In some cases, "the rules" seem like an overwhelming force, an extension of the institution of security that results in passenger apathy. As Portlander grumbled, "I know I can't change it, so why bother?" However, discourses about the rules overshadow places where passengers can assert agency. Although some passengers confessed feeling constrained by and unempowered to change airport security protocols that make them uncomfortable, TSA policy changes over time suggest that passenger voices do matter.

Even in complex bureaucratic systems like the TSA, policies and practices evolve. In airport security, adjustments arguably come most often in response to security threats, but also after news coverage, customer demand, and legal action. Modified screenings for children emerged after several high-profile media exposés on pat-downs involving minors. Furthermore, as a direct result of congressional mandates instigated by voters and advocacy groups, the TSA addressed some privacy concerns related to advanced imaging. While these examples do not mean that policy directly follows customer demand, they do suggest that passenger interests and voices can help effect change when funneled through channels with clout, whether those channels are news coverage, civic engagement, or advocacy groups.

From a social justice perspective, passengers should know that they do have rights in security settings, although the rights are not always clearly presented. There is, for example, a TSA civil rights policy, which none of the passengers I spoke with knew existed.[12] Passengers should understand their rights so that they know when TSO behavior is unacceptable and when they should take action in response to experiences that make them uncomfortable or upset.

Even for well-publicized protocols like opting out of AIT, TSOs may try to steer passengers toward their preferred screening modality. Therefore, passengers should realize that, for better or worse, they need to insist on their rights, the way Sammy did when traveling with her medical equipment. And they should communicate with the TSA, clearly and directly, about interactions that appear untoward or cause undue stress.

In fact, complaining is vitally important to effecting change. The TSA uses low numbers of complaints as evidence of tacit consumer approval, assuming that "if people aren't complaining, then they must be satisfied." However, my research and consumer polls (e.g., Gallup, U.S. Travel Association) suggest that it might be more accurate to describe consumers as ambivalent than as satisfied. For instance, reports in 2012 showed that fewer than forty thousand passengers lodged a formal complaint with the TSA—less than 1 percent of passengers who flew that year—and the TSA promoted that as evidence of success and consumer satisfaction.[13] However, the low rate of complaints strongly contrasts with consumer polls, which rated the TSA abysmally.

Low numbers of complaints may have more to do with passengers not knowing how to log a complaint or not having had time to do so during the course of travel. The TSA actually has an entire complaint section on its website, where you can lodge grievances related to, among other things, civil rights, screening procedures, and customer service/professionalism.[14] Just be sure to record as many details as possible, including the name of the TSO involved and the date, time, and specific location of the incident you are reporting. You are also allowed to take photos and videos. In some instances, passengers have complained and requested a review of security surveillance recordings (either through general complaint mechanisms, media coverage, or lawsuits), and the TSA has apologized and offered compensation.

Passengers should consider taking action to address philosophical and political concerns with stakeholders outside of the airport as well—for instance, on matters related to civil rights and invasion of privacy. As the recently attempted Screening with Dignity bill showed, change is often accomplished in response to lawsuits and congressional mandates. Formally contacting your representatives, political officials, and advocacy groups can help change security protocols.

Evolving security will help not only the nearly two million people who fly commercially in the United States every day, but also the nearly fifty thousand security officers who have to deal with us.

Pro Travel Tip #17:

Share Your Story

In this book, I've shared the experiences of many travelers and TSOs. My goal was never to tell the definitive story of communication, identity, and emotion in airport security, but to tell *a* story about the people I interviewed and met in security. I know there are many other voices and experiences out there, and I would love to know *your* story too. If you'd like to share your experiences with traveling through or working in airport security, please visit the website www.101patdowns.com and drop me a line.

> While this book is definitely about airport security, the takeaways regarding communication, emotion, and identity go beyond the checkpoint. Have you ever wondered why, for instance, people have such different views of law enforcement officers? Some folks think of them as lifesaving heroes, and others think of them as "pigs," "citation writers," or "donut eaters." And likewise officers view community members in different ways—perhaps as citizens, noncitizens, or potential criminals? Taking a discursive view— that is, considering the personal, organizational, and societal discourses that shape our perspectives—can show us how people develop their opinions and frame others. Like TSOs, law enforcement officers have a responsibility to protect the public at large and may be less attuned to individual experiences.
>
> Like airport security interactions, law enforcement situations can be highly emotional, and they involve steep power differentials between officers and community members. But unlike airport security, the potential consequences of mismanaged emotional situations can be deadly. So understanding how emotions and identity are shaped by discourses and how they influence communication is a vital way to reduce conflicts and misunderstandings that can escalate to violence.

Similarly, we can take ideas about identity, emotion, and communication to the doctor's office. In health care settings, roles and experiences are situated in a robust historical and discursive landscape, with doctors positioned as one of the ultimate authorities, routinely with control over life and death. The role of the patient is constructed with less (but perhaps growing) agency. But these roles are situated in a constantly changing context due to new health care laws and the influx of publicly accessible but confusing health care information. Consider how, during the COVID-19 crisis, dynamic circumstances changed the nature of patient care, changing office practices for social distancing, reinforcing telemedicine, and introducing much controversy about the utility of wearing masks.

Thinking about health care interactions in terms of identity performances can help us understand why some medical experiences are more challenging than others. Like TSOs, physicians are trained to exhibit particular emotions—they stay calm in order to manage their patients' fears, for instance, and cultivate neutrality in the face of suffering and grief so as not to cross professional boundaries. However, this historically important emotion management sometimes blocks opportunities for compassionate communication and impedes relationships with patients. A growing body of research indicates that bedside manner is a vital element of doctor-patient communication. Acting with compassion and empathy rather than stoicism is a key element.

Likewise, patients portray certain types of identities. Many of us are probably guilty of behaving stereotypically in medical history interviews—lying about how much we exercise or drink, ahem—in order to seem more like ideal patients. We might also consider how health care structures—intimidating insurance processes, strange smells and noises, limiting visitation policies—shape how we feel and communicate at the doctor's office.

Appendix

Security Checkpoint Transportation Security
Officer Stations/Positions and Descriptions

Travel document center The podium near the front of the passenger line. The TSO here is responsible for checking that boarding passes and identification documents are legitimate.

Divestiture officer Officer who stands in the checkpoint area, typically near or between lines where passengers are depositing items into the X-ray baggage scanner and preparing to go through advanced imaging screening. This officer gives reminders to passengers regarding how to prepare for the screening—for example, by removing their shoes and belts and placing laptops and large electronics in separate bins.

Walk-through metal detector To keep people from going through the metal detector without permission, an officer stands near the metal detector and directs passengers through it or, more likely, into the AIT. This person also calls for "assists" when passengers want to opt out of imaging.

X-ray baggage screener X-ray technology screens luggage, looking for contraband. The TSO observing the screen will occasionally call for a "bag check" for suspicious artifacts.

Advanced imaging technology monitor Every AIT machine has an officer who directs passengers inside it. This officer gives directions, gets passengers into the correct positions, and then directs them out of the machine to collect their luggage or, if necessary, to receive more screening.

Floater Officer who floats between positions, refilling stacks of bins, observing security, and performing pat-downs when required.

Exit monitor Officer who sits where arriving passengers depart the terminal and monitors the exit to make sure that passengers do not double back and that no one sneaks into the terminal without screening.

Behavior detection officer Officer specially trained to observe behavior and emotional displays. Behavior detection officers observe the security line and interactions, typically from the front of the security line near the travel document checkers. These officers are trained to spot differences in behavior within crowds.

Notes

INTRODUCTION

1. I do not recommend convertible airplanes. Shawna Malvini Redden, "Southwest Flight 812: I Prefer My Plane Without a Sunroof, Thanks," *The Bluest Muse*, April 2, 2011, http://www.bluestmuse.com/2011/04/southwest-flight-812-i-prefer-my-plane/.

2. Corkscrews *are* technically allowed, but not if they have a knife attachment, no matter how small or dull.

3. Eliott C. McLaughlin, "Holiday Travel Stokes Sex Crime Victim's TSA Pat-Down Fears," CNN, December 22, 2010, https://www.cnn.com/2010/TRAVEL/12/21/tsa.patdown.sex.crime.victims/index.html.

4. Tracy, "Becoming a Character for Commerce."

5. Daunt and Harris, "Forms of Dysfunctional Customer Behaviour."

6. Beisecker, "Patient Power in Doctor-Patient Communication."

7. Malvini Redden, "How Lines Organize Compulsory Interaction."

8. Wieland, "Ideal Selves."

9. LeGreco and Tracy, "Discourse Tracing."

10. *Saturday Night Live* regularly comments on TSA policy, including a 2010 sketch parodying late-night phone sex commercials. The skit poked fun at enhanced pat-downs with the tag line "It's our business to touch yours." Soraya Roberts, "'SNL' TSA Skit Parodies New Pat-Down Policy That Has Critics Complaining About Invasiveness," *New York Daily News*, November 22, 2010, https://www.nydailynews.com/entertainment/tv-movies/snl-tsa-skit-parodies-new-pat-down-policy-critics-complaining-invasiveness-article-1.452751.

    In an even more outrageous tone, the creators of the adult cartoon *South Park* ridiculed the TSA in an episode titled "Reverse Cowgirl," which showcases gendered battles about toilet seats. After a woman theatrically dies from falling in the commode, the "Toilet Security Administration" is created to monitor the use of toilets in public and private spaces. While crass, the episode pointedly condemns the TSA as frivolous, its officers as sexually deviant, and the public as resigned to government intrusion into their most private of practices. Jacob Kleinman, "South Park New Episode Takes on TSA, Toilet Seat Gender War," *International Business Times*, March 15, 2012, https://www.ibtimes.com/south-park -new-episode-takes-tsa-toilet-seat-gender-war-video-425858.

11. The project involved ethnographic exploration in airport security at eighteen international airports over the course of several years. A full participant, I took 133 one-way flights, typically passing through security multiple times per trip (Spradley, *Participant Observation*). I spoke with passengers and TSOs during security interactions. I spent approximately 115 hours in the field, not including travel time, mostly focused on security and writing thick descriptions (Geertz, *The Interpretation of Cultures*). I conducted approximately two hundred informal ethnographic interviews and formal interviews with thirty-one passengers and sixteen TSOs, each averaging an hour (Tracy, *Qualitative Research Methods*). Additionally, I conducted "discourse tracing," which involves attending to personal-level data such as observations and interviews to explicate local, contextual communication, while also keeping in mind organizational-level information such as organizational policies and societal discourse that emphasizes larger social narratives (LeGreco and Tracy, "Discourse Tracing"). I defined September 11, 2001, as the "rupture point" for my case and combed through twenty years of TSA history, policy changes, and news articles, with close focus on the first thirteen years of the TSA's existence. All quotations in this book are direct, edited only for clarity with notations. All passenger, crew, and TSO interviewee names are pseudonyms. For more details about the project, see Malvini Redden, "How Discourses Cast Airport Security Characters."

1. GOLDEN AGE TO SECURITY THEATRE

1. Note that some airports, like San Francisco International and Orlando International, maintain private security companies, but they are required to implement TSA protocol.

2. Robert Pear, "A Nation Challenged: Flight Safety Legislation; Congress Agrees To U.S. Takeover For Air Security," *New York Times*, November 16, 2001, http://www .nytimes.com/2001/11/16/us/nation-challenged-flight-safety-legislation -congress-agrees-us-takeover-for-air.html.

3. Approximations of the TSA workforce fluctuate between forty-five thousand and sixty thousand, and they were generally lower during the TSA's formative years.

4. In March 2013 the TSA announced that small pocket knives with blades 2.36 inches long or less would be allowed on flights, along with certain types of sporting equipment like hockey sticks, billiard cues, and up to two golf clubs. However, in April 2013 the TSA announced delays in the implementation of the new rules, which were ultimately canceled in light of vociferous complaints by flight attendant lobbying groups. Andrew Bender, "TSA Cancels Decision Allowing Knives on Planes," *Forbes*, June 6, 2013, https://www.forbes.com/sites /andrewbender/2013/06/06/tsa-cancels-decision-allowing-knives-on-planes/ #5f2ce63ce55a.

5. In 2000, 599,563,678 passengers flew domestically in the United States. In 2010, 629,537,593 people flew domestically. U.S. Department of Transportation, Research and Innovation Technology Administration, Bureau of Transportation Statistics, 2013; U.S. Committee on Appropriations, "Department of Homeland Security Appropriations Bill 2012, Report to Accompany H.R. 2017," http://www .gpo.gov/fdsys/pkg/CRPT-112srpt74/pdf/CRPT-112srpt74.pdf.

6. Jessica Dickler, "Post 9/11 Travel: What Airport Security Costs Us," CNN, September 8, 2011, http://money.cnn.com/2011/09/08/pf/911_travel/index.htm.

7. In 2020, as of the writing of this book, the TSA's budget is $7.8 billion. Pekoske, "Examining the President's FY 2020 Budget Request."

8. Charles Kenney, "Airport Security Is Killing Us," *Business Week*, November 18, 2012, http://www.businessweek.com/articles/2012-11-18/how-airport-security-is -killing-us.

9. Mueller, "Embracing Threatlessness."

10. Koerner, *The Skies Belong to Us*.

2. "MY HOUSE, MY RULES"

1. Malvini Redden, "How Lines Organize."

2. I do end up going downstairs to watch the check-in lines, only to have airline personnel assume I'm a corporate shill sent to watch them or competition trying to steal ideas.

3. Kemeny and Shestyuk, "Emotions, The Neuroendocrine and Immune Systems."

4. TSOs receive substantial training in emotion management—specifically, they learn to suppress their reactions to difficult passenger behavior and stressful situations, and to simulate negative, intimidating expressions of emotions to keep passengers in line.

5. Ashforth and Kreiner, "'How Can You Do It?'"; Rivera, "Emotional Taint."

6. Entry-level TSOs typically make between $25,000 and $40,000 per year and enjoy federal health and retirement benefits. "What Is TSA?," FederalLawEnforcement.org, https://www.federallawenforcement.org/tsa/.

7. As discussed in chapter 2, immediately following the September 11, 2001, terrorist attacks, as the TSA was being formed, airport security was still a private business largely sponsored by the airline industry.
8. Hareli and Rafaeli, "Emotion Cycles."

3. FEAR AND LOATHING

1. Gross, "Emotion Regulation"; Kemeny and Shestyuk, "Emotions, the Neuroendocrine and Immune Systems."
2. Amanda Ripley, "Airport Screeners Dress for Respect," *Time*, June 17, 2008, http://content.time.com/time/nation/article/0,8599,1815529,00.html.
3. Cialdini, *Influence*.
4. Malvini Redden, "How Lines Organize."

4. IS THAT A SALAMI IN YOUR PURSE?

1. "TSA Issues Guidelines to Help Passengers through Security," TSA, https://www.tsa.gov/news/press/releases/2002/04/30/tsa-issues-guidelines-help-passengers-through-security-and-expands.
2. Colin Campbell, "TSA Stops Woman at BWI Airport with Gun-Shaped Heels, Bullet Straps," *Baltimore Sun*, March 1, 2016, https://www.baltimoresun.com/news/crime/bs-md-bwi-gun-shoes-20160301-story.html.
3. See Scarduzio and Malvini Redden, "The Positive Outcomes of Negative Emotional Displays."
4. Jeff intimates that the unmarked gold block was contraband. However, TSO regulations state that you can travel with gold bars, as long as they are worth less than $1 million.
5. Charles C. Mann, "Smoke Screening," *Vanity Fair*, December 20, 2011, http://www.vanityfair.com/culture/features/2011/12/TSA-insanity-201112.
6. In recent years the TSA has also added experience requirements such as a year as a security guard or certification as an X-ray technologist.
7. "Civil Enforcement," TSA, https://www.tsa.gov/travel/civil-enforcement.

5. "ONE SHOE, TWO SHOES"

1. Pre-COVID-19 pandemic, by the way.
2. Fun fact: Airport floors can promote athlete's foot and the spread of disease via fecal matter tracked in on peoples' shoes.
3. Michael Elliot, "The Shoe Bomber's World," *Time*, February 16, 2002, http://content.time.com/time/world/article/0,8599,203478,00.html.
4. "TCRA Offering Socks to Passengers," *Johnson City Press*, February 7, 2003.
5. Kitty Bean Yancey, "Fliers Bare Their Souls on Checkpoint Woes," *USA Today*, July 21, 2006, http://usatoday30.usatoday.com/travel/flights/2006-07-20-checkpoint-woes_x.htm.

6. Keith L. Alexander, "TSA Intends to Lace Up Its Shoe Policy," *Washington Post*, December 21, 2004, http://www.washingtonpost.com/wp-dyn/articles/A15183 -2004Dec20.html.

7. John Ward Anderson and Karen DeYoung, "Plot to Bomb U.S.-Bound Jets Is Foiled," *Washington Post Foreign Service*, August 11, 2006, http://www.washingtonpost.com /wp-dyn/content/article/2006/08/10/AR2006081000152.html.

8. In fact, even *writing* about the sounds is making my chest tighten.

6. NO CRYING OVER STOLEN SHAMPOO

1. DQ Wilber, "TSA to Maintain Its Ban on Liquids and Gels," *Washington Post*, August 24, 2006, http://www.washingtonpost.com/wp-dyn/content/article/2006 /08/23/AR2006082301676.html.

2. Anderson and DeYoung, "Plot to Bomb U.S.-Bound Jets."

3. Roger Yu, "Not Following Baggies Rules Can Bog Down Lines," *USA Today*, November 7, 2006, http://usatoday30.usatoday.com/money/biztravel/2006-11 -06-vignettes-usat_x.htm.

4. Joe Sharkey, "Turns out There's a Reason for Those 3-Ounce Bottles," *New York Times*, September 11, 2007, http://www.nytimes.com/2007/09/11/business /11road.html.

5. Joe Sharkey, "Some Volatile Opinions about Volatile Liquids," *New York Times*, September 18, 2007, http://www.nytimes.com/2007/09/18/business/18road .html.

6. See Williams and Sizemore, *Biologic, Chemical, and Radiation Terrorism Review*.

7. I don't correct Peter's timeline here, but the liquids and gels limitations didn't start until a few years later.

8. "TSA Travel Tip: Traveling with Alcohol," *TSA Blog*, June 21, 2019, https://www.tsa .gov/blog/2019/06/21/tsa-travel-tip-traveling-alcohol.

7. NAKED SCANNERS ARE FOR PERVERTS

1. Nick Bunkley, "Would-Be Plane Bomber Is Sentenced to Life in Prison," *New York Times*, February 16, 2012, https://www.nytimes.com/2012/02/17/us/would-be -plane-bomber-sentenced-to-life.html.

2. Scott Shane, "Inside Al Qaeda's Plot to Blow Up an American Airliner," *New York Times*, February 22, 2017, https://www.nytimes.com/2017/02/22/us/politics /anwar-awlaki-underwear-bomber-abdulmutallab.html; Ginger Allen, "Female Passengers Say They're Targeted by TSA," *CBS DFW*, February 3, 2012, http://dfw .cbslocal.com/2012/02/03/female-passengers-say-theyre-targeted-by-TSA.

3. "Technology," TSA, https://www.tsa.gov/sites/default/files/resources/technology _factsheet.pdf.

4. The National Council on Radiation Protection recommends limiting lifetime exposure to ionizing radiation, which can potentially cause cancer and other physiological damage. Moulder, "Risks of Exposure."

5. Since the inception of the TSA, female passengers have complained about being singled out for more pat-downs and scans than their male counterparts. Steven Frischling, "TSA Technologies, Security Theater, and Oversight Failure," *Flying with Fish* (blog), July 16, 2012, http://boardingarea.com/blogs/flyingwithfish/2012 /07/16/tsa-technologies-security-theater-oversight-failures.

6. Bianca Bosker, "100 Body Scans From Security Checkpoint Leaked," *Huffington Post*, November 16, 2010, https://www.huffpost.com/entry/100-body-scans-from -secur_n_784317.

7. Joel Johnson, "One Hundred Naked Citizens: One Hundred Leaked Body Scans," *Gizmodo*, November 16, 2010, https://gizmodo.com/one-hundred-naked-citizens -one-hundred-leaked-body-sca-5690749.

8. U.S. Department of Homeland Security, "DHS/TSA/PIA-032 Advanced Imaging Technology," December 2015, https://www.dhs.gov/publication/dhstsapia-032 -advanced-imaging-technology.

9. U.S. Department of Homeland Security, "Advanced Imaging Technology," https:// epic.org/foia/dhs/bodyscanner/appeal/TSA-AIT_ScannerFactSheet.pdf.

10. Colloquial evidence that is often repeated by TSOs suggests that going through AIT exposes passengers to less radiation than a cell phone call or a few minutes at altitude. While this may be true, far greater are the potential dangers to TSOs who work around the machines day in and day out.

11. Moulder, "Risks of Exposure."

12. "Whole Body Imaging Technology and Body Scanners," Electronic Privacy Information Center, http://epic.org/privacy/airtravel/backscatter.

13. Mehta and Smith-Bindman, "Airport Full-Body Screening."

14. Moulder, "Risks of Exposure," 726.

15. Michael Grabell, "Europe Bans X-ray Body Scanners Used at U.S. Airports," ProPublica, November 15, 2011, https://www.propublica.org/article/europe-bans-x -ray-body-scanners-used-at-u.s.-airports.

16. "Whole Body Imaging."

17. Leezel Tanglao, "Airport Baby Pat-Down Out of Line? TSA Says Agents Followed Procedure in Kansas City," ABC News, May 11, 2011, http://abcnews .go.com/US/kansas-city-airport-baby-pat-extreme-tsa-agents/story?id= 13576190.

18. Caroline Costello, "TSA Eases Security Procedures for Seniors," *SmarterTravel*, March 15, 2012, http://www.smartertravel.com/blogs/today-in-travel/tsa-eases -security-procedures-for-senior-travelers.html?id=10788878.

19. Jay Blackman and Kari Huus, "TSA to Remove Controversial Full-Body Scanners," NBC News, January 18, 2013, http://www.nbcnews.com/travel/TSA-remove -controversial-full-body-scanners-1B8038882.

20. Jason Edward Harrington, "Dear America, I Saw You Naked. And Yes, We Were Laughing. Confessions of an Ex-TSA Agent," *Politico*, January 30, 2014, https:// www.politico.com/magazine/story/2014/01/tsa-screener-confession-102912.

21. Michael Grabell and Christian Salewski, "Sweating Bullets: Body Scanners Can See Perspiration as a Potential Weapon," ProPublica, December 19, 2011, https:// www.propublica.org/article/sweating-bullets-body-scanners-can-see-perspiration -as-a-potential-weapon.

22. Farah Naz Khan, "Is That Airport Security Scanner Really Safe," *Scientific American*, December 18, 2017, https://blogs.scientificamerican.com/observations /is-that-airport-security-scanner-really-safe/.

8. MEETING RESISTANCE

1. "National Organization Calls for End to Invasive TSA Screening Methods," National Sexual Violence Resource Center, November 24, 2010, http://www.ncdsv .org/images/NSVRC_NatlOrgCallsEndInvasiveTSAScreeningMethods_11-24 -2010.pdf.

2. J. Bumgardner, "Woman Guilty After Refusing TSA Patdown," KXAN News, July 22, 2011.

3. Charles Krauthammer, "Don't Touch My Junk," *Washington Post*, November 19, 2010, http://www.washingtonpost.com/wp-dyn/content/article/2010/11/18 /AR2010111804494.html.

4. We Won't Fly, https://www.facebook.com/wontfly/.

5. Foucault, *The History of Sexuality*.

6. Associated Press, "TSA Pats Down 4-Year-Old after She Hugs Grandmother," Yahoo News, April 26, 2012, https://news.yahoo.com/tsa-defends-pat-down-4-old -kan-airport-231522461.html; "Traveling with Children," TSA, https://www.tsa .gov/travel/special-procedures/traveling-children.

9. RISK-BASED SECURITY

1. Nic Robertson and Paul Cruickshank, "Heightened Concerns in Europe over Potential Terrorist Attack," CNN, October 12, 2010, https://www.cnn.com/2010 /WORLD/europe/10/12/europe.terror.threat/index.html.

2. If you forget, lose, or do not have photo identification, the TSA can ask you to complete a different identity verification process in some cases.

3. Charles C. Mann, "Smoke Screening," *Vanity Fair*, December 20, 2011, http://www .vanityfair.com/culture/features/2011/12/TSA-insanity-201112.

4. "TSA Behavior Detection and Analysis Program," TSA, https://www.tsa.gov/news /press/testimony/2013/11/14/tsa-behavior-detection-and-analysis-program.

5. SPOT training details, including the SPOT checklist and rating form—the "SPOT Referral Report"—were deemed Sensitive Security Information until a source leaked it to the *Intercept*. Jana Winter and Cora Currier, "Exclusive: TSA's Secret Behavior Checklist to Spot Terrorists," *Intercept*, March 27, 2015, https://theintercept .com/2015/03/27/revealed-tsas-closely-held-behavior-checklist-spot-terrorists/.

6. Sensitive Security Information is "information that, if publicly released, would be detrimental to transportation security as defined by Federal regulation 49 C.F.R. part 1520." "Sensitive Security Information," TSA, https://www.tsa.gov/sites /default/files/ssi_best_practices_guide_for_non-dhs_employees.pdf. Part of my commitment to research ethics was to complete my study accessing information in ways that any passenger might—exploring security as a ticketed passenger but not causing any disruptions, not probing TSOs for any sensitive information. During interviews, if TSOs seemed hesitant to share information, I reiterated that they were under no obligation to speak with me, and if they felt uncomfortable, they could skip to another topic or stop the conversation altogether. Any sensitive information that appears in this book was offered freely or inadvertently, or found publicly online. Any information an officer or interviewee specifically asked me to omit was deleted and not included in any published document.

7. T. Smith, "Next in Line for TSA? A Thorough 'Chat-Down,'" NPR, August 16, 2011, http://www.npr.org/2011/08/16/139643652/next-in-line-for-the-tsa-a-thorough -chat-down.

8. "TSA Behavior Detection Officers Will Be Retrained after Profiling Complaints," CNN, August 23, 2012, http://edition.cnn.com/2012/08/22/travel/TSA-officers /index.html?hpt=hp_t2.

9. Bruce Schneier, "Airport Security: Israel vs. the United States," *Schneier on Security*, July 3, 2007, http://www.schneier.com/blog/archives/2007/07/airport_securit_7.html.

10. Federal Bureau of Investigation, "Statement Regarding United States vs. Trey Scott Atwater," February 17, 2012, https://archives.fbi.gov/archives/elpaso/press -releases/2012/statement-regarding-united-states-vs.-trey-scott-atwater-1.

11. Bart Jansen, "TSA 'Chat Downs' Investigated at Boston's Logan Airport," *USA Today*, August 13, 2012, https://abcnews.go.com/Travel/tsa-chat-downs -investigated-bostons-logan-airport/story?id=16998085.

10. EVEN PILOTS HAVE PAT-DOWNS

1. "Crewmember Identity Verification Program to Begin Testing," TSA, April 1, 2011, https://www.tsa.gov/news/releases/2011/04/01/crewmember-identity -verification-program-begin-testing.

2. "U.S. Airline Flight Attendants to Get Expedited Airport Screening in Second State of Known Crewmember Program," TSA, July 27, 2012, https://www.tsa.gov/news /releases/2012/07/27/us-airline-flight-attendants-get-expedited-airport -screening-second-stage.

3. National Institute for Occupational Safety and Health, "Aircrew Safety and Health," Centers for Disease Control and Prevention, https://www.cdc.gov/niosh /topics/aircrew/cosmicionizingradiation.html.

4. Lindsay Beyerstein, "TSA: Pilots' Junk Off Limits, Flight Attendants' Fair Game," *In These Times*, November 22, 2010, http://inthesetimes.com/working/entry/6691 /pilots_junk_off-limits_to_tsa_flight_attendants_fair_game_sexism/.

5. Lilit Marcus, "Flight Attendant Flees TSA after Being Caught with 70 Pounds of Cocaine," *Condé Nast Traveler*, March 24, 2016, https://www.cntraveler.com/stories /2016-03-22/flight-attendant-flees-tsa-after-being-caught-70-pounds-cocaine.

6. Department of Justice, U.S. Attorney's Office, Southern District of New York, "Flight Attendant Pleads Guilty to Airport Security Violations and Unlicensed Money Transmitting," July 10, 2018, https://www.justice.gov/usao-sdny/pr/flight -attendant-pleads-guilty-airport-security-violations-and-unlicensed-money.

7. Mateusz Maszczynski, "Controversial Changes to Known Crewmember Program Will Now No Longer Go Ahead," *Paddle Your Own Kanoo*, August 27, 2019, https:// www.paddleyourownkanoo.com/2019/08/27/controversial-changes-to-the -known-crewmember-program-will-now-no-longer-go-ahead/.

8. Aviation Security Advisory Committee, "Report of the Aviation Security Committee on Insider Threats," TSA, July 19, 2018, https://www.tsa.gov/sites/default/files /asacinsiderthreatreport_072018.pdf.

9. Kylie Bielby, "GAO: TSA Needs Strategic Plan to Counter Insider Threats to Aviation," *Homeland Security Today*, February 11, 2020, https://www.hstoday.us /subject-matter-areas/airport-aviation-security/gao-tsa-needs-strategic-plan-to -counter-insider-threats-to-aviation/.

11. ON THE FRONT LINES

1. Ashforth, Harrison, and Corley, "Identification in Organizations."

2. Following Wieland, I suggest that "a focus on ideal selves draws attention to the social pressures involved in identity construction and considers how identity workers maintain and repair their identities so that they align with these ideals." Wieland, "Ideal Selves," 512.

3. In 2018 TSA director David Pekoske announced a slight adjustment to this call, changing the TSA creed from "Not on My Watch!" to "Not on Our Watch!" See https://www.tsa.gov/sites/default/files/tsa_strategy.pdf.

4. Gioia and Chittipeddi, "Sensemaking and Sensegiving."

5. Benefiel, *Soul at Work*.

6. Tracy, "Locking Up Emotion."

7. Wrzesniewski, McCauley, Rozin, and Schwartz, "Jobs, Careers, and Callings."

8. Pratt, "The Good, The Bad, and the Ambivalent."

9. Intriguingly, the TSA's VIPR program (Visible Intermodel Prevention and Response), which positions the TSA as expanding its role to all transportation systems, would include screenings for bus and trains as well. Christopher Elliott, "The TSA Wants to be Everywhere in 2013—Here's Why We Shouldn't Let It," *HuffPost*, January 2, 2013, https://www.huffpost.com/entry/the-tsa-wants-to-be -every_b_2393332.

10. And yes, if this sounds familiar, you might recognize a similar line of argument used to explain how once "normal" people in Nazi Germany enacted atrocities against Jews. They were just following orders and enforcing "the rules."

12. LEMMINGS AND SHEEPLE

1. Foucault, *Discipline and Punish*.

2. Gross, "Emotion Regulation."

3. Nigel Duara, "John Brennan, Man Who Stripped in Front of TSA, Found Not Guilty," *Huffington Post*, July 19, 2012, https://komonews.com/news/local/man -who-stripped-nude-for-tsa-found-not-guilty-11-22-2015.

4. Cialdini, *Influence*; Weick, *Sensemaking*.

13. NICE TSOS FINISH LAST

1. Incidentally, I interviewed some passengers who talked about service sometimes being worse at smaller regional airports where TSOs "take themselves too seriously."

2. Tracy and Tracy, "Emotion Labor at 911."

3. Collinson, "Identities and Insecurities," 539.

4. Hareli and Rafaeli, "Emotion Cycles."

14. THE TRAVELING UNICORN

1. Libby Zay, "Woman Screams the TSA 'Molested' Her After Pat-Down," *Harrold's Blog*, June 2, 2011, http://harrolds.blogspot.com/2011/06/osama-laughed-woman -screams-tsa.html.

2. If you ever see an "SSSS" written on your boarding pass, congrats, you've been flagged. The acronym stands for "secondary security screening selection" and might indicate that you've been flagged for previous challenging behavior, you're on someone's radar for strange travel patterns, or you're on an itinerary that includes a "high-risk" country. Some might also suggest it indicates illegal racial

profiling. Ben Lucky, "Everything You Need to Know About Getting an 'SSSS' on Your Boarding Pass," *One Mile at a Time*, May 12, 2019, https://onemileatatime .com/what-does-ssss-on-boarding-pass-mean/.

15. TRAVELING WITH IDENTITY BAGGAGE

1. Harriet Baskas, "TSA Pat-Down Leaves Traveler Covered in Urine," NBC News, March 25, 2011, http://www.nbcnews.com/id/40291856/ns/travel-news/t/tsa-pat -down-leaves-traveler-covered-urine/.
2. Jane Allen, "Prosthetics Become Source of Shame at Airport Screenings," ABC News, November 23, 2010, https://abcnews.go.com/Health/Depression/tsa -medical-humiliations-extra-pain-airports-people-prosthetic/story?id=12227882.
3. Katie Rogers, "TSA Defends Treatment of Transgender Air Traveler," *New York Times*, September 22, 2015, https://www.nytimes.com/2015/09/23/us/shadi -petosky-tsa-transgender.html.
4. Trans people talk about how this "anomaly" language is used to surveil and examine their genitalia.
5. A ProPublica report in 2019 found that 5 percent of civil rights complaints filed from January 2016 to April 2019 related to the screening of trans people, despite trans people making up less than 1 percent of the population. The government is usually protected from lawsuits, but federal law permits people to sue officers who conduct searches and arrest people. In August 2019 a U.S. Court of Appeals for the Third Circuit overturned previous rulings that protected the TSA and its employees from lawsuits. While the TSA argued that its employees are just screeners who examine passengers and their belongings, the court noted that those employees are now called "officers" and wear uniforms and badges to that effect. Allowing passengers to sue these officers enables recourse for those who are assaulted, wrongly detained, or faced with fabricated charges. "Judges Say Travelers Can Sue TSA over Screen Mistreatment," AP News, August 30, 2019, https://apnews.com /de76f18824324fd282e6d55aed19d6bd.
6. Drew Jones, "TSA Apologizes to Native American Traveler after Agent Snaps Braids, Says 'Giddyup!' during Pat-Down," *Washington Post*, January 17, 2020, https://www.washingtonpost.com/travel/2020/01/17/tsa-apologizes-native -american-traveler-after-agent-snaps-braids-says-giddyup-during-pat-down/.
7. Alexandra Deabler, "Renowned Mali Musician Claims TSA Left Custom-Made Instrument 'in Pieces,' Calls Alleged Incident Racist," Fox News, February 7, 2020, https://www.foxnews.com/travel/mali-musician-tsa-custom-made-instrument-in -pieces.
8. Nacos, "The Portrayal of Female Terrorists."
9. Crenshaw, "Mapping the Margins."

10. "Kimberlé Crenshaw on Intersectionality," Columbia Law School, June 8, 2017, https://www.law.columbia.edu/news/archive/kimberle-crenshaw -intersectionality-more-two-decades-later.

11. Brenda Medina and Thomas Frank, "TSA Agents Say They're Not Discriminating Against Black Women, But Their Body Scanners Might Be," ProPublica, April 17, 2019.

12. See the CROWN Act website, https://www.thecrownact.com/about.

13. Current TSA policy allows trans passengers to be patted down by an officer of their same gender expression. Previously, the TSA enforced pat-downs according to sex assigned at birth or whatever was noted on government identification documents.

14. Laurie Baratti, "Woman Suing TSA for Sexual Assault Following Pat-Down," *Travel Pulse*, February 11, 2020, https://www.travelpulse.com/news/airlines /woman-suing-tsa-for-sexual-assault-following-pat-down.html.

15. Screening with Dignity Act of 2018, H.R. 6659, 115th Congress (2018), https://www .congress.gov/bill/115th-congress/house-bill/6659/text.

16. Taylor Romine and Chandelis Duster, "Black Women Sue Golf Course That Called Cops Alleging They Were Playing Too Slowly," CNN, April 23, 2020, https://www .cnn.com/2020/04/23/us/black-women-lawsuit-golf-course/index.html.

17. Malvini Redden and Scarduzio, "A Different Type of Dirty Work."

CONCLUSION

1. Weick, *Sensemaking*.

2. This is especially odd because during the writing of this book in spring 2020, conservative groups around the country were storming state capitols to protest COVID-19 related stay-at-home and mask-wearing orders, arguing they curtailed civil rights. And yet, the TSA conducts far more rights violations every day without any fuss.

3. Michael Elliot, "The Shoe Bomber's World," *Time*, February 16, 2002, http://www .time.com/time/world/article/0,8599,203478,00.html.

4. Mark Duell and Michael Zennie, "Saudi Teen's Wild Week after He Leads Oregon Police on Grand Theft Auto Chase and Then Forced down a Flight to Texas with Smoking and a Song about Osama Bin Laden," *Daily Mail*, February 23, 2012, http://www.dailymail.co.uk/news/article-2105029/Continental-Airlines -passengers-hold-smoking-Saudi-Yazeed-Mohammed-Abunayyan-shouting-Allah -great.html; Jim Scholz, Matt Hosford, and Genevieve Shaw Brown, "Rant on American Airlines Flight Ends With Flight Attendant in Hospital," NBC News, March 9, 2012, https://abcnews.go.com/Travel/flight-attendant-rant-sends -american-airlines-flight-back/story?id=15886557; Jim Avila, Matt Hosford, and Christina Ng, "Jetblue Pilot Yelled about Sept. 11," ABC News, March 28, 2012,

http://abcnews.go.com/US/jetblue-pilot-yelled-sept-11-restrained/story?id=16017810.

5. Collinson, "Identities and Insecurities."
6. Tracy and Trethewey, "Fracturing the Real-Self ↔ Fake-Self Dichotomy." This quote is regularly attributed to Aristotle in a longer passage: "We are what we repeatedly do. Excellence, then is not an act but a habit." However, the exact language is likely from American philosopher and historian William James Durant in his book *The Story of Philosophy*, which captures the spirit, if not the exact words, of Aristotle.
7. Grandey, "When 'the Show Must Go On'"; Ekman and Friesen, *Unmasking the Face*.
8. Hareli and Rafaeli, "Emotion Cycles."
9. See Sekerka, Vacharkulksemsuk, and Garland, "Positive Emotions," and Garland, Fredrickson, Kring, Johnson, Meyer, and Penn, "Upward Spirals of Positive Emotions."
10. Fredrickson and Losada, "Positive Affect."
11. Hosford, "Head of TSA, John Pistole, Defends Advanced Patdowns," ABC News, November 17, 2010, http://abcnews.go.com/Politics/tsas-pistole-defends-advanced-patdowns-capitol-hill/story?id=12172503.
12. "Civil Rights for Travelers," TSA, https://www.tsa.gov/travel/passenger-support/civil-rights.
13. In more recent years, the rates of complaints are slightly higher. In 2017, 1.37 passengers complained about airport security for every 100,000 that flew. Gary S. Becker, "TSA Complaint Data Reveals Airport Screening Trends," *Security Debrief*, March 16, 2018, http://securitydebrief.com/2018/03/16/tsa-complaint-data-airport-screening/.
14. "Complaint," TSA, https://www.tsa.gov/contact-center/form/complaints.

Bibliography

Ashforth, Blake E., and Glen E. Kreiner. "'How Can You Do It?': Dirty Work and the Challenge of Constructing a Positive Identity." *Academy of Management Review* 24, no. 3 (1999): 413-34.

Ashforth, Blake E., Spencer H. Harrison, and Kevin G. Corley. "Identification in Organizations: An Examination of Four Fundamental Questions." *Journal of Management* 34, no. 3 (2008): 325-74.

Beisecker, Analee E. "Patient Power in Doctor-Patient Communication: What Do We Know?" *Health Communication* 2, no. 2 (1990): 105-22.

Benefiel, Margaret. *Soul at Work, Spiritual Leadership in Organizations.* New York: Church Publishing, 2005.

Cialdini, Robert B. *Influence: Science and Practice.* 4th ed. Boston: Pearson Education, 2009.

Collinson, David. L. "Identities and Insecurities: Selves at Work." *Organization* 10, no. 3 (2003): 527-47.

Crenshaw, Kimberlé. "Mapping the Margins: Intersectionality, Identity Politics, and Violence Against Women of Color." *Stanford Law Review* 43 (1990): 1241.

Daunt, Kate L., and Lloyd C. Harris. "Exploring the Forms of Dysfunctional Customer Behaviour: A Study of Differences in Servicescape and Customer Disaffection with Service." *Journal of Marketing Management* 28, no. 1-2 (2012): 129-53.

Ekman, Paul, and Wallace V. Friesen. *Unmasking the Face: A Guide to Recognizing Emotions from Facial Clues.* Malor Books, 2003.

Foucault, Michel. *Discipline and Punish: The Birth of the Prison.* New York: Vintage, 2012.

———. *The History of Sexuality: An Introduction.* New York: Vintage, 1990.

Fredrickson, Barbara L., and Marcial F. Losada. "Positive Affect and the Complex Dynamics of Human Flourishing." *American Psychologist* 60, no. 7 (2005): 678.

Garland, Eric L., Barbara Fredrickson, Ann M. Kring, David P. Johnson, Piper S. Meyer, and David L. Penn. "Upward Spirals of Positive Emotions Counter Downward Spirals of Negativity: Insights from the Broaden-and-Build Theory and Affective Neuroscience on the Treatment of Emotion Dysfunctions and Deficits in Psychopathology." *Clinical Psychology Review* 30, no. 7 (2010): 849-64.

Geertz, Clifford. *The Interpretation of Cultures*. New York: Basic Books, 1973.

Gioia, Dennis A., and Kumar Chittipeddi. "Sensemaking and Sensegiving in Strategic Change Initiation." *Strategic Management Journal* 12, no. 6 (1991): 433-48.

Grandey, Alicia A. "When 'the Show Must Go On': Surface Acting and Deep Acting as Determinants of Emotional Exhaustion and Peer-Rated Service Delivery." *Academy of Management Journal* 46, no. 1 (2003): 86-96.

Gross, James J. "Emotion Regulation: Affective, Cognitive, and Social Consequences." *Psychophysiology* 39, no. 3 (2002): 281-91.

Hareli, Shlomo, and Anat Rafaeli. "Emotion Cycles: On the Social Influence of Emotion in Organizations." *Research in Organizational Behavior* 28 (2008): 35-59.

Kemeny, Margaret E., and Avgusta Shestyuk. "Emotions, the Neuroendocrine and Immune Systems, and Health." In *Handbook of Emotions*, 3rd ed., edited by Michael Lewis, Jeannette M. Haviland-Jones, and Lisa Feldman Barrett, 661-75. Guilford Press, 2008.

Koerner, Brendan I. *The Skies Belong to Us: Love and Terror in the Golden Age of Hijacking*. New York: Broadway Books, 2014.

LeGreco, Marianne, and Sarah J. Tracy. "Discourse Tracing as Qualitative Practice." *Qualitative Inquiry* 15, no. 9 (2009): 1516-43.

Malvini Redden, Shawna. "How Discourses Cast Airport Security Characters: A Discourse Tracing and Qualitative Analysis of Identity And Emotional Performances." PhD diss., Arizona State University, 2013.

———. "How Lines Organize Compulsory Interaction, Emotion Management, and 'Emotional Taxes': The Implications of Passenger Emotion and Expression in Airport Security Lines." *Management Communication Quarterly* 27, no. 1 (2013): 121-49.

Malvini Redden, Shawna, and Jennifer A. Scarduzio. "A Different Type of Dirty Work: Hidden Taint, Intersectionality, and Emotion Management in Bureaucratic Organizations." *Communication Monographs* 85, no. 2 (2018): 224-44.

Mehta, Pratik, and Rebecca Smith-Bindman. "Airport Full-Body Screening: What Is the Risk?" *Archives of Internal Medicine* 171, no. 12 (2011): 1112-15.

Moulder, John E. "Risks of Exposure to Ionizing and Millimeter-Wave Radiation from Airport Whole-Body Scanners." *Radiation Research* 177, no. 6 (2012): 723-26.

Mueller, John. "Embracing Threatlessness: Reassessing U.S. Military Spending." In *American Grand Strategy and Seapower*, edited by Michael Gerson and Alison Lawler Russell. Conference report CRM D0025988.A2/Final, August 4, 2011. http://politicalscience.osu.edu/faculty/jmueller/CNApart.pdf.

Nacos, Brigitte L. "The Portrayal of Female Terrorists in the Media: Similar Framing Patterns in the News Coverage of Women in Politics and in Terrorism." *Studies in Conflict & Terrorism* 28, no. 5 (2005): 435–51.

Pekoske, David. "Examining the President's FY 2020 Budget Request for the TSA." Department of Homeland Security, Transportation Security Administration, April 2, 2019. https://www.tsa.gov/news/testimony/2019/04/02/examining-presidents -fy-2020-budget-request-transportation-security.

Pratt, Michael G. "The Good, the Bad, and the Ambivalent: Managing Identification among Amway Distributors." *Administrative Science Quarterly* 45, no. 3 (2000): 456–93.

Rivera, Kendra Dyanne. "Emotional Taint: Making Sense of Emotional Dirty Work at the US Border Patrol." *Management Communication Quarterly* 29, no. 2 (2015): 198–228.

Scarduzio, Jennifer A., and Shawna Malvini Redden. "The Positive Outcomes of Negative Emotional Displays: A Multi-Level Analysis of Emotion in Bureaucratic Work." *Electronic Journal of Communication* 25, no. 3/4 (2015). http://www.cios.org /ejcpublic/025/3/025305.html.

Sekerka, Leslie E., Tanya Vacharkulksemsuk, and Barbara L. Fredrickson. "Positive Emotions: Broadening and Building Upward Spirals of Sustainable Development." *The Oxford Handbook of Positive Organizational Scholarship* (2012): 168–77.

Spradley, James P. *Participant Observation*. Long Grove IL: Waveland Press, 2016.

Tracy, Sarah J. "Becoming a Character for Commerce: Emotion Labor, Self-Subordination, and Discursive Construction of Identity in a Total Institution." *Management Communication Quarterly* 14, no. 1 (2000): 90–128.

———. "Locking Up Emotion: Moving Beyond Dissonance for Understanding Emotion Labor Discomfort." *Communication Monographs* 72, no. 3 (2005): 261–83.

———. *Qualitative Research Methods: Collecting Evidence, Crafting Analysis, Communicating Impact*, 2nd ed. Hoboken NJ: Wiley Blackwell, 2019.

Tracy, Sarah J., and Angela Trethewey. "Fracturing the Real-Self ↔ Fake-Self Dichotomy: Moving Toward 'Crystallized' Organizational Discourses and Identities." *Communication Theory* 15, no. 2 (2005): 168–95.

Tracy, Sarah J., and Karen Tracy. "Emotion Labor at 911: A Case Study and Theoretical Critique." *Journal of Applied Communication Research* 26 (1998): 390–411.

Weick, K. E. *Sensemaking in Organizations*. Thousand Oaks CA: Sage Publications, 1995.

Wieland, Stacey M. B. "Ideal Selves as Resources for the Situated Practice of Identity." *Management Communication Quarterly* 24, no. 4 (2010): 503–28.

Williams, Mollie, and Daniel C. Sizemore. *Biologic, Chemical, and Radiation Terrorism Review*. Treasure Island FL: StatPearls Publishing, 2020. https://www.ncbi.nlm.nih.gov/books/NBK493217.

Wrzesniewski, Amy, Clark McCauley, Paul Rozin, and Barry Schwartz. "Jobs, Careers, and Callings: People's Relations to Their Work." *Journal of Research in Personality* 31, no. 1 (1997): 21–33.

Index